AF795119

COMMUNICATION, DEVELOPMENT AND CIVIL SOCIETY

By the Same Author :

Communication Planning for Socio-Economic Development (edited along with *Ranjit Singh*)

Media and Development : Themes in Communication and Extension. (edited along with *M.R. Dua*)

Third Revolution in Indian Perspective—Contemporary Issues and Themes in Communication

Rural Press—Problems and Prospects, (edited along with *Rajeshwar Dyal*)

Media Policy and Nation Building—Select Issues and Themes (with *Vir Bala Aggarwal*)

National Media Policy (edited along with *Rajeshwar Dyal*)

Media and Market Forces—Challenges and Opportunities (edited along with *Rajeshwar Dyal*)

Communication Technology, Media Policy and National Development

Communication and Development—The Challenge of the Twenty-first Century

Handbook of Journalism and Mass Communication (with *Vir Bala Aggarwal*)

Handbook of Reporting and Communication Skills : Companion volume to Handbook of Journalism and Mass Communication

---

About the Author

V.S. Gupta, former Professor. Haryana Agricultural University, is currently associated with the Department of Journalism as an expert for post-graduate and doctoral programmes, and also as a member of Board of Studies, Research Advisory Committee and Academic Council. As the zonal/country representative for Asian Media Information and Communication Centre (AMIC), Singapore, from 1991 to 1999, he organised a number of regional seminars and national colloquiums. He was awarded UNDP Fellowship and was selected for Journalist Fellowship Award.

Prof. Gupta has written, jointly and singly, twelve books, and a number of manuals and monographs.

COMMUNICATION, DEVELOPMENT AND CIVIL SOCIETY

Essays on Social Development and Civil Society

by

V. S. GUPTA

CONCEPT PUBLISHING COMPANY, NEW DELHI-110059

All rights reserved. No part of this work may be reproduced, stored in a retrieval system or transmitted in any form or by any means, electronic, mechanical, photocopying, microfilming, recording or otherwise, without the prior written permission of the copyright owner and the publisher.

ISBN : 81-8069--050-4 (HB)

First Published 2004

© V.S. Gupta

Published and Printed by
Ashok Kumar Mittal
Concept Publishing Company
A/15-16, Commercial Block, Mohan Garden
New Delhi-110059 (India)

Phones : 25351460, 25351794
Fax : 091-11-25357103
Email : publishing@conceptpub.com

PREFACE

The second edition of this book builds on the framework provided by the earlier edition of my book—*Communication and Development : The Challenge of the Twenty-first Century*. This edition of the book retains the essential elements of the subjects—communication and development. The second edition has been updated, data made available as a result of the Census of India 2001 has been used at most of the places. A number of chapters have been enlarged and several new aspects included.

The book has been written at a time when the Tenth Five Year Plan has been launched and development objectives are being defined not just in terms of increases in GDP or per capita income but in broader terms of enhancement of human well-being. The planning strategy of the country now takes note of the experience which shows that often there is no direct correspondence between economic attainments of a society and the quality of life. There is renewed emphasis on governance for human development. The recent score card developed to indicate the progress and quality in India's governance puts on record areas of concern and challenges—criminalisation of public life, politics of vote bank, recourse to competitive populism, bloated bureaucracy and several others. Consequently, the process of development suffers. New challenges emerge. An effort has, therefore, been made to discuss most of the issues impinging on the development process and prospects.

The book has been revised, enlarged and updated so as to conform to the course contents of development communication subject for the students of mass communication in the Indian universities. The curricula developed by several university departments, as well as the UGC Curriculum Development Committee, have been taken into view. In fact concepts like human development, human rights, civil society and several others, without which no discussion on development issues would be considered complete, have also been included.

While writing this book, I have tried to use all the good and the latest information on the subject. The ideas of leading scholars—individuals as well as institutional thinking—have been incorporated so as to enrich the contents of the book. Some of the institutions and the authors whose books I have consulted are : a number of reports—particularly the World Development Reports and the Human Development Reports being brought out by the World Bank and the UNDP for the past several years; writings of the Nobel Laureate Amartya Sen specially his book, *India : Economic Development and Social Opportunity;* and of course books and monographs brought out by AMIC, particularly the issues of *Media Asia.* Likewise UNESCO, UNFPA and several other international organisations have brought out useful publications and reports on sectoral subjects under their jurisdiction. These publications have helped me build perspective on different issues. I must also mention at least the major titles from which I have drawn data, information and ideas UNDP's *Human Development Report 2000* on Human Rights and Human Development, *World Banks' World Development Reports* for the period 1998-2001, *Knowledge for Development, Entering the 21st Century,* and *Attacking Poverty.* The two publications of the Planning Commission : *Approach Paper to the Tenth Five Year Plan (2002-2007)* and the first *National Human Development Report 2001* have been equally helpful.

The two chapters, Development Planning in India, and Civil Society and Good Governance—which were written for presentation at the Indian Institute of Advanced Study, Shimla for a seminar I had coordinated in November 2001 and for the trainees of NANA Group at the Indian Institute of Mass Communication last year, have been reworked and included in this publication with the hope that these chapters will certainly enhance the utility of the book.

V.S. Gupta

ACKNOWLEDGEMENTS

I must acknowledge my debt of gratitude to :—

1. Vijaya Menon, former Secretary General, AMIC, Singapore—an institution builder and a visionary whose lasting contribution to the discipline of media research, studies and dissemination will remain ever lasting; and

2. Ashok Mittal, the publisher—more of a friend whose counsel in matters of publishing and academics has helped me publish a number of books.

V.S. Gupta

CONTENTS

LIST OF TABLES

LIST OF ABBREVIATIONS

ADO	Agriculture Development Officer
AIR	All India Radio
AMIC	Asian Media Information and Communication Centre
BBC	British Broadcasting Corporation
BPL	Below Poverty Line
C-DOT	Centre of Development of Telematics
CNN	Cable News Network
COL	Commonwealth of Learning
CSE	Centre for Science and Environment
CSO	Civil Society Organization
DPAP	Drought Prone Area Programme
ERNET	Education and Research in Network
FAO	Food and Agriculture Organisation
FES	Friedrich Ebert Stiftung
GDP	Gross Development Product
GNP	Gross National Product
HDI	Human Development Index
HYV	High Yielding Variety
IARI	Indian Agricultural Research Institute
ICPD	International Conference of Population and Development
IGNOU	Indira Gandhi National Open University
INSAT	Indian National Satellite
IPDC	International Programme of Development Communication

IRDP	Integrated Rural Development Programme
KCP	Kheda Communication Project
MFALA	Marginal Farmers and Agricultural Labour Agency
NAMEDIA	Non-Aligned Media
NGOs	Non-Governmental Organisations
NHDR	National Human Development Report
NHRC	National Human Rights Commission
NIMME	National Institute of Multi-Media Education
NICNET	National Information Centre Network
NPG	National Performance Gap
ORT	Oral Rehydration Therapy
PHC	Public Health Centre
RNI	Registrar of Newpapers of India
SAC	Space Application Centre
SEWA	Self Employed Women Association
SFDA	Small Farmers Development Agency
SITE	Satellite Instructional Television Experiment
STD	Sexually Transmitted Diseases
STV	School Television
UNDP	United Nations Development Programme
UNESCO	United Nations Educational Scientific and Cultural Organization
UNICEF	United Nations International Children's Emergency Fund
VLW	Village Level Worker
VO	Voluntary Organization
WHO	World Health Organization

1

INTRODUCTION AND OVERVIEW

The following excerpt from the Introduction—New Directions in Development Thinking—of the World Development Report 1999-2000—*Entering the 21st Century,* is a fair representation of the contemporary thinking on development issues :—

> The principal goal of development policy is to create sustainable improvements in the quality of life for all people. While raising per capita incomes and consumption is part of that goal, other objectives—reducing poverty, expanding access to health services, and increasing educational levels—are also important. Meeting these goals require a comprehensive approach to development.

One of the twentieth century's hallmark achievements has been its consistent support to, and advocacy for, concepts like human development, human rights, intergenerational equity and capability building. A round of World Conferences deliberated on finding practical ways of solving global problems in a range of areas such as education (1990), environment and development (1992), human rights (1993), population and development (1994), natural disaster reduction (1994), social development (1995) and advancement of women (1995). These conferences were also responsible for formulating a number of key developmental objectives : sustainable development, empowerment of women, environmental protection, education for all, and role of civil society in good governance. It is precisely these issues and concepts, primarily in the Indian context and in the Indian situation, that this book discusses. More than that, it also seeks to establish linkages between development issues and the communication process.

Pathway to Development Planning

India embarked on the process of development planning in 1951 in the backdrop of call of Jawaharlal Nehru, who reminded the country of the tasks ahead which included the ending of poverty and ignorance and disease and inequality of opportunity. Let us see to what extent we have succeeded in the quest for the above goals.

Since independence, India has made significant progress in several areas of economic and human development. Food production has gone up to provide adequate levels of food security; infrastructure development has been satisfactory; a vast pool of trained human resources has been developed; a vast network of development institutions has been established and a high level of technological development in areas like Information Technology has taken place.

However, implementation of the Five Year Plans, particularly in terms of delivery of social sectors has been inadequate. About 260 million persons or about 26 per cent of population still continue to be below the normative poverty line. Population growth continues to be still high, and unsustainable; a little less than half of women still illiterate; infant mortality rates are high. As the Recent Score Card of India's governance developed in the *National Human Development Report 2001;* says : Some of the *Challenges and Concerns* in the areas of Political Governance are : Criminalisation of public life, politics of vote bank, communal violence and corruption and recourse to competitive populism. These concerns constitute formidable bottlenecks in India's progress and accomplishment of goals enshrined in the Five Year Plans.

India's Millennium Missions 2020— President Dr. APJ Abdul Kalam, as Principal Scientific Adviser to the Government of India in his Convocation Address to the Indian Institute of Management, Lucknow in March 2001 identified five areas where India had core competence for an integrated action. Dr. Kalam said : We have many challenges. Nearly 300 million people who are below the poverty line have to join in the mainstream of good life. Hundred per cent literacy, health for all, multiple industrial and agricultural productivity and lifestyle with value system has to emerge. He wants India to improve its place in the indices of world competitiveness.

Competitiveness has been defined as, 'the ability of a national economy to achieve sustained high rates of economic growth'. In that order of ranking Singapore is 1, USA 2, Hong Kong 3, UK 8, Germany 25, and India 59. The world competitiveness is defined as a combination tringle consisting of progressiveness of industry, technology push and governmental deregulation status. Dr. Kalam suggests five areas where India has core competence for an integrated action and can transform the nation to a developed country. These five areas are :

- ***Agriculture and Food Processing***—With a target of 360 million tonnes of food and agriculture production.
- ***Reliable and Quality Electric Power***— For all parts of the country.
- ***Education and Health Care***
- ***Information Technology***
- ***Strategic Sectors***—Nuclear Technology, Space Technology and Defence Technology.

Dr. Kalam feels the nation needs leaders who can command the change for transformation of India into a developed nation embedded with knowledge society in twenty years.

Kerala with education and better health-care can bring down the population growth rate and provide better quality of life to the people.

India has the potential and capability of emerging as one of the front-ranking nations of the world. What it needs is a political leadership with a vision, imbued with a sense of purpose to take the country to a place and position commensurate with the talent and genius of its people. This calls for a dispassionate discussion of policies and issues involved. These basic issues are : Development Planning, Poverty Alleviation Programmes, Literacy and Education, Health and Population Issues, Human Rights, Environmental Protection, Civil Society and Good Governance. This work looks at these issues in the contemporary perspective and establishes a linkage between communication, development and civil society.

Overview

The book has been divided into two thematic sections. The first section comprises three chapters : Development Planning in India, Development Communication— Definitions and Concepts, and the Indian Communication Landscape.

Development Planning in India discusses the process of economic and social development in the country in the context of fundamental changes ever since the policy of liberalisation was ushered in during 1991. The chapter takes a look at the planning process at a time when the policy regarding the Tenth Five Year Plan is being firmed up. The launching of the Tenth Plan; and the publication of two valuable documents by the Planning Commission—*Approach Paper to the Tenth Five Year Plan (2002-2007)* and the first-ever *National Human Development Report 2001,* in March 2002; has provided the government, the planners, administrators and the academics with an opportunity to critically look at *afresh* the shifting paradigms, changing concepts about a whole lot of issues—human development, enhancement of human well-being and quality of life, educational attainments, health attainments, demographic concerns, and governance for human development. Apart from presenting the thrust areas of the Five Year Plans in a summary form the chapter discusses Social Sector Development and the Human Development Approach, because development of social sectors has become integral part of the development strategies.

Human Development identifies three dimensions of well being :

- ***Longevity***—the ability to live long and healthy life;
- ***Education***—the ability to read, write and acquire knowledge;
- ***Command over Resources***—the ability to enjoy a decent standard of living and have a socially meaningful life.

The changing trends in the international development thinking, symbolised by the publication of Human Development Reports by the UNDP since its inception in 1990 has been adequately reflected in the message of the Tenth Plan. More and more policy makers in many countries are reaching the conclusion that to be valuable and legitimate, development progress must be people-centred, equitably distributed and environmentally and socially sustainable. The Message of the Plan is, therefore, in consonance with the above thinking when the Approach Paper says : Economic growth cannot be the only objective for national planning, and indeed over the years, development objectives are being defined not just in terms of increase in GDP or per capita income but broader in terms of enhancement of human well-being.

The chapter on Development Communication—Definitions and Concepts—apart from looking at evolution of the terms development and communication, also enlists the milestones during 1990s in the journey on road to development : setting up of national institutions in areas like women empowerment, human rights and consumer protection; policies, programmes and legislations. A major step towards decentralisation and devolution of power at the grassroots level two 73rd and 74th Constitutional Amendment Acts was passing of relating to Panchyati Raj institutions. Another important milestone in this direction was attention being paid to alternative development paradigm and its various synonyms. The paradigm and the terms associated with it became quite popular in the literature on development studies. The seven sins of Development Planners, referred to by Mahbub-ul Haq in his book *The Poverty Curtain* (1976) are as valid today as when these were formulated by the author more than twenty-five years earlier. Two aspects added in this chapter are features of development communication and importance of participation, which in spite of the lip service accorded to it, remains more a rhetoric than reality.

The chapter takes note of the conceptual broadening in the notions of human well-being and deprivation. The notion of well-being has shifted away from just material attainments, or the means for development, to outcomes that are either desirable in themselves or desirable because of their role in supporting better opportunities for people. Similarly poverty is viewed not only in terms of lack of adequate income, but as a state of deprivation spanning the economic and social context of the people. This has resulted in renewed focus on development indicators in the area of education and health attainments—critical for capacity building.

Interestingly, in his search for references for the present work, the author came across several of the forgotten but well-preserved and valuable monographs, books and articles on the subject. One of it was the UNESCO monograph No. 101 in the series—Reports and Papers on Mass Communication—*Communication Technology and Development*—a slim, but by all means a scholarly work. The monograph says : Development, both as a process, a generic notion and as a concept referring to several specific evolutionary or revolutionary phenomena, has been used since the Second World War to describe four broad types of phenomena :

1. Modernization, nationalism and political development;
2. Economic development and technological diffusion;
3. Imperialism and underdevelopment; and
4. Revolution, liberation and human development.

During the 1950s and 1960s, modernization, nationalism and political development were the dominant approaches to development and nation-building, specially among the political scientists, sociologists and social psychologists in the United States. The new paradigm, however, puts man at the centre of development with the objective of creating good conditions for all to enjoy a long, healthy, and creative life. Human development is the end-economic growth and social sector development are the means. Development of social sectors has become integral part of the recent development strategies.

The fourth chapter takes an overview of the media landscape and the contemporary trends and discusses a wide range of media, extending from Oral, Traditional forms of Communication to Mass Communication—Print Media, Electronic Media, Internet and Civil Society, and finally, changing trends in contemporary media. Interestingly even today, in spite of the vastly expanding media of mass communication, oral and interpersonal communication, both through spoken words—continue to enjoy predominant position, particularly in rural areas. There is now greater realization that because of our emphasis on material culture, we have not been responsive to the fact that evolution of mankind has also fostered great oral civilizations. The fact remains that the rich cultural heritage of our society is preserved through oral cultures of which myths, legends, tales, epic poems and ballads constitute important parts. Traditional forms of communication—folk theatre, folk tales, religious discourses—continue to be sources of entertainment and dissemination of information. The mass media has made people aware of the unexpected wealth of folk and tribal music and exposed folk artists to the cultural diversity of the country.

The chapter also discusses in detail the role and contribution of the community press in a country like India where rural population still constitutes a predominant majority. The concept of community newspaphers is not new. Small media has proved to be successful all over the world. In the Indian context many communication scholars use the terms—community press, rural press, local newspapers and small newspapers interchangeably which only goes on to show that community press essentially comprises of small newspapers serving non-metropolitan areas, small towns and villages. Several other aspects of print media, not discussed in the previous edition of the book—concentration of newspapers, ownership pattern help develop an over all picture of the print media in the country.

The recent years have witnessed exponential growth in media industry, particularly in electronic and satellite communication, internet communication and rapid advances in communication technology. The communication landscape in the country has been undergoing major changes largely due to technological developments during the last two decades. Use of computers has revolutionised the process of collection and dissemination of information. Convergence is yet another technological revolution profoundly impacting the communication scenario. Internet is being widely used by corporate houses, educational institutions, inter-governmental organisations, NGOs and voluntary bodies. The new technology, in fact, is being increasingly used for networking and reaching out to the people in distress and during emergencies. The section on changing trends in contemporary media takes note of frivolity which is fast becoming a practice with metropolitan media. A newly launched newspaper in a metropolitan town includes all news, from the state of nation to the state of *fashion*, with the later dominating its newspages; perhaps indicates the coming state of affairs—none too happy for the coverage of development issues presently confronting the country.

The second section comprises chapters on development issues : rural development, literacy and education, health and population, human rights, environmental protection and civil society and good governance.

Rural development continues to be the *sine qua non* of development planning in the country. Rural development, in the broad sense of the term, holds key to all economic progress—whether in industrial or agrarian sectors. The approach to rural development programmes has however been bureaucratic rather than participatory. Rural development plans were generally prepared at the national and state headquarters and passed on to local level offices of the government for execution. Consequently, quite often there was a mismatch between what the people wanted and what they got from the government.

Apart from looking at the rural development, poverty alleviation and welfare programmes including employment generation programmes in rural areas, the chapter establishes linkages between rural development and media. Media strategies for rural development will be essentially based on localness of approach nd dissemination of culturally appropriate and user-friendly technology. These strategies will have to be innovative, realistic and fine tuned to meet the aspirations of the people. As the well known agricultural scientist M.S. Swaminathan rightly suggests the rutal development network including the *gram sewaks* would need to be served by the mass communication media, particularly the radio, television and the language press, research and extension worker, the education system and the drive for technical literacy.

Rural Press serves as a link between policy makers, development bureaucracy and farmers and also as a second line of conversion of scientific knowledge into information for utilization in the field situation. The rural newspaper also, with its simple language and content, reinforces the reading habit. The rural newspapers, which are in contact with grassroots levels, are aware of local problems and shall be able to communication in the language and the idiom that the people understand.

Equally important, for the dissemination of information to the rural community, are the local radio stations. The thrust of Farm and Home Programmes established by the All India Radio, is on increasing production of cereals, oilseeds, pulses, vegetables, fruits as well as on the role of panchayats in rural development. Radio is still the cheapest, fastest and the farthest reaching technique for beginning a communication process. As against radio, which still retains popularity in the rural areas, television is increasingly becoming a medium for entertainment. Krishi Darshan programme on television has failed to create the desired impact on rural audience.

The communication perspective for rural development takes note of summaries of research projects in agricultural information. These case studies of communication support to agriculture were a part of research projects assigned to the trainees in the Post-graduate Diploma Course in Agricultural Journalism on media related issues. These studies clearly prove that, contrary to popular impression about marginalisation of radio, it continues to serve the village community effectively through its farm broadcasts. Studies on radio show that in an era of computer and information technology, the farmers still depend on radio for the dissemination of farm news and technologies. The course, introduced at the Haryana Agricultural University in 1996 as a Distance Education Programme for the faculty of agricultural universities and development workers of the states from all over the country, aimed at imparting insight in communication process and build up necessary skills in development communication. The course had drawn participants from Andaman and Nicobar to Tamil Nadu, Karnataka, Tripura and several other states.

A brief section on transfer of technology to rural areas expresses a note of caution because new agricultural technologies bring many ecological problems such as salinity, soil erosion, surface and ground water pollution. Development of technology in isolation from users creates more problems resulting in ecological imbalance and degradation of natural resources.

The Approach Paper to Tenth Five Year Plan says : Our performance in the field of education is one of the most disappointing aspects of our developmental strategy. Out of approximately 200 million children in the age group 6-14 years, only 120 million are in schools and net attendance in the primary level is only 66 per cent of the enrolment. This is completely unacceptable and the Tenth Plan should aim at radical transformation in this situation. *Education for All* must be one of the primary objectives of the Tenth Plan.

The observations of the Nobel Laureate Amartya Sen are equally telling : There is one field in which India has clearly done worse than *even* the average of the poorest countries in the world, and that is elementary education.... India has been left behind in the field of basic education even by countries which have not done better than India in many other developmental achievements, such as Ghana, Indonesia, Kenya, Myanmar (Burma), Philippines, Zimbabwe, and Zambia (*India : Economic Development and Social Opportunity*, 1995).

It is widely perceived that education is critical for economic and social development. It is crucial for building human capabilities and for opening opportunities. Without education development can neither be broad based nor sustained. Gray Becker in *Human Capital* (1993) says : Since human capital is embodied knowledge and skills, and economic development depends on advances in technical and scientific knowledge, development presumably depends on the accumulation of human capital. The education system should provide both a solid basis for future learning and essential skills for living a constructive life within society. In an era where technological progress is sweeping the society, literacy and education play a pivotal role in enabling it to adopt and accept technology quickly. It has been established that in India a one-year increase in the average number of years of primary schooling of the work force would raise output by 23 per cent. In Bangladesh the average salary of a secondary school educated woman was about seven times than that of a woman with no primary education.

The rapid obsolescence of knowledge requires individuals to make special efforts to stay up-date. The World Development

Report 1998-98, *Knowledge for Development* says : *Knowledge is critical for development,* because everything we do depends upon knowledge. Simply to live we must transform the resources we have into things we need, and that takes knowledge. And if we wish to live better tomorrow than today, if we want to raise our living standards as a household or as a country and preserve our common environment, we must do more than simply transform more resources in ways that generate even higher returns of our efforts and investments. That too takes knowledge, and in ever greater proportion to our resources.

New Information and Communication Technologies (NICTs), also termed as New Learning Technologies, offer valuable opportunities to expand educational infrastructure and improve the quality of instruction, and to increase the cost-effectiveness of the present education systems. The open learning system, popularly known as distance education, has brought about a virtual revolution in education. In case NICTs are suitably harnessed, not only to expand educational opportunities but also to improve quality of education even at the school level it will not be long before India attains hundred per cent educational level for its propulation of over one billion.

The chapter, Health, Population and Communication Strategies, underline the importance of the willing acceptance and participation of the people for the successful implementation of health and population programmes, enhancing reproductive facilities for women—an aspect which had been ignored for years. At a time when public sector health institutions have been found grossly incapable of meeting the requirement of the public at large, civil society organisations can make valuable contribution to this important sector of nation building. The situation in the health and population sector continues to pose serious challenges to the government and policy planners in the country, also because public spending on health has been declining for years.

The country adopted the National Population Policy 2000, which has the long term objective of achieving population reduction by 2045 at a level consistent with the requirement of sustainable economic growth, social development and environmental protection. The population welfare programmes will succeed only if movement for empowerment of women and female literacy are strengthened. It is impossible to conceive the successful implementation of a vast national programme of family welfare without the cooperation of local bodies, particularly panchayati raj institutions, voluntary and non-governmental organisations. No government can build a society, whereas voluntary action can. The voluntary bodies have more freedom to articulate their point of view, raise consciousness, motivate and mobilise people.

The chapter also stresses the urgent need of streamlining and improving the health care services at the PHCs rather than privatising the health care system.

The United Nations High Commissioner for Human Rights, Mary Robinson in a special contribution to the Human Development Report 2000—*Human rights and human development,* says : Simply stated, universality of human rights means that human rights must be the same everywhere and for everyone. By virtue of being human, every individual is entitled to inalienable rights and freedoms. These rights ensure the dignity and worth of the human person and guarantee human well-being.

Human rights and human development share a common vision and a common purpose to secure the freedom, well-being and dignity of all people everywhere. Prof. Amartya Sen, in the first chapter of the above Report charts out seven key features needed for a better approach to securing human rights. The seven features have been listed in the concluding portion of the relevant chapter.

The Preamble to the Indian Constitution, Fundamental Rights and Directive Principles, which together have been described as forming the core of the Constitution reflects the basic principles of the Universal Declaration of Human Rights. The Indian citizens have been assured of liberty of thought, expression, belief, faith and worshsip. The National Human Rights Commission was constituted with a former Chief Justice of India as its chairman after the Protection of Human Rights Act was enacted in 1993. The Commission has been urging policies in the economic and social sector that are truly responsive to the needs of the most vulnerable in the society. It is now generally accepted that there is a correlation between the Human Development Index and respect for human rights.

The Human Development Report stresses that media can mobilise public opinion by spreading awareness of human rights policies and highlighting violations. In many countries the media is already a major force for reporting and demanding accountability. Cyber networks have brought attention to rights, disseminating information on good practices and on rights violations. Educating policy makers, the army, the police and other groups about human rights is essential for creating a human rights culture.

Futureless growth —The Human Development Report, 1996 defines futureless growth as a situation where the present generation squanders resources needed by future generations. Rampant and uncontrolled economic growth in many countries is laying waste to forests, polluting rivers, destroying biodiversity and depleting natural resources. This damage and destruction is increasing, driven overwhelmingly by demand in the rich countries, inadequate conservation in the developing countries and the pressure of poor people pushed into marginal lands in poor countries.

In sum, Development that perpetuates today's inequalities is neither sustainable nor worth sustaining. That, by and large, sums up the focus of the chapter on Environmental Protection. The Overview of the Indian environmental situation signifies the same sorry state of affairs : rivers are under severe pressure because of increase in the drinking water requirement and also for irrigation purposes; and use of water in industries; quality of air in most Indian towns and cities has gone down because of increased vehicles and a large number of industries. Yamuna is the most polluted river in the country. A major source of air pollution in rural areas is caused by burning of unprocessed cooking fuels in homes—it is estimated that indoor pollution in India's rural areas is responsible for the five hundred thousand premature deaths.

Excessive exploitation of forests has decimated seriously our forest resources. Deforestation leads to the destruction of wild life habitats. It is now being increasingly realised that demography is not merely a question of numbers of people. When the carrying capacity of planet earth reaches the point of exhaustion, as is the case with countries like India, China and Indonesia, an environmental disaster is waiting to happen any moment.

The World Summit on Sustainable Development (WSSD) held at Johannesburg from 26 August–4 Septemper 2002 established a clear link between poverty, inequality and planet safety. The UN Secretary General Kofi Annan pointed out : The choice is not between environment and development, as some have framed the issue. Development that does not sensibly manage the environment will prove short-lived. One would heartily agree with the Nobel Laureate Amartya Sen when he calls for public action for environmental protection. The Judicial Activism on the part of the Indian judiciary including the Supreme Court has been a redeeming feature of the otherwise sorry state of affairs. The concluding chapter on, Civil Society and Good Governance, traces the emergence of modern concept of civil society, its potential and the contribution to the system of good governance, and the recognition it has gained for its essential role.

The new concept of civil society, which has gained greater popularity ever since the break up of the former Soviet Union in the late 1980s, implies that ordinary people have an important role in societal development. As the opening chapter in the special issue of Media Asia (29 : 1) on, *Media and Civil Society,* states : Each society today has a vast array of formal organisations that are autonomous from the state and the market. In addition there are innumerable informal, local and small and spontaneous efforts by individuals and small groups which contribute towards the larger public good. The totality of these initiatives could be labelled 'civil society'. Thus civil society is diverse, pluralistic, and heterogeneous. Another simpler definition is : non-governmental, not-for-profit, independent nature of organisations that allow for broad citizen partnership. In India, the increasing role of non-governmental organisations, voluntary bodies and other organs of civil society in advocacy and policy formulation has introduced a new element in democratic governance. In the contemporary society, policy formulation cannot be left to governments alone.

There has been deep anxiety about the poor score card regarding good governance in the country. The National Human Development

Report 2001 finds a number of concerns and challenges in the areas of Economic, Political and Civil Governance where major policy initiatives are needed. The Report admits issues like corruption, criminalisation of public life, politics of vote bank, competitive populism and the use of money-power, particularly during elections are compromising decisive political action. Other issues, equally serious are, lack of accountability and transparency.

It is hoped that the civil society as a movement and as a collective entity—NGOs, VOs and CSOs will succeed where the political leadership is reluctant to act.

REFERENCES

India 2002, (A Reference Annual), Publications Division, Ministry of Information and Broadcasting, Government of India, New Delhi.

Kunczik Michael, (1992) *Development and Communication,* Friedrich-Ebert Stiftung, Bonn.

Media Asia, (2002), *Media and Civil Society,* AMIC, Singapore.

Planning Commission, (2001) *Approach Paper to the Tenth Five Year Plan (2002-2007),* Government of India, New Delhi.

Planning Commission, (2002) *National Human Development Report 2001,* Government of India, New Delhi.

Shariff, Abusaleh (1999) *India : Human Development Report,* National Council of Applied Economic Research, New Delhi.

UNDP, (2000) *Human Development Report 2000,* Oxford University Press.

World Bank, (1998-1999) *World Development Report 1998-99, Knowledge for Development,* Oxford University Press.

World Bank, (2000) *World Development Report 1999/2000, Entering the 21st Century.* Oxford University Press.

World Bank, (2000) *World Development Report 2000-2001,* Attacking Poverty. Oxford University Press.

2

DEVELOPMENT PLANNING IN INDIA

The process of economic and social development in India has been undergoing fundamental changes ever since the policy of liberalization was ushered in during 1991. It is now being realised that economic growth alone cannot be the only objective for national planning. Over the years development objectives are being defined not just in terms of increases in GDP or per capita income but in broader terms of enhancement of human well-being. This includes not only an adequate level of consumption of food and other types of consumer goods but also access to basic social services specially education, health and availability of drinking water and sanitation.

At a time when the Tenth Five Year Plan (2002-2007) has been firmed up and the target is to make India one of the ten fastest growing developing countries in the world, there is also a deepening concern that the country has not done too well in several areas. The Approach Paper to the Tenth Plan points : More than half of the children 1-5 years old in rural areas are under-nourished, with girl children suffering even more severe malnutrition, as many as 60 per cent of the rural households and about 20 per cent of urban households do not have a power connection. Land and forest degradation in the rural areas, and over-exploitation of ground water is seriously threatening sustainability of food production.

The Approach Paper, released by the Planning Commission in September 2001, outlines the direction that the Indian economy is likely to take during the first few years of the new millennium. It lays down future guidelines, which are broadly indicative for the country to adopt on road to development, and also makes a frank appraisal of the deficiencies and weaknesses in the system of governance, which works as a roadblock in country's progress towards higher levels of economic growth.

The Approach Paper is a forward looking document which not

only articulates the hopes and aspirations of the people but also takes into account the concerns and difficulties faced by them in their quest for living with dignity in the present and hope for the future.

It also discusses the role of the government in the sphere of economic and social development and says: It is now generally recognized that the government in the past tended to take on too many responsibilities, imposing severe strains on its limited financial and administrative capabilities and also stifling individual initiative. An all-pervasive government role may have appeared necessary at a stage where private sector capabilities were underdeveloped, but the situation has changed dramatically in this respect. This is not to say that the government has no role to play or only a minimalist role, in promoting development. On the contrary, government has a very important role but a different one from one that was envisaged in the past. There are many areas, e.g. social sectors—where its role will clearly have to increase. There are other areas, e.g. infrastructure development, where gaps are large and private sector cannot be expected to step in significantly. In these areas the role of the government may have to be restructured. Redefining the role of the government to reflect the changed circumstances facing the economy must be an important aspect of future strategy.

Social sector development has been the *raison d'etre* of planning in India. The Directive Principles of the State Policy, enshrined in the Constitution, form the social premises of planning in the country. The founder Chairman of the Planning Commission, set up in 1950, was Jawaharlal Nehru, who had identified the major task before the nation as of, 'the ending of poverty and ignorance and disease and inequality of opportunity.' It was towards this end that the objectives of the planning process were largely addressed.

The First Plan (1951-56) laid emphasis on agriculture, irrigation, power and transport so as to provide an infrastructure for rapid industrial expansion in future. The Second Plan (1956-61) was a big leap forward. It laid special emphasis on industrialization, increased production of iron and steel, heavy chemicals including nitrogenous fertilizers and development of heavy engineering and machine-building industry. The Third Plan (1961-66) aimed at securing a marked advance towards self-sustaining growth. Its immediate objectives were to secure an increase in the national income of over five per cent per annum, achieve self-sufficiency in food grains and increased agricultural production to meet the requirements of industry and exports; expand basic industries like steel, chemicals, fuel and power; utilize fully the manpower resources of the country and ensure substantial expansion in employment opportunities; establish progressively greater equality of opportunity and bring about reduction in disparities of income and wealth and a more even distribution of economic power.

The situation created by the Indo-Pakistan conflict in 1965, two successive years of severe drought, devaluation of the currency, general rise in prices and erosion of resources available for Plan purposes delayed the finalization of the Fourth Five Year Plan. Instead, between 1966 and 1969, three Annual Plans were formulated within the framework of the draft outline of the Fourth Plan.

The Fourth Plan (1969-74) aimed at accelerating the tempo of development and reducing fluctuations in agricultural production as well as the impact of uncertainties of foreign aid. It sought to raise the standard of living through programmes designed to promote equality and social justice. The Plan laid particular emphasis on improving the condition of the less privileged and weaker sections especially through provision of employment and education. The major objectives of the Fifth Plan (1974-79) were to achieve self-reliance and adopt measures for raising consumption standards of people living below the poverty line. This Plan also gave high priority to bringing inflation under control and to achieving stability in economic situation.

Removal of poverty was the foremost objective of the Sixth Plan (1980-85). The strategy adopted was to move simultaneously towards strengthening infrastructure for both agriculture and industry. Stress was laid on tackling inter-related problems through a systematic approach with greater management, efficiency and intensive monitoring in all sectors and active involvement of people in formulating specific schemes of development at the local level and securing their speedy and effective implementation.

The Seventh Plan (1985-90) emphasized policies and programmes, which aimed at rapid growth in food grains production, increased employment opportunities and productivity within the framework of basic tenets of planning: growth, modernization, self-reliance and social justice. To reduce unemployment and consequently, the incidence of poverty, special programmes like *Jawahar Rozgar Yojna* were launched in addition to the existing programmes. Due recognition was accorded to the role small scale and food processing industries can play in this regard.

Human Development as Focus for Planning— In keeping with the process of economic reforms and restructuring of the economy, the Eighth Plan (1992-97) recognized the need for a re-orientation of planning. The Eighth Plan emphasized (a) human development as the main focus of planning; (b) a large economic space for private sector; (c) physical and social infrastructure development by public sector (allowing at the same time the private sector to participate) and (d) a greater role to the market to infuse economic efficiency even in the working of public sector.

The Ninth Five Year Plan (1997-2002) was launched in the fiftieth year of India's Independence. The specific objectives of the Ninth Plan were: (i) priority to agriculture and rural development with a view to generating adequate productive employment and eradication of poverty; (ii) accelerating the growth rate of economy with stable prices; (iii) ensuring food and nutritional security for the vulnerable sections of society; (iv) providing basic minimum services of safe drinking water, primary health care facilities, universal primary education, shelter, and connectivity to all in a time-bound manner; (v) containing the growth rate of population; (vi) ensuring environmental sustainability of development process through social mobilization and participation of people at all levels; (vii) empowerment of women and socially disadvantaged groups as agents of socio-economic change and development; (viii) promoting and developing Panchayati Raj Institutions (PRIs), cooperatives and self-help groups; and (ix) strengthening efforts to build self-reliance.

Tenth Five Year Plan Launched— India embarked on its Tenth Five-Year Plan from 1 April 2002. The aim is to set a higher growth rate of the economy at 8 per cent per annum during the period 2002-07. Development planning of over fifty years has raised economic status of the country. India is now almost self-sufficient in food, has a strong and diversified industrial base, and possesses world's largest pool of skilled manpower. It has accomplishments to its credit in the fields of space, nuclear and missile technology as well as information technology. Encouraging progress has also been made in other dimensions. The percentage of the population in poverty has continued to decline. Population growth has decelerated below 2 per cent for the first time in four decades. Literacy has increased from 52 per cent in 1991 to 65 per cent in 2001 and the improvement is evident in all States. Sectors such as software, entertainment and IT enabled services to have emerged as new sources of strength creating confidence about India's potential to be competitive in the world economy.

Social Sector Development —The term social sector is often used to refer to education, health and nutrition sectors. According to K. Seeta Prabhu, Head, Human Development Resource Centre at the UNDP, India Country Office, the term has not been formally defined and thus has come to acquire several connotations. One of the definitions of social sector is related to human development as against human resource development. The UNDP defines Human Development Approach as the process of enlarging people's choices. The concept encompasses empowerment, co-operation, equity in basic capabilities and opportunities, sustainability and security. In this approach people occupy centre stage, and measures such as education, health and nutrition are emphasized for their intrinsic value and their role in enhancing the basic capabilities of people. The emergence of the concept of human development can be traced to efforts by economists such as Amartya Sen who defines standard of living in terms of functioning and capabilities rather than in terms of commodity possessions. This approach emphasizes acquisition of education, health and nutrition, which is considered as an essential human right. However, in the Approach Paper the social infrastructure segment includes education, health and nutrition in addition to rural water supply. The document rationalizes the premise of social development by including rural water supply under the social infrastructure as drinking water problem is a governance issue and has a bearing on the quality of life, that large majority of people in the rural areas experience every-day.

In terms of human development objectives, education is an end in itself, not just a means to an end. Education, which is basic human right, is critical for economic and social development. It is crucial for building human capabilities and for opening opportunities. Without education, development can be neither broad based nor sustained.

Amartya Sen and Jean Dreze in one of their books— *India Economic Development and Social Opportunity*, point out that education and health can be seen to be valuable to the freedom of a person in at least five distinct ways :

1. ***Intrinsic importance***—Being educated and healthy are valuable achievements in themselves, and the opportunity to have them can be of direct importance to a person's effective freedom.
2. ***Instrumental personal roles***—A person's education and health can help him or her to do many things—other than just being educated and healthy—that are also valuable. They can, for instance, be important for getting a job and more generally for making use of economic opportunities.
3. ***Instrumental social roles***—Greater literacy and basic education can facilitate public discussion of social needs and encourage informed collective demands. These in turn can help expand the facilities that the public enjoys, and contribute to the better utilization of the available services.
4. ***Instrumental process roles***—The process of schooling can have benefits even aside from its explicitly aimed objectives, namely formal education. For example, the incidence of child labour is intimately connected with non-schooling of children, and the expansion of schooling can reduce the distressing phenomenon of child labour so

prevalent in India. Schooling also brings young people in touch with others and thereby broadens their horizons.

5. ***Empowerment and distributive roles***—Greater literacy and educational achievements of disadvantaged groups can increase their ability to resist oppression, to organize politically, and to get a fairer deal.

Despite concerted efforts India continues to record high levels of morbidity, especially among infants, children, the elderly and women. The burden of short duration and major morbidity fall on the vulnerable section of the population, including wage labourers, minorities and the low-income groups. In his Convocation Address at the All India Institute of Medical Sciences in July 1998, the Prime Minister Atal Bihari Vajpayee said that our record in health care was far from edifying. He called for radical reform in both health care and medical education systems to ensure that the advances in medicine and the vast infrastructure for health care created over the past five decades were made accessible to the masses at affordable cost.

In this context, the Approach Paper says: Improvement in the health status of the population has been one of the major thrust areas in social development programmes of the country. This was to be achieved through improving access to the utilization of Health, Family Welfare and Nutrition Services with special focus on under-served and underprivileged segments of population. There will have to be a continued commitment to provide essential primary health care, emergency life saving services, services under the National Diseases Control programmes and the National Family Welfare programme free of cost to individuals based on their needs and not on their ability to pay. At the same time, suitable strategies will have to be evolved, tested and implemented for levying and collecting user charges from people above poverty line and utilizing funds obtained for improving the quality of health care services.

The Tenth Plan stresses the reorganisation and restructuring of existing health care infrastructure, at primary, secondary and tertiary levels, so that they have the responsibility of serving population residing in a well defined geographical area and have appropriate referral linkages with each other. At the same time it is essential that there is appropriate delegation of powers to PRIs so that there is local accountability of the public health care providers. The problems relating to poor performance need to be sorted out locally.

The major nutrition-related public health problems currently are chronic energy deficiency, micronutrient deficiencies, such as anemia due to iron and folic acid deficiency, Vitamin A deficiency, Iodine deficiency disorders and associated health hazards. Nutritional problems need to be tackled across a broad front. There need to be a continued increase in food grain production to meet the needs of the growing population. This increase should be more in the case of coarse grain production to meet the energy requirements of BPL families at lower cost. Efforts have to be made to check the sluggish trend in per capita availability of pulses and increase pulse production, improve affordability of pulses and increase consumption. Similarly, increased availability of vegetables at affordable cost throughout the year in urban and rural areas is desirable to address nutritional needs of the population.

Message of the Plan

That there has been a paradigm shift in attempting to tackle problems of social sector development is clear from the following enunciation relating to objectives of the Tenth Plan:

> Economic growth cannot be the only objective for national planning and indeed over the years, development objectives are being defined not just in terms of increases in GDP or per capita income but broader in terms of enhancement of human well-being. This includes not only an adequate level of consumption of food and other types of consumer goods but also access to basic social services especially education, health, availability of drinking water and basic sanitation. It also includes expansion of economic and social opportunities for all individuals and groups, reduction in disparities, and greater participation in decision-making. The Tenth Plan must set

suitable targets in these areas to ensure significant progress towards improvement in the quality of life of all our people.

Even after fifty-five years of independence, development issues—alleviation of poverty, eradication of illiteracy and ignorance, health and population—continue to be major areas of national concern. Today development does not mean merely economic growth. Therefore, development objectives are being redefined not just in terms of increase in gross domestic product or per capita income but in broader terms of enhancement of human well-being and quality of life. The new paradigm of development puts man at the centre of development planning with the objective of creating good conditions for all to enjoy a long, healthy and creative life.

Human development is the end—economic growth and social sector development are the means. Higher economic growth is for producing more goods and services and for generating employment, and for reducing poverty, while social development is essential for the well-being or improving the quality of life. Development of social sectors has become integral part of the recent development strategies. More investment in social sectors such as health, education and nutrition sustains economic growth. However, social sector development also cannot be sustained in the absence of economic growth.

National Human Development Report 2001

The publication of the National Human Development Report 2001 by the Planning Commission in March 2002 would, by all means, be considered a landmark step towards giving new direction to the process of development during the Tenth Five Year Plan. The report focuses on the issues of governance for human development. The Deputy Chairman, Planning Commission, Mr. K.C. Pant rightly points out in the Foreword to the Report: Human Development has to reflect and address the social concerns and processes that underline the various outcomes. It has also to recognize the local constraints and aspirations of the people. The Foreword also points out that process of development should be assessed in terms of what it does for an average individual and adds: The process of development has to be seen in terms of the benefits and opportunities that it generates for people and how these are eventually distributed—between men and women, the well-off and deprived and across regions. Experience shows that, often, there is no direct correspondence between economic attainments of a society and the quality of life.

Economic Attainments and Quality of Life

It becomes necessary, therefore, to have a framework and evolve development strategies that forge and strengthen the link between the two, and encourage the most effective and efficient use of available resources for furthering the well-being of the people.

Human development identifies the three dimensions of well-being:—

1. ***Longevity***— the ability to live long and healthy life;
2. ***Education***—the ability to read, write and acquire knowledge; and
3. ***Command over resources***— the ability to enjoy a decent standard of living and have a socially meaningful life.

It is, therefore, axiomatic as the report states that the choice to live a healthy life, free from illness and ailments, and of a reasonable life span are critical attributes in the notion of personal well-being. Longevity and a life free of morbidity is, thus, a valued end in itself and moreover, it is crucial for other valued human attainments. Similarly, apart from its intrinsic value, education in the present day context, is perhaps among the most important means for individuals to improve personal endowments, build capability levels, overcome constraints and in the process enlarge their available set of opportunities and choices for a sustained improvements in well-being. It is a critical means to empowerment and to bring about a social, economic and political inclusion of the marginalised segments in the mainstream of society.

Human development is the process of enlarging people's

choices, by expanding human functionings and capabilities. Human development thus also reflects human outcomes in these functionings and capabilities. It represents a process as well as an end.

Capabilities Essential for People—At all levels of development the three essential capabilities are for people to lead a long and healthy life, to be knowledgeable and to have access to the resources needed for a decent standard of living. But the realm of human development extends further: other areas of choice highly valued by people include participation, security, sustainability, guaranteed human rights— all needed for being creative and productive and for enjoying self-respect, empowerment and a sense of belonging to a community. In the ultimate analysis, human development is development of the people, for the people and by the people.

The concept of human development is closely related to sustainable development. The World Development Report 1999-2000, *Entering the 21st Century* says: Sustainable development has many objectives. Raising per capita incomes is only one among many such objectives. Improving quality of life involves more specific goals: better health services and educational opportunities, greater participation in public life, a clean environment, intergenerational equity and more. Outcomes of policies based on consensual, participatory and transparent processes, are more easily sustained. Institutions of good governance that employ such processes are critical for development and should encompass partnership among all elements of civil society.

The National Human Development Report 2001 discusses in detail Economic Attainments and Well-being, Health Attainments and Demographic concerns including mortality and health indicators and several other aspects including well-being of elderly, children, crime and violence against women. The chapter on governance for Human Development gives a valuable score card on India's governance comprising achievements, concerns and challenges.

The Report, which is an attempt to map the state of human development, reiterates the three critical dimensions of well-being, stated earlier in the chapter. It is, however, felt that with more than five decades gone after independence and more than a decade spent for experiments with liberalization, such a report should have emerged earlier. At least three state governments—Madhya Pradesh, Sikkim and Rajasthan have already brought out their state development reports. The Report, which is comprehensive and detailed, brings out the attainments of states also. Kerala's achievement appears to be impressive, with the lowest rural urban disparities in the country. Kerala is followed by Himachal Pradesh. Haryana which has one of the worst juvenile as well as adult sex ratios, shows a balanced development with significant gaps in rural and urban attainments. Punjab shows balanced development on most indicators except in the case of the infant mortality.

REFERENCES

Approach Paper to the Tenth Five Year Plan (2002-2007), Planning Commission, Government of India, New Delhi (September, 2001).

Draze, Jean and Sen, Amartya (1995), *India: Economic Development and Social Opportunity,* Oxford University Press.

India 2002, Publications Division, Ministry of Information & Broadcasting, Government of India (2002).

National Human Development Report 2001, Planning Commission, Govt. of India, New Delhi.

Prabhu, K. Seeta (2001) *Economic Reform and Social Sector Development,* Sage Publications, New Delhi.

3

DEVELOPMENT COMMUNICATION
Definitions and Concepts

The evolution of the term 'development' has had a fascinating history about itself. It has been open to large number of definitions, connotations and interpretations. The term has engaged and invited a multidisciplinary approach because of the vastness of the canvas it encompasses within its ambit.

In its broadest sense, 'development' tends to be an umbrella under which several phenomena—varying from human and spiritual development to economic and community development, as well as technological development have become related. Defining 'development' is not an easy task. It has been interpreted in various ways by sociologists, economists and development planners. They defined the term according to their own frame of reference. Modernisation, social change and enhancing quality of life are often used in one way or the other in explaining the term. In all cases development suggests some amount of improvement, self-reliance, uplift and progress as also awareness and self-awareness to some extent.

Development has become the global 'civil religion' during the past more than 40 years—a battle cry for all nations rich or poor, strong or weak. It is a long and complex evolutionary process—more a process of social change rather than merely generation and accumulation of material resources.

Our understanding and perceptions about the process of development have undergone radical changes during the last 40 years. The earlier thinking about development during the sixties was dominated by Rostow's theory of economic growth. Researchers looked upon development as economic growth in stages without emphasizing the need for structural changes in society, and without indicating which sectors of the population in a developing country should receive the attention of planners and policy makers. The theory of economic growth, propounded by W.W. Rostow pointed out the following stages of economic growth :

1. the traditional and stagnant low per capita stage;
2. the transitional stage in which pre-conditions for growth are laid down;
3. the "take-off" stage marking the beginning of the process of economic growth; and
4. the industrialized, mass production and consumption stage, which makes for self-sustaining growth.

This approach emphasised capital accumulation, growth of labour force and the technological progress as the principal components of economic growth. It was assumed that economic growth in per capita Gross National Product would spread the benefits throughout the economy and eventually reach all groups. The theory failed to explain economic backwardness of many countries, particularly those who inherited it as a part of colonial legacy and it was not sufficiently sensitive to poverty. Rostow assumed that people in developing countries would respond rationally to economic incentives. The theory also assumed that once leading sectors of industry were advanced, their advantages would trickle down to the other sectors of economy.

The dominant thinking about development during this period was that, capital intensive technology imported from advanced countries, would lead to economic growth, industrialization and increase in per capita income—which by itself would lead to improvement in the living standards of the population. This paradigm of development was influenced by the western model—emphasis on industrialization—hydroelectric dams, huge steel mills and manufacturing industries. The development was essentially capital and technology intensive with agriculture receiving low priority. The planning for economic growth—which was synonym with development—was devised and executed by central government. Development was quantified only in terms of aggregate or per capita basis. The thinking was encapsulated in terms of "growth-first-and-let-equality come later", and trickle down theories.

The opening years of the seventies saw a number of studies, new methods of analysis and new concepts which helped enhance understanding of development process, development policies and policies of development assistance. The causes which led to under-development of economies in the Third World countries were redefined. The western models of development assumed that main causes of underdevelopment lay within the underdeveloped nation rather than any external factors responsible for it. Some of these were : traditional peasantry unresponsive to technological changes, fatalistic character of the population, land tenure system, etc.

In an illuminating essay on, World Bank's Concept of Development, J.H. Adler records the evolution of World Bank's notion on the process of economic development—how the concept of development process, has continuously changed, with new radical departures forcing revisions and modifications of some parts of what appeared to be firmly established doctrine. The period 1962-68 was that of Revision of Convictions during which agriculture and industry were identified as sectors deserving more attention; the announcement in 1963 that the Bank would be willing to finance educational projects constituted indeed a "new departure". According to Adler : The change resulted from the—obviously belated—recognition that under some conditions acceleration of the growth rate required not only an increased supply of capital, but also of other factors, especially skills. The Bank's willingness to provide financial support for education also reflected the previously mentioned view that development was inevitably slow; investment in education was accepted as yielding net returns with a high present value even if its full benefits could be expected only after a long gestation period.

The early and mid-1960s saw a change in World Bank's view and recognition of the complexity of development process. The period from 1968 onwards saw sharpness of break with earlier attitudes. Development was taken as a process of social change. It was being increasingly recognised that chances of attaining an orderly process of development were closely related to the effectiveness of measures *to distribute the gains of development equitably*; or atleast reasonably equitably among income groups, regions and sectors. This implies, for instance that in the formulation of a strategy for agricultural development the makers of development policy and providers of development finance must pay attention to the small and subsistence farmer and his participation in the development process.

One of the important conclusions regarding evolution of the World Bank's view on the process of economic development during some twenty years is : There is no short-cut to development—neither via industrialization, nor via import substitution, infrastructure investment, or education. On the contrary, the only firm conclusion that emerges from twenty years of observation, analysis and action is that the path to development is far longer and much more arduous than it appeared to be when the conscious drive towards development, and development aid, began some twenty years ago.

Today the World Bank takes into consideration not only social change, but also includes cultural, ethical and spiritual issues to understand more intimately the development process. Unthinkable a few years ago, leading religious leaders from around the globe reached a landmark accord with the World Bank in 1998 to put moral and social values back into the financial grants balance sheets. So far the World Bank had ignored the importance of such values in development projects because it had focused primarily on economic parameters.

Entering the 21st Century, World Development Report 1999-2000, takes note of new directions in development thinking, outlook for comprehensive development and the shifting landscape at the dawn of the 21st century. The Report agrees that with nearly 1.5 billion people living on less than $ 1 a day and more than 2 billion on less than $ 2 a day, the task is indeed daunting.

After over 50 years of seeking to reduce poverty and disease and educate the poor, the World Bank admitted that many of its past policies were misguided and it needed help to succeed in the future.

The Report painted a bleak picture of a developing world which has fallen even further behind rich nations despite the efforts by the World Bank and others to make the world a better place to live.

It also said that in many ways the Bank had failed in its mission to improve conditions of poverty, disease and poor education in the developing world. Simple solutions—investments in physical and human capital, for instance, and unfettered markets—will not work in isolation, the report said, admitting its past focus had been misguided. Governments, the private sector, civil society and donor organisations need to work together in support of broad based development.

The conceptual framework for development of the past 50 years ... tended to focus too heavily on the search for a single key to development, the report noted. When a particular key failed to open the door to development in all times and places, it was set aside in search for a new one. Projects like building dams—something the World Bank was prolific in, during the 1950s and 1960s—can carry hidden costs and harm communities through population dislocation and other cultural and environmental problems. The Report says : Trickle-down economics—the practice of cutting taxes for the rich hoping it would benefit the poorer in society—does not work.

But whatever policies were used over the past 50 years, one thing is certain : poverty continues to rise. Today 1.5 billion people live on an income of less than $ 1 a day, up from 1.2 billion people in 1987. The report forecast the number living at that lowest of incomes would reach 1.9 billion by 2015. The gap between the rich and the poor has also widened.

The delegates of the developing nations at the United Nations Conference on Human Environment at Stockholm in 1972 attempted to look at the problems of underdevelopment with a fresh perspective.

The work of two leading economists, E.F. Schumacher, who initiated a new philosophy of development with his book *Small is Beautiful*, and Andre Gunder Frank, who considered capitalism as the main cause of exploitation and inequality caused considerable rethinking about development.

The eminent communication scholar, Everett M. Rogers, has documented this process of rethinking about development in his book *Communication and Development—Critical Perspectives* (1976), as under :

> We summarize these newer conceptions of development by defining development as a widely participatory process of social change in a society, intended to bring about both social and material advancement (including greater equality, freedom, and other valued qualities) for the majority of the people through their gaining greater control over their environment (Rogers, 1975).

Thus, the concept of development has been expanded and made much more flexible, and at the same time more humanitarian, in its implications.

Rogers, at the same time, takes note of change in thinking as to the definition of development in the previous seven years. According to the earlier definition: Development is a type of social change in which new ideas are introduced into a social system in order to produce higher per capita incomes and levels of living through more modern production methods and improved social organization (Rogers with Svenning, 1969). Rogers's approach to development articulated human concerns, as against economic concerns, and the emphasis shifted from GNP to distribution of fruits of development to all segments of society. The approach was participatory which underlined the importance of values such as equality and freedom. The approach was basically communication approach as compared with Rostow's authoritarian model of capitalism and industrialization.

Nothing highlights the rethinking on development as forcefully as the regret expressed by Professor Tinbergen, who propounded GNP as measure of progress. Tinbergen says : The use of GNP is steering the society with a wrong compass. GNP gives, imperfectly and somewhat deceptively, a measure of the aggregate value of national goods and services. It conceals the distribution of wealth and gives a deceptive picture of social health. Since the computation of GNP is not accompanied by a computation of Gross Destruction of Basic Resources (GDBR)—soil degradation, pollution of water and the atmosphere, depletion of mineral resources, the entry of toxic wastes in the food chain, and so on—it is a faulty indicator of economic health. Similarly, balance of payments, in an export-led-growth system gives a highly distorted picture of the internal purchasing power of national currencies.

Economic growth can no longer be defined as merely raising the GNP and per capita income. A major share of benefits of economic development is appropriated by the upper sections of the society, leaving the masses where they were or even worse off. In developing countries, thus, theories of development have produced greater benefits for the more advanced sectors of the community than for the marginal sectors resulting in the widening of gap between the rich and the poor. It was, therefore, felt that in case the benefits of development were to be equitably distributed, the focus has to be on people and societies and the Third World countries have to evolve their own pathways to development.

The 1990s have seen the setting up of quite a few progressive institutions, formulation of several useful social policies and the passing of a few progressive bills. Some of these institutions, policies and programmes and legislations/judgemnts are :–

Institutions

1. National Commission on Women in 1992 under the NCW Act, 1990.
2. National Human Rights Commission set up in 1994, under the Protection of Human Rights Act, 1993.
3. Consumer Protection Courts.

Policies

1. Draft National Policy on Women formulated in 1996.
2. National Plan of Action for children (1992) and the National Plan of Action for the Girl Child (1991-2000).
3. Ratification of the Convention on the Elimination of All Forms of Discrimination Against Women in 1993.

Programmes

1. Mahila Samriddhi Yojana (MSY) launched in 1993.
2. Joint Forest Management (JFM) of the Ministry of Environment and Forests.

Legislations/Judgements

1. SC/ST Prevention of the Atrocities Act of 1990.
2. 73rd and 74th Constitutional Amendment Acts of 1993.
3. The National Environment Tribunal Act, 1995.
4. The Workmen's Compensation (Amendment) Act, 1995 which substantially increases the rates of compensation for occupation injuries.

Man at the Centre of Development

The World Development Reports, which the World Bank brings out every year, particularly the two reports *Knowledge for Development*, 1998-99 and *Entering the 21st Century*, 1999-2000; the Human Development Reports by the UNDP since its launch in 1990 and the reports of a number of international agencies such as UNESCO—*Learning : The Treasure Within*, and a number of international conferences such as—UN Conference on Environment and Development in Rio in 1992, the International Conference on Population and Development in Cairo in 1994, and the World Summit for Social Development in Copenhagen in 1995 consider that people are the most valuable resources and the real wealth of a nation. The new paradigm puts man at the centre of development with the objective of creating good conditions for all to enjoy a long, healthy, and creative life. Human development is the end-economic growth and social sector development are the means. Higher economic growth is for producing more goods and services and for generating employment, and for reducing poverty, while social development is essential for the well-being or improving the quality of life. Development of social sectors has become integral part of the recent development strategies. More investment in social sectors such as health, education and nutrition sustains economic growth, however, social sector development also cannot be sustained in the absence of economic growth.

The failure of the dominant paradigm led to re-thinking about alternative strategies. The opening up of China, and her record of performance also had its impact on these strategies. One of the pioneering efforts in this direction is *The Poverty Curtain* (1976) of Mahbub-ul Haq. Haq, who passed away recently, would be remembered as Founder and Chief Architect of UNDP's Annual Human Development Reports (1989-95). In order that development efforts spread to vast majority of population, Haq favoured drastic restructuring of political and economic power relationship. Haq suggested : Growth in GNP often does not filter down, what is needed is a direct attack on poverty; the market mechanism is often distorted by the existing distribution of income and wealth, and is generally an unreliable guide to setting national objectives; new development strategies must be based on the satisfaction of basic human needs rather than on market demand; and development styles should be such as to build development around people rather than people around development.

Some of the observations made by Haq in the above book, published more than twenty-five years back, are valid even today. Writing about the Seven Sins of Development Planners, he says :

> Development planners are quite fond of making a distinction between planning and implementation. When hard pressed, they generally argue that while development planning is their responsibility, its implementation is the responsibility of the entire political and economic system. This is no more than a convenient alibi. A good development plan often comes with a realistic blueprint for its own implementation. It must contain specific recommendations on all the detailed policies, institutional reforms, administrative framework and well conceived projects which are necessary for its successful implementation. It should also be based on realistic political assumptions. The planners should keep evaluating the plan constantly during the course of its implementation so that timely corrections can be made in its direction. (p. 21)

Another Development

Today considerations such as human aspects of development, linked to the improvement in quality of life and equitable distribution of national income are imperative. Several significant initiatives, in transversing this distance from the concept of economic growth to human aspects of development emphasising participatory approach and fulfilment of basic needs of people are briefly recapitulated here.

The Dag Hammarskjold Foundation, Uppsala in its report : *What Now? Another Development (1975)* summarizes the basic new directions : Development of every man and woman—of the whole man and woman—and not just the growth of things, which are merely means. Development geared to the satisfaction of needs beginning with the basic needs of the poor who constitute the world's majority; at the same time, development to ensure the humanization of man by the satisfaction of his needs for expression, creativity, conviviality and for deciding his own destiny.....Another development requires transformation of socio-economic and political structures that have long been identified. They include such fundamental steps as agrarian reforms, urban reforms, reforms of the commercial and financial circuits, redistribution of wealth and means of production as well as the redesigning of political institutions through, *inter alia*, decentralization with a view to ensuring democratization of the political and economic decision making power, promoting self-management and curbing the grip of bureaucracies. As history shows, few of these transformations can be achieved without changing the power structure itself.

During the 1990s alternative development paradigm has been receiving greater attention and importance. There may be several reasons for this. The world of alternative development is not a 'literary world'. The alternative development philosophy is that as development is people-centred, genuine development knowledge is also people's knowledge and what counts is local rather than abstract expert knowledge. Alternative development paradigm has several synonyms—appropriate development, participatory development, people-centred development, human-scale development, people's self-development, autonomous development, holistic development. Certain popular terms associated with alternative development are : grassroots movements, NGOs, empowerment, democratization, citizenship, human rights, development ethics. However the paradigm of alternative development, which has become quite popular has been criticised on account of being diffused, which lacks a clear cut theoretical base.

The Sarvodaya Movement in Sri Lanka since its inception in 1958 has aimed at securing the common man's participation to the maximum possible level in the developmental exercise. The movement is dedicated to the resurgence of human values.

One of the remarkable aspects in the Sarvodaya Rural Development strategy is the 'discovery of an intelligible language to open up the *development dialogue* with the people'. It has been the experience of the workers of Sarvodaya Movement that the planning aspect in this strategy is the discovery of an intelligible language to open up the development dialogue with the people. The planners who came from outside, whether with the seal of authority and power of the Central Government in their hands or other accredited representatives from International and National Organisations never understood what the rural people meant by the term 'development'. The planners had their own definitions which the common villager did not understand. This language of the rustic villagers, on the other hand, was not understood by the planners and administrators.

In the words of Ariyaratne 'a serious attempt to discover an intelligible language common to both was never made'.* The Sarvodaya Movement took note of the increasing disparity between the understanding of common people as to what development was about and the expectations of the privileged in society pertaining to development. In case of the common man development as related to him is directly concerned with the satisfaction of his basic human needs.

* Dr. A.T. Ariyaratne, the well known social thinker and founder President of Sarvodaya Shramadana Movement of Sri Lanka was presented the Gandhi Peace Prize-1996 by the President Dr. Shankar Dayal Sharma on 1 January, 1997.

Since people have lost faith in the highly advertised big government plans coming down from bureaucrats, they are getting attracted to the movement, knowing very well that it is a non-governmental voluntary effort. Some of the Sarvodaya principles which are considered to be important for a national development effort and which encourage common man's approach to development are :

1. While the fundamental human rights of every individual should be ensured without exception in the eyes of the law, the principal aim of any development effort should be to fulfil without delay the social, economic, cultural and spiritual aspirations of that segment of the society which stands lowest in it.
2. National development plans in the village should be drawn up, implemented and evaluated with the fullest participation of the people of the village.
3. National development should have its beginning within the village itself. All development plans should be made with the village taken as the unit. Development in respect of constituencies and the districts should be undertaken by the coordination of those village units. We call this 'development from the village upwards'.
4. The primary goal of local production activities should be to utilize the human and material resources available in the village, to meet the needs of the village people themselves.
5. Use should be made of appropriate village technologies and organizational structures which the villagers themselves can control.

Sustainable Improvement in Quality of Life

The disquiet with the concept of development led to several major efforts; one such effort was the report of the Brundtland Commission, *Our Common Future*. The report made it obvious that the contents of economic growth would have to change and even the consumption of material goods should be according to the scale of sustainability. The concept of sustainability has emerged from our awareness of the disastrous consequences of avaricious and unchecked exploitation of nature and our acknowledgement that its resources are limited. It is the basis of the survival of the environment, of society and that of the individual.

Development Tasks

Today development is invariably linked with other related issues—poverty, environment, literacy, population pressures and human rights. The issues related to development require interdisciplinary knowledge and inter-sectoral understanding of problems as well as integrated plans for action. As Nobel leaureate Amartya Sen points out: Equally important is to link the strategies of development to some thing more fundamental, in particular the ends of economic and social development. Why do we seek development? What can it achieve, if fruitful? How are the successes and failures of policies including the reforms of traditional policies to be judged?

On the first Independence Day Jawaharlal Nehru had laid down broadly the parameters within which development had to be pursued—the ending of poverty and ignorance and disease and inequality of opportunity. In this context, Sen says : Economic growth is important but it is valuable precisely because it helps to eradicate deprivation and to improve capabilities and the quality of life of ordinary people. We must not make the mistake—common in some circles—of taking the growth rate of GNP to be the ultimate test of success, and of treating the removal of illiteracy, ill health and social deprivation, as—at best—possible means to that hallowed end. The first and the most important aspect of Nehru's listing of what we have to do is to make clear that the elimination of illiteracy, ill health, and other avoidable deprivations are valuable for their own sake—they are the tasks that we face. The more conventional criteria of economic success (such as a high growth rate, a sound balance of payments, and so forth) are to be valued only as means to deeper ends. It would, therefore, be a mistake to see the development of education, health care, and other basic achievements only or primary as expansions of human resources—the accumulation of human capital—as if people were just the means of production and not its ultimate end. The bettering of human life does not have to be justified by showing that a person with a better life is also a better producer.

The theories and perspectives of development from economic growth to equitable distribution of benefits of development to sustainable development and enhancement of quality of life and development as a part of human rights philosophy has been a most rewarding and exhilarating study of contemporary society. We shall continue to study various aspects of development in the context of specific subjects. Equally important would be to spell out role of communication in development and some of the important aspects of Development Communication.

The definition of development given by the North-South Commission has been broader than merely alleviation of poverty. Development means more human dignity, safety, justice and equality. The elimination of existing strong inequalities within society is central to successful processes. Equality is the value which is of decisive importance to successful modernisation which also means democratisation leading to breaking up of old social structures based on inherited positions.

Depending on national priorities the goals of development would naturally be different for different countries—one child family in China, creating computer culture in Singapore, ORT, clean drinking water and rural roads in India. Development in any particular country comprises those programmes and projects which receive top priority in the planning process of that country.

The new paradigm of development does not envisage the role of communication as that of magic multiplier of development, however, it is certainly envisaged to play a facilitative role in the process of development.

Although it may appear to be a truism, the importance of communication to human life cannot be overemphasised; for without communication no society can exist, no social structures would survive and flourish. Communication not only means to communicate or pass on information—it also means community participation. The basic features of communication are :

(a) Communication is a process for transmission of ideas, thoughts and feelings from one person to another;

(b) Communication is persuasive and seeks to obtain desirable response to what is being transmitted;
(c) Communication is a two-way process both vertically and horizontally, in a spirit of 'give and take' or 'send or receive'.

Wilbur Schramm who was one of the foremost scholars recognised the important role that communication could play in the development of Third World countries. His landmark book, *Mass Media and National Development, The Role of Information in the Developing Countries*, is the first major treatise on the subject. His introduction to the above book : The Human Meaning of Underdevelopment, which describes the two families—the Ifes living in West Central Africa and the Bvanis in South Asia, has been written with rare sensitivity and concern for human and social problems and challenges faced by the society in these countries. Schramm argues :

1. knowledge is better than ignorance;
2. health is better than disease;
3. to eat is better than to be hungry;
4. a comfortable standard of living is better than poverty;
5. to participate actively in one's nation is better than to be isolated from it.

The analysis of the problems of underdevelopment in the study provides us with an illuminating overview about the role communication can play in national development. Some of the important conclusions of the study are reproduced below :

1. National development moves very slowly in a climate where innovation is feared and distrusted, where fatalism leads men to believe they can do very little about their situation, where men do not believe in the dignity of labour and have little wish to better their lot...... this climate is to be modified. Wherever dangers or opportunities need to be reported, decisions need to be made, new knowledge

needs to be taught—there information flows. Efficiency of communication is a consideration in determining the speed and smoothness of national development.

2. The whole information system, not a particular channel or a combination of channels, needs to be planned to fight the battle of development.
3. A developing country should try to make it as easy as possible to establish and maintain local media, such a small town newpapers and local radio stations. Local media are of great importance in social and economic development, not only because they are in a better position to know and serve the particular needs of a region, but also because they make it easier for more people to have access to media and therefore to take part in public affairs.
4. A developing country should try to establish a cooperative relationship between the organs of government responsible for its mass media development and education and other related activities. The development of education and literacy in a country has such an intimate relationship to media development that it is almost impossible to separate the two.

It is this anxiety as well as optimism that the potential of communication be utilised to further the cause of development, which has stimulated efforts to define and put in practice the concept of development communication. Since both the areas of study—development and communication by themselves elicit a large number of opinions, analysis, studies, any precise definition of development communication has eluded the communication and development scholars and experts. There has, however, been a broad agreement that development communication is primarily oriented to the needs of the people, implies a grassroots approach, and is decentralised and participative.

Development Communication

Development communication defies precise definition. It has been variously considered as a concept, approach, an ideal or even a philosophy. It also underlines certain amount of ideology, that of use of communication for development.

The term development journalism first cropped up around 1967 to define a notion of journalism according to which reporting events of national and international significance should be constructive in the sense that it contributes positively to the development of the country concerned. Its main focus should not be on day-to-day news but on long term development processes. Western models of journalism are seen as not transferable to developing countries (Michael Kunczik, *Concepts of Journalism*).

Whereas the two terms, development journalism and development communication are generally used by the communication scholars interchangeably, Shelton Gunaratne in paper—Old Wine in a New Bottle : Public versus Developmental Journalism in the US has said : Developmental Journalism has its roots in development communication which goes back to the work of agricultural extension carried out by large land grant state universities in the United States. Eventually it developed into a coherent doctrine.

The term development journalism as such was coined and introduced to international discussion at the Philippines University of Los Banos. In the early 1970s, the DEPTH-News a pioneer agency in development journalism defined it as "investigative reporting applied to the problems of development. It is not sunshine journalism."

Development communication emerged as a field of study during the post-World War II years when the countries of Asia, Africa and Latin America were asserting their right to independence, self-reliance and economic development. Its genesis is generally traced to the introduction and application of Agricultural Extension, also termed as Extension Education in most of the developing countries in early 1960s. The importance of communication as a tool to motivate and persuade people for eliciting positive response to various development programmes took shape. The use of Agricultural Communication became popular in some of the developing countries, giving rise to the use of the term (Rural Communication) in due course. It was soon realised that communication input cannot be confined to the development of agricultural aspects alone and also that apart from rural areas, urban areas also needed improvement and development. It was essentially an interplay of some of these factors that led to the emergence of the term development communication.

It is significant that the University of Philippines at Los Banos (which was the first University in the world to have Development Communication courses), retitled its Master's Degree programme in agricultural communication, as an M.A. in Development Communication. Thus, development communication is something with which the developing countries are already familiar in different forms like agricultural extension education or rural communication. The origins of development communication are, therefore, embedded in the practical efforts and situations of the developing countries in their tasks of changing the lifestyles, and improving the economic conditions of the people.

It is, however, more than agricultural extension education or rural communication. It does not restrict itself merely to the development of rural areas, nor is it concerned with agricultural development alone. It is oriented towards development whether it be in rural or urban areas or in agriculture, family planning, industrial production sectors.

One of the originators of the concept, Nora Quebral of the Los Banos University defines development communication as "the art and science of human communication applied to the speedy transformation of a country and the mass of its people from poverty to a dynamic state of economic growth that makes possible equality and the larger fulfilment of the human potential."

The above definition has been generally referred to, in any discussion about development communication by several media experts. Development communication uses communication media to help bring about socio-economic upliftment of the people in a way which is compatible with its humanistic goals. Quebral says : The very phrasing of development communication indicates its orientation towards goals, not to means. Its goals are inherent in the meaning given to development. Some of the more qualitative are the enhancement of quality of life, unfolding of human personality and humanisation of the individual. The humanistic goals, as well as the multifaceted nature of development (economic, social, political and cultural aspects) predict a wider scope for the study of the practice of development communication.

Mercado defines development communication as an "incremental process which starts with the diffusion of new information and technology which stimulates people to bring about conditions in the environment favourable to maximum productivity and the improvement of the general well-being." Rosario-Braid says that development communication requires communication personnel to go beyond their traditional roles. "The communicator's role will be that of enabling people to express their aspirations through available media and to assist them in attaining greater productivity." She says that in a broad sense, development communication is "the identification and utilization of appropriate expertise in the development process that will assist in increasing participation of intended beneficiaries at the grassroots level."

Funtions of Development Journalism

The function of development journalism is not merely to keep a watch on government actions, but to promote the development of the country. Peter Golding wrote that development journalism could promote national progress by :

(1) stressing the educational function of news by raising the awareness of events and issues;
(2) producing stories about social needs or problems in the hope of stirring up government action; and
(3) highlighting self-help projects that can be implemented by other communities and reporting on obstacles to development.

Essential Features of Extension Education

According to experts in the area of extension education and human resource development, development communication should have certain essential features as under :

1. Development communication is purposive and the intention here is to help in socio-economic development.
2. It is based on study of audience's characteristics and environment.
3. It views people not as independent atoms but being connected to each other in networks where a good many decisions are made by clusters of individuals. Many communication strategies at village level are based on this premise.
4. It aims at educating people, not simply passing along information to them.
5. It takes into account a variety of media forms, both human and non-human and mass media. An appropriate combination of mass media and inter-personal communication channel is considered more suitable. Use of localised medium with control in the hands of users seem quite befitting as in local radio, local television or community newspapers, etc.
6. Formative (during the process of production of communication materials) and summative evaluation are a must to gain constructive feedback about effectiveness of the communication process.

Development communication is said to cover every subject under the rubric "development" be it agriculture, environment, health care, literacy and education. A number of media experts have given many definitions ranging from simple to more elaborate.

According to J.F. Jamias, development journalism is characterized by the following five formalistically defined criteria :

1. Purposefulness (goal oriented)
2. Pragmatism (judged by results)
3. Relevance (to the development of the country)
4. Mass orientation (by addressing common problems)
5. Scientific outlook of development journalists.

The basic purpose of development journalism, as with other forms of journalism, is to inform, educate and entertain. Since people need basic information about the development programmes and plans envisaged by various departments of the government, information should be presented in an interesting and intelligible manner so that the intended beneficiaries are fully aware of all aspects.

Equally important function of development journalism is to investigate, analyse and interpret such plans. In the past, development journalism has been criticised for its tendency to depend wholly on government organisations, media officers, and others who, in the name of development news, tried to make propaganda even about those programmes which were not really useful for the people. Development news is not PR handout which presents list of success stories achieved by government in different areas. In a country like India where even after 52 years of independence, there are visible pockets of poverty and distress there would always be need for in-depth study and analysis of the failures, as well as successes.

Development journalism should seek to create an enabling environment, which through increased and accurate information facilitates the development process itself. It makes the expert knowledge available where it is needed and provides a forum for exchange of views and discussion. As Wilbur Schramm says : It is generally the increasing flow of information that plants the seeds of change. It is also the widened background of information that furnishes the climate for "nationness" itself. By making one part of a country aware of other parts...by making possible a nationwide dialogue on national policy, by keeping the national goals and national accomplishments always before the public, modern communication can help separate development into truly national developments.

Public Journalism

In my quest for understanding the very many nuances and dimensions of development journalism, I came across a review regarding emerging concept of public journalism in the United States which is very similar to the concept of development journalism that the West denounced during the debate on the New World Information and Communication Order.

Shelton Gunaratne, Professor of Mass Communication at the Moorhead State University in the above paper* refers to several research studies and postulates that public confidence in news dropped sharply (Between 1988 and 1993 people's confidence in television news dropped from 55 to 25 and newspapers news from 50-20 per cent) because journalism in all forms ignores its obligations to effective public life and the failure has been a major contributor to the resultant malaise in public life. Journalism should be, and can be, a primary force in the revitalization of public life.

The terms public journalism, civic journalism and community journalism have been used interchangeably. He quotes Lambeth from his paper, Review of good news, social ethics and the press, about new forms of civic journalism constituting some combinations of the following :

1. Careful, timely and sensitive listening to public needs,
2. Systematic consultation of the public by means of polls and focus groups,
3. Journalist-organized dialogue with panels of resource specialists chosen for their differing expertise and perspectives,
4. Media sponsored public fora designed to deliberate on key issues,
5. Continuity of in-depth reporting on issues chosen independently by journalists for their fidelity to citizen concerns,
6. Occasional cooperative projects by newspapers, radio and/ or television newsrooms.

Communication and Participation

Since the very inception of planning process in India, participation of people in development programmes has been the sheet anchor

---

* "Old Wine in a New Bottle : Public versus Developmental Journalism in the USA," Shelton Gunaratne in *Asia Pacific Media Educator*, Vol. I :1, September, 1996.

of the development policy of the central and state governments. In recent years, however, the term participation has become an important part of the development lexicon. In spite of the enormous importance attached to this concept the term has not been clearly conceptualized. It is, therefore, becoming more of a rhetoric.

A common element in the lexiographic meanings of participation is the centrality of "sharing", e.g. entitling policy holders to a share of company's additional profits or like workers participation—the involvement of employees at levels in the policy making decision of a company. In the absence of genuine sharing of the benefits of development programmes, participation is being more and more sloganised rather than being implemented earnestly.

Communication, of course, is one of the key elements to achieve participation. The new development communication perspectives underline community orientation—community radio, community listening groups, etc., self-management and self-reliance, voluntary action and a right to participate in planning, implementation and decision making. This, however, does not mean that planners, managers and experts have no role to play in executing the development programmes. It is important that knowledge, experience and view point of the local people be given due consideration before decisions are arrived at. The beneficiaries of the development programmes be not considered as passive recipients, they should rather be taken as stake holders in the success of development process.

Whereas participation as a part of communication process has been enthusiastically accepted in most of the countries, participation of the people at grassroots level remains generally very low. In the case of mass media particularly as we shall see in subsequent chapters—participatory communication is a difficult task. Since administrators fear that participation may generate more expectations than may be ordinarily met, they see an element of risk in involving people in the development process.

The close relationship between development, participation and communication was appropriately conveyed by the UNESCO. Director of Communication Division in his Key Note address at the AMIC 25th Anniversary Conference held at Singapore in June

1966; as under :

> The struggle against poverty, education for all, the preservation of the environment, the fight against AIDS, the promotion of human rights and of a culture of peace, all these great and noble causes for which the international community is mobilizing its human, intellectual and financial resources, will remain idle words if the people directly concerned in the rural areas and in the suburbs of the megalopolis; do not themselves consider these causes as their own. Therefore, they should be given the means and the skills to participate in the communication process, in order to voice their opinions and aspirations through their own media or, at least, through media with which they can identify. There is no development without participation, as there is no participation without communication. Development, participation and communication form part of a continuum.

There is today widespread agreement that development can be sustainable and long-lasting only if people's participation is made central to the development process. However, there is considerable difference of opinion on the very concept of participation and also on the ways of achieving it. Participation in development is now being sought the world over, not because it is a fad but because there has been a consensus on the usefulness of participation in development projects. It is considered a *sine qua non* for sustainable development. However people's participation remains more a rhetoric than reality.

It is generally accepted that the most difficult part in the process of development planning is to ensure the involvement of the villagers at the panchyat level because participation of people cannot be taken for granted. Generally the poor and the backward avoid taking part in the deliberations of village panchayats because of lack of confidence, hesitation in articulating their point of view and general scepticism about the benefits accruing to them from the development plans. It is in such situations that communication can make a significant contribution. On such occasions an awareness generation programme will be in order to motivate people to participate in the planning process. It needs to be stated, however, that the usual one way communication strategies like posters, distribution of printed material, use of traditional media may be useful in creating awareness, but that may not be enough. While mass media may generate curiosity, additional efforts, usually with the help of inter-personal channels of communication, will be necessary to ensure mobilisation, involvement and participation of the people.

REFERENCES

Adler, H. J. (1973). The World Bank's Concept of Development. In : *Development and Planning*, Bhagwati, J.N. and Eckaus, R.S. (eds.). The MIT Press, Cambridge, Massachusetts.

Ariyaratne, A.T. (1980). *Collected Works*, Vol. II, Sarvodaya Research Institute, Sri Lanka.

Birendra Kumar and B.S. Hansra (2000) *Extension Education for Human Resource Development.* Concept Publishing Company, New Delhi.

Entering the 21st Century, World Development Report, 1999-2000. The World Bank, Washington.

Kunazik, Michael (1988). *Concepts of Journalism, North and South.* Friedrich-Ebert-Stiftung, Bonn.

Many Voices, One World (1980). Report of the International Commission on the Study of Communication Problems, London, Kogan Page/UNESCO.

Nederveen, Pieterse J. (2001) *Development Theory : Deconstructions/Reconstructions.* Vistaar Publications, New Delhi.

Rogers, E. M. (1976). *Communication and Development—Critical Perspectives.* Sage Publications, London.

Schramm Wilbur (1964). *Mass Media and National Development. The Role of Information in the Developing Countries.* Stanford University Press and UNESCO, Paris.

4

INDIAN COMMUNICATION LANDSCAPE
Contemporary Trends

India, with over one billion population, is a land of contrasts, a plural and a multi-lingual society. It has a wide range of communication media, extending from oral communication, to inter-personal methods of communication to satellite broadcasting, from a two-page broad sheet in a regional language printed on a treadle so common in small towns and villages even now, to multi-edition dailies printed through facsimile printing process. It has the second largest broadcasting service in the world, a burgeoning television and cable TV system and now the emerging multi-media and internet revolution in the urban areas. It also has one of the largest film industries in the world.

Oral Communication

In the ancient Indian society, religious, philosophical and cultural discourse was characterised by oral communication. Cradle of an ancient civilisation, India has also been a rich repository of traditional forms of communication. For thousands of years the Indian religious and social landscape was dotted with saints and scholars, wandering monks, priests and preachers who would move from one place to another and disseminate thoughts and ideas on various aspects of life, religion and social behaviour. Interestingly, even today vast congregations of men and women are frequently organised where modern day *gurus* and *rishis* expound religious discourses. These programmes receive fillip from the audio-visual media when these are further disseminated through different TV channels. This pattern of communication—a communication experience in itself—oral, inter-personal aided by the gadgets of electronic technology—extensive public address system, closed circuit TV has all the attributes and characteristics of the Indian communication process encompassing elements from the ancient to the modern media of communication.

Speech is beyond doubt the most important vehicle of human communication. The culture of the Indian nation has been predominantly oral. The spoken word always had a sanctity of its own. It was revered as the source of knowledge and inspiration for good conduct. Before the advent of printing technology, traditional beliefs were disseminated orally. In ancient days oral communication was the only technique available to the religious preachers and philosophers for propagating their point of view.

Large masses of people were illiterate. The general masses were not aware of the advantages of literacy or education. Their outlook towards life was determined by fate and accident of birth. In such a situation the oral tradition of communication was harnessed to perpetuate ideas in support of the *status quo* and the social system prevailing at the time. The Brahmin priests used highly sanskritised language which carried an aura of scholarship and erudition. The religious teachings were confined to the elite, far beyond the access of the general masses.

Although the means of transport were primitive, communication by religious preachers was still possible. These religious preachers who were known as *parivrajakas* (wandering monks) travelled from and between various centres of pilgrimages and delivered discourses on religious matters, epics and scriptures. It will be interesting to point out the difference in the methods and use of language by the preachers of Brahminism and Buddhism. Whereas, the Brahmin priests used sanskritised, literary and scholarly language, the Buddhist method of communication was through local language. People were therefore more receptive to the Buddhist mode of communication.

During the modern times Mahatma Gandhi was one of the most successful practitioners of oral communication. In order to communicate his plans of action during freedom struggle his views and philosophy, Gandhi was not contented with his writings alone. He spoke with conviction and sincerity of purpose; his expressions were chosen with utmost care. His words and sentences were most appropriately chosen to convey his meaning. He used *Padayatra* (literally journey by foot; but also included journey by train) and prayer meetings for establishing direct and personal rapport with his listeners.

The other interpersonal channel which carried Gandhiji's message to the people was his regular prayer meeting. Silent prayer was followed by singing of hymns and chanting of *Ramanam* by the audience. These prayer meetings ended with a brief statement by Gandhiji on some vital issue. The regular national and international media looked forward to these statements from the greatest leader of the Indian freedom movement. Thus, the prayer meetings became a very potent means for the dissemination of the Gandhian ideas on politics, economics, village uplift, untouchability, *ahimsa*, *satyagraha* and *swadeshi* (Vilanilam, 1987).

Today, in spite of the vastly expanding media of mass communication, interpersonal communication through spoken words continues to enjoy a predominant position particularly in villages; the extension workers, political and opinion leaders rely on spoken word communication for the dissemination of the desired message and putting across their point of view.

The Dag Hammarskjold Foundation in one of its publications : *About Understanding–Ideas and Observations on Cross-cultural Communication,* succinctly discusses the significance of oral civilizations. It says : Because of our emphasis on material culture, we have not been responsive to the fact that evolution of mankind has also fostered great oral civilizations. These cultures do not express themselves to the same extent in stone or other physical materials; their cultural testimony lies in transient sound symbols of musical instruments or the human voice.... Oral culture is preserved in the form of proverbs, riddles, songs and stories. In addition, there are myths, legends, tales, epic poems and ballads. The story tellers, the old men and women, were professional in their craft. The tales and legends became the common spiritual heritage of many tribes.

It is, therefore, time we appreciate the rich cultural heritage that the oral cultures of our society has bequeathed to us.

Traditional Forms of Communication

> Even where modern media have penetrated isolated areas, the older forms maintain their validity, particularly when used to influence attitudes, instigate action and promote change. Extensive experience shows that traditional forms of communication can be effective in dispelling the superstitions, archaic perceptions and unscientific attitudes that people have inherited as part of tradition, and which are difficult to modify if the benefits of change are hard to demonstrate. Practitioners of the traditional media use a subtle form of persuasion by presenting the required message in locally popular artistic forms. This cannot be rivalled by any other means of communication.
>
> — *Many Voices, One World*

The traditional forms of communication constitute a potential source for conveying messages for economic and social development. Communities and individuals have utilized a wide range of media—local fairs, puppet shows, street theatre, folk songs and ballads for social purposes and as a support to local development schemes for health and family welfare campaigns, for creating political awareness.

In India, the most effective means of communication, specially in villages continue to be the traditional forms—folk theatre, folk tales, and of course, religious discourses. Folk forms which have been traditionally used as a means of disseminating information are diverse in nature and include different combinations of drama, dance, song, mime, story telling and puppetry.

India has a rich tradition of using folk media for nation building activities; even during the freedom struggle folk songs were used to popularise *satyagrah* and conveying political messages. Gurudev Rabindranath Tagore, in his famous *swadeshi samaj* speech in July 1904 advocated the use of *Jatra*, festivals and songs in order to reach the rural masses. Likewise, the eminent Tamil poet Subramanyam Bharathi started using folk music to invoke patriotic feelings. Folk tunes were used to popularise songs on glories of spinning-wheel, need to boycott British goods and other diverse themes associated with the freedom struggle. Even during the recent parliamentary elections, *Jatra* was one of the popular modes used for campaigning.

The relevance of traditional form of communication—*Nukkad Natak* (street plays) was brought in bold relief when this form was utilised in states like Orissa, Uttar Pradesh and Bihar to apprise the rural population of the Kargil conflict during 1999. In this day and time, when there has been exponential growth in broadcast media and means of transport and travel are within the reach of common man; one is confronted with a sense of dismay that there would be some people in the rural areas of the country who would be still ignorant of the national happenings in the country. These street plays were perhaps one of the few successful channels to inform the people of various aspects of the conflict as also the valour and sacrifices made by the Indian soldiers. The plays were equally successful in instilling a feeling of patriotism in the audience.

The outcome of various researches has established the importance of folk media in development communication. Traditional uses of folk media have been primarily for entertainment, social communication and religious activity. These media have an element of motivational and persuasive communication. There have been sporadic efforts to involve folk media for conveying development messages through mass media agencies. These efforts have not gone very far as a number of traditional media experts have expressed the view that presenting messages through folk media which is spectator-oriented would alienate these media from their basic philosophy and cultural setting.

Radio and television have added new dimensions to folk music, making different styles known outside their language area. The mass media have made people aware of the unexpected wealth of folk and tribal music and exposed musicians to the cultural diversity of India and folk musical styles live again for millions to be heard and viewed over a vast media network for all times. They have created a new interest in folk music, not only among the musicians and sophisticated audiences, but also among the people themselves.

The effect of the renewed interest in folk forms among urban circles, brought about partly by the mass media agencies has given stimulus to folk music of different regions.

Much of social usage of folk medium has been related to preindustrial societies in which cultural expression has been primarily oral and essentially localized. Traditional performing arts are functional and interpersonal, have a contextual base and would be able to carry the message of change, development and growth. However, there have been differing opinions in India on the wisdom of using mass media to broadcast folk media for social and development purposes. Successful publicity through folk arts depends on a happy synthesis of writing skill (at the script level) and theatre skills (at the performance level).

However, creative or innovative talent in the governmental organisations is lacking. There is a severe dearth of talent and imagination also. That's why the productions remain essentially ineffective.

Interpersonal Communication

Interpersonal communication has been classified as 'word of mouth communication that occurs in face-to-face interaction between two or more individuals'. Some of the characteristics of interpersonal channels are : message flow tends to be two-way, amount of feedback readily available is high; are more effective when the attitude change is the goal of the source. Since the modern means of mass communication had not been in place till such time as printing was invented in the 15th century in Europe, vast majority of people lived within the context of their small village or tribal community with interpersonal communication being the main form of social contact. The International Commission for the Study of Communication Problems in its report, *Many Voices, One World—Communication and Society, Today and Tomorrow*, says : Such interpersonal communication has been ever present, unceasing and specially within a small community, unrivalled in its importance. In the past it must have served to strengthen the values of comradeship and cooperation to counterbalance the fragmentation imposed by subjection to external authority. In any case, it has always had a socializing dimension, encouraging work, harmonious group living, banding together in the struggle against natural forces and in collective decision making. It remains an irreplaceable facet of human communication.

Interpersonal communication usually occurs in social situations, whereas the mass media inform decisions, interpersonal contacts support and legitimate them. Interpersonal influence is a two-way communication, the audience can talk back and convince itself. It is flexible, it is more trustworthy. If a goal of interpersonal communication is to achieve a changed attitude, to this end as a rule interpersonal communication is more effective than mass communication. The great advantage that the mass communication has over interpersonal communication is that of multiplier factor in circulating messages and information. With the rapid proliferation of mass media in India, the mass communication process is reaching out to larger number of people. However, the number of people to whom the mass communication process reaches out cannot be ascertained, and from whom the feedback is not immediately available. In the mass communication process, the active participation of the recipients is comparatively small. In this context, Melkote refers to Schramm as under : Only when communication can build itself into the social structure, is it going to show any real hope of extensive results. Only when media channels can mix with interpersonal channels and with organisation in the village, are you going to have the kind of development you will like.

The communication system in the People's Republic of China is a good example of this model. The mass media in this country work with and through a complex web of interpersonal channels and groups, feeding people with information they need and at the same time can feedback to the party cadres.

Several communication scholars have emphasized the more effective use of interpersonal communication in combination with media channels, in situations which call for reaching people with new ideas and persuading them to utilize these innovations.

It, however, needs to be stated clearly that efficient use of media to bring about social change must take into account adequate knowledge of local culture. The new practices sought to be introduced should generally conform to the societal norms of the group or the unit. In India interpersonal channels, in combination with mass media, have been used effectively for conveying social and political messages to the people. This in fact is the most favoured communication method of reaching to millions of people in the shortest possible time. In the recent parliamentary elections this combination—political and public rallies were organised in large numbers including street corner meetings in towns and villages; and the news—at times even live coverage through television, was successfully utilised to get across to the people from all sections of society.

MASS COMMUNICATION

Mass communication, or communication through mass media, has been an ever-evolving process since the invention of printing by Gutenberg in the 15th century in Germany. Several historians believe that the modern age of communication dates from the invention of printing. Printing was initially used for dissemination of knowledge and ideas through books.

Print Media

In a country like India of subcontinental dimensions and with a population excceeding one billion, press plays a vital role of building public opinion by way of dissemination of information to the people. Uncensored news, fearless editorial criticism, and other articles published in the newspapers and magazines influence the day-to-day governance of the country to a great extent. The significance of the press, as one of the pillars of democracy and the freedom it enjoys have contributed to the consistent growth of print media in the country. Today, the people have access to a wide range of publications, published in different languages with various periodicities and catering to diverse interests, virtually at their doorsteps.

James Augustus Hicky's *Bengal Gazette* or *Calcutta General Advertiser* appeared on January 29, 1780 and is today recognized as India's first formal newspaper. The *Bombay Gazette* out of which grew *The Times of India*, came on the scene in 1838. The Indian press has grown greatly since then with its role to inform the people, all the people it can reach, and not just the governors, of whatever may be in the public interest. By publishing such information or 'news', the 'Fourth Estate' informs or creates public opinion, thereby holding all in authority accountable for their acts of omission or commission and setting, day by day, an agenda for public discourse and debate aided by such informed comments on events as it may make or publish.[1]

According to an assessment by the Anthropological Survey of India a decade ago, incredible extent of India's pluralism is revealed by the statistics: 4599 separate communities in India with as many as 325 languages and dialects in 12 distinct language families and 24 scripts.

The 45th Annual Report of the Registrar of Newspapers for India—*Press in India 2001*, says: Newspapers were published in as many as 101 languages and dialects during 2001. Apart from English and 18 other principal languages, listed in the Eighth Schedule of the Constitution, newspapers were also published in 82 other languages, dialects and in a few foreign languages. The total number of newspapers registered with the Registrar of Newspapers of India (RNI) as on 31 December 2000 was 49,145.[2]

Over the past few decades, the Indian press has witnessed a three-tier growth. The mainline English language newspapers, published mostly from the metropolitan centres and state capitals, constitute the upper crust of the press. The English language press, catering to less than 5 per cent of the readers has a major share of advertising revenue because it is seen by the advertisers as aimed at the upper class clientele credited with purchasing power.

Leading Hindi and regional language newspapers, which during the past more than a decade have registered phenomenal increase in circulation, constitute the second tier of the Indian press. The statistics show that the domination of English language papers from non-metropolitan areas is fast eroding. The regional language press is increasingly making use of advanced means of telecommunication and printing technology.

The third tier of the Indian press is constituted of the small newspapers, mostly in Hindi and Indian languages are brought out from district centres, having grassroots contacts. This segment of print media has progressed rapidly because of the three factors—gradual spread of literacy, rise in people's purchasing power and increasing level of political and general awareness and interests in the affairs of the country.

The Indian press, by far the freest press in South Asia, pluralistic, multi-lingual, continues to be largely urban-oriented. More so the metropolitan press; and the newspapers coming out from the national capital are Delhi centric. The press in English language is elitist, geared to the commercial culture, obsessed with garnering the maximum share of advertising revenue. Issues concerning rural development are not given adequate coverage.

Interestingly community press in India bears a close resemblance to the weekly newspapers in the United States of America. A reference about weekly newspapers in the book, *Understanding mass media*—says:

> ***Weekly Newspapers***—Sometimes called the community, or grassroots press, the weeklies were once exclusively rural or suburban publications. They ranged from suburban papers that featured lifestyle stories (for example, on apartment living or how to fund day-care centres) to small country papers dominated by local events and subscribers' correspondence. During the 1980s, an increasing number of new urban weeklies were founded. Some concentrate on their own neighbourhoods; other sophisticated, cosmopolitan publications that review such topics as politics and the arts. Alternative news weeklies such as *New York's Village Voice* and the *Boston Phoenix* are mainly supplemental reading for people who are already informed about news and public affairs from other media.

One of the major characteristics of the print media in India is that it tends to concentrate in certain important cities and towns as under:

(i) Metropolitan Cities (Delhi, Calcutta, Mumbai and Chennai),
(ii) State Capitals (other than the Metropolitan Cities),
(iii) Union Territory Capitals,
(iv) Other Big Cities, and
(v) Small Towns.

The following table* shows concentration of newspapers during 2000.

Table 4.1 : Concentration of Newspapers During 2000

(Language & Place wise)

Language	*Metropolitan Cities*	*State Capitals*	*Union Territories*	*Bigger Cities*	*Smaller Towns*	*Total*
English	4437	1091	218	1064	365	7175
Hindi	3130	3898	86	7181	5390	19685
Assamese	10	119	0	25	66	220
Bengali	1108	84	5	609	837	2643
Gujarati	223	290	2	917	534	1966
Kannada	33	1028	0	316	291	1668
Kashmiri	0	1	0	0	0	1
Konkani	4	2	0	1	0	7
Malayalam	54	299	4	572	502	1431
Manipuri	0	39	0	0	6	45
Marathi	478	13	2	1507	717	2717
Nepali	8	16	0	3	38	65
Oriya	24	178	3	292	217	714
Punjabi	156	5	59	506	153	879
Sanskrit	13	6	2	22	10	53
Sindhi	26	21	0	47	12	106
Tamil	1364	32	33	399	137	1965
Telugu	70	359	2	456	313	1200
Urdu	661	980	2	841	364	2848
Bilingual	955	498	43	841	507	2844
Multilingual	160	74	16	176	116	542
Others	47	156	3	46	119	371
Total	**12961**	**9189**	**480**	**15821**	**10694**	**49145**

**Press in India* 2001.

The newspapers are categorised in three groups, which are further sub-divided into sub-groups :

(i)	**Big Newspaper**	A newspaper with a circulation of more than 75,000 copies per publishing day.
	Sub-groups	(i) Those having a circulation of one lac copies and above. (ii) 75,001 - 99,999 copies.
(ii)	**Medium Newspaper**	A newspaper with a circulation between 25,001 and 75,000 copies per publishing day.
	Sub-groups	(i) 50,001-75,000 copies, (ii) 25,001 - 50,000 copies.
(iii)	**Small Newspaper**	A newspaper with a circulation upto 25,000 copies per publishing day.
	Sub-groups	(i) 15,001- 25,000 copies, (ii) 5,001 - 15,000 copies. (iii) 2001 - 5000 copies. (iv) upto 2000 copies.

Community Press

As would be seen from the above discussion, there is no official categorization of the press as community press, as such. It is, however, understood that the community press would generally exclude newspapers published from metropolitan cities (except for neighbourhood newspapers) and in terms of circulation these would be small or medium newspapers, mostly in regional languages. Interestingly some newspapers, which pioneered community journalism in the country have now progressed to the big newspaper category.

The following broad definitions of community press would be more indicative in nature, rather than a precise formulation:

(i) ***Community Newspapers***— Newspapers that are located outside the capital and their focus is more on local news. However, in terms of both readership and influence, they could well match up to some of their national counterparts.[3]

(ii) ***Rural Papers***—The concept of community newspapers is not new. Small media has proved to be successful all over the world, in both urban and rural areas. Community newspapers need to be in the vernacular and need to have immediate relevance to the local community. In a country like India where there are so many diversely different communities with unique needs, cultures and interests, community newspapers can be powerful tool, speaking out people's thoughts, sharing their problems and finding local solutions.[4]

(iii) ***District Papers***—The spread of the dailies and other papers to the interior of the country has been noticeable in the past two decades. It goes without saying that the dailies which have come up in the smaller centres, other than the metros, state capitals and the bigger cities outside the capital cities, are mostly in the small category.[5]

(iv) ***Neighbourhood Newspapers***— Another trend visible during the last decade has been the growth of neighbourhood newspapers in urban areas catering to a specified territorial area of the metropolitan cities. Such neighbourhood papers have become successful both in terms of readership and garnering advertisement revenue.

Therefore, the broad parameters of definition and context of community press in the country would be as under.

The newspapers, catering to rural as well as urban areas, coming out mostly from district towns (and also in some cases from bigger cities), targeted to a well defined readership and limited area would generally fall within the perview of community press. The community press would certainly not be a part of the nationally circulated big newspapers. Neighbourhood newspapers coming out from metropolitan towns, but targeted to readership of a specified area have also been listed within the parameters of community newspapers.

It also needs to be noted that in the Indian context many communication scholars use the terms community press, rural press, local newspapers and small newspapers interchangeably which only goes on to show that community press essentially comprises of small newspapers serving primarily non-metropolitan areas, small towns and villages.

In his introduction to an important book on the subject—*Five Successful Asian Community Newspapers,* the AMIC Secretary General Vijay Menon, uses the term 'rural and community press' and 'rural newspaper'.

It would be difficult to pinpoint specifically the background as to how the community press started in the country. However, newspaper publishing in India came of age during the freedom movement in the nineteenth century. During that period, because of various factors including low literacy and limited population in capital and big cities, the circulation and spread of even national level papers was not very high.

The press in India has expanded rapidly, both in numbers, as well as in circulation only after independence. The total number of newspapers in 1956 was 6570 as against 49,145 in 2000. The circulation has also shown an impressive growth from 92 lacs to 12.7 crores during 2000, registering a fourteen time increase over the period.

The frequency of community press ranges from a daily newspaper to weekly and monthly publications.

According to the figures supplied by the RNI for the year 2000, 10,694 newspapers are published from smaller towns. These newspapers are published from all states and union territories in the country in English and 18 languages mentioned in the Schedule of the Constitution and a large number of dialects.

Community newspapers certainly constitute an important segment of the print media in the country. In this context the following comments of an eminent Indian scholar are relevant even today :

> Sometimes it has been asked whether the host of small district newspapers which have come out in recent years serve any useful purpose. They are said to confine their attention mainly to local complaints and disputes. I have regarded these district papers as of immense value, for, they focus the attention of the

> local population on local development efforts and assist in creating interest in the local affairs. I personally know of a number of cases in which these small newspapers have exercised considerable influence on local administration and have helped to build local opinion on political and economic issues. If development requires local participation, these district papers have to play an important role in mobilizing local effort. It may be conceded that all of them are not motivated by the highest ideals, and some of them may be instruments of local politicians, but as a whole they are of great assistance to local development. Political decentralization and establishment of *Panchayati Raj* have created a new political structure in local administration. The *Zila Parishads* and *Panchayat Samitis* have been entrusted with wide powers in the spheres of local administration and local development. The small district newspapers have the same significance in local affairs as provincial papers in state matters and metropolitan papers in national problems.[6]

A small district newspaper provides a forum to articulate the urges of the common man. It takes up local issues and immediate requirements, affecting the people. It gives greater importance to the problems agitating the ordinary people; unemployment, scarcity of agricultural inputs, the law and order situation at the village level etc. It is best suited to act as the second level of conversion of scientific knowledge into information in a usable form for the benefit of the ultimate clientele—the farmers.

One of the important recommendations made in the Report of the International Commission for the Study of Communication Problems, also popularly known as *Many Voices, One World,* testifies to the important role of the community press:

> The development of a community press in rural areas and small towns would not only provide print support for economic and social extension activities. This would also facilitate the production of functional literature for neo-literates as well.

In all the provinces and in all languages there have been publications, which have created impact through increase in readership and circulation. Several of the community newspapers, which started as small newspapers, have become important state newspapers with multiple editions from different centres of the states.

The respectability and importance which the community newspapers enjoy in the country is testified by the following reference:

> While the so-called national English press caters to a well defined, homogenous segment of society—the urban English-speaking elite, which hails from a common socio-economic background—the readers of the Indian language press cover the widest spectrum of literates from first generation readers like rickshaw pullers to village school teachers whose families have been newspaper readers for generations. Having to satisfy such a mixed readership, the language daily is alert to problems at the grassroots while not closing its eyes to the world beyond the village or the district to which it caters.[7]

Table 4.2 indicates most widely read, circulated and dominant newspapers in the Indian languages.

There is no law that restricts activities related to the publishing of newspapers in general or that of community newspapers in particular.

A study of ownership pattern of newspapers in 2000 reveals that individuals owned the majority of them in the country. Out of 49,145 newspapers registered up to 2000, individuals own 37,945 of them (77.21 per cent), followed by Societies and Associations (4,894 or 9.96 per cent), Joint Stock Companies (2,189 or 4.45 per cent), Firms and Partnerships (1,695 or 3.45 per cent), Trust, (907 or 1.85 per cent) and others (741 or 1.51 per cent). The remaining 774 newspapers (1.51 per cent) were owned by the Central and State Governments as shown in Table 4.3.

Table 4.2 : States with Dominant Newspapers

State	*Newspapers*	*In per cent*		*Languages*
		Share in total circulation	*Share in total readership*	
A.P.	*Eenadu*	55	92	Telugu
Gujarat	*Gujarat Samachar*	38	58	Gujarati
	Sandesh	30	47	Gujarati
Karnataka	*Prajavani*	26	57	Kannada
Kerala	*Malayala Manorama*	42	63	Malayalam
	Mathrubhumi	31	54	Malayalam
Punjab	*Punjab Kesri*	37	50	Hindi
Rajasthan	*Rajasthan Patrika*	34	50	Hindi
Maharashtra	*Navakal*	*8*	*27*	Marathi
	Lokmat	6	26	Marathi
Tamil Nadu	Dinathanthi	18	66	Tamil
	Dinamani	7	20	Tamil
West Bengal	*A.B. Patrika*	4	45	Bengali

Source : ABC: Vidura, Jan.-March 1999.

Table 4.3 : Ownership of Newspapers

Form of Ownership	*Number of Newspapers*	*Percentage of Total*
Individuals	37,945	77.21
Joint Stock Companies	2,189	4.45
Firms/Partnerships	1,695	3.45
Trusts	907	1.85
Societies/Associations	4,894	9.96
Government (Central/State)	774	1.57
Others	741	1.51
Total	49,145	100

Source : *Press in India* 2001.

Electronic Media

Over the years and particularly so during the preceding two decades, India has developed a fairly extensive electronic media infrastructure. Radio and television, and cable television since the advent of gulf war in 1991, have seen exponential growth in terms of reach and impact. Presently, All India Radio network comprises 208 radio stations and 327 transmitters and provide radio coverage to a population of 98.8 per cent spread over 90 per cent area of the country. The flagship of Doordarshan—the Primary channel—operates through a network of 1042 terrestrial transmitters of varying powers to make available TV signals to over 87 per cent of population*.

Radio, which continues to be a very important medium, has not matched the growth of television. It is indeed a sad commentary on the priorities of government media planners in our country that radio, which has been the most widely used medium for development purposes, is cost effective and has the capacity to reach large audiences, has been marginalised.

The well-known radio personality, Mark Tully making a comparison between radio and TV says : Radio, as a means of mass communication is friendly and has a far bigger reach. When you are listening to radio, you are personally involved, your mind is working. This is because mind is picturising the piece of information being communicated. In television, it is like spoon feeding your audience. The pictures are there before you and voice over is nothing more than captions to a series of visuals.

There could not have been more unequivocal and categorical assertion about utilitarian qualities of radio than what has been stated in the UNESCO report on communication—*Many Voices, One World*. In developing countries, radio is the only medium that can really be labelled mass where a large proportion of the population can be reached by radio broadcasts and possesses the means to receive them. No other medium now has the potential to reach so many people so efficiently for information, educational, cultural and entertainment purposes. Radio can be used easily and economically to reach outlying regions and for communication in the many vernacular, often unwritten languages, existing in developing countries. Almost all countries have a certain capacity to produce radio programmes in line with their political needs, cultural patterns and basic values.

In the above context, one cannot help recalling the observations made by the Working Group on Autonomy for Akashvani and Doordarshan that India should have given first priority to the

* *India* 2002.

development and densification of radio for at least next 10-15 years. Radio is far cheaper and the availability of cheap transistors has made it ubiquitous.

In the beginning of the nineties, the sudden arrival of satellite channels had affected the popularity of radio and it remained virtually dead, at least in urban areas. With the opening of FM channels, introduction of new programmes and application of latest technologies, the radio is fast coming back in the reckoning.

Radio continues to be most frequently used mass medium in development programmes. Development broadcasting originated primarily to carry information on agriculture and rural development, health and family welfare. Some of the important programmes where AIR has been making significant contribution are : radio support for distance education programmes launched by universities, schools and other organisations, pulse polio immunisation campaign, and in the broadcast of Radioscope, National Science Magazine started since April 1995. These programmes, as well as others concerning rural development and other sectors, would come up for detailed discussion in the respective chapters.

Radio is essentially a people oriented medium, a medium of the poor man, who is central to all the development strategies of the national and state governments. It is non-elitist and is ideally suited for dissemination of information at the local/community level. It would, therefore, be appropriate to briefly refer to India's experience in setting up the first local radio station at Nagercoil in 1989.

Television made its beginning in the country as a modest pilot project in September 1959; when the President Dr. Rajendra Prasad inaugurated the Experimental Television Service, operated from improvised studio. The programmes were telecast twice a week for a duration of one hour each and the signals were limited to 25 km from Delhi. The regular service with a news bulletin was started in 1965.

It would be interesting to recall, in retrospect the delay in starting television in India was due to the general feeling in the government that television was a luxury, a status symbol with limited utility and, therefore, could not be treated on priority for allocation of funds in a poor country like India where the need was pressing for more important necessities for the people. However, the role of television from the very beginning as an aid to education and social change was clearly recognised. There was also a realization of the immense potential of television as an instrument of rapid socio-economic transformation.

Today Doordarshan, the National Television Service in India, is also one of the largest terrestrial networks in the world. The flagship of Doordarshan—the Primary Channel—operates through transmitters of varying powers to make available TV signals for over 87 per cent of population. Doordarshan uses a large number of transponders of the Indian National Satellite. During 2000-2001 Doordarshan earned more than Rs. 637 crores as revenue through commercial advertisements.

To meet the regional aspirations, there are at present 11 regional language satellite channels on Doordarshan. Since the footprints of INSAT satellites cover the whole country, regional language programmes are available throughout the country regardless of one's place of residence.

The Satellite Instructional Television Experiment (SITE) in 1975, was primarily undertaken to experiment with television through satellite communication to broadcast special programmes in 2400 villages in six states aroused wide international interest. Subsequently the Ninth Asian Games in 1982 proved to be a significant milestone in the growth of Indian television because it heralded the introduction of colour television in the country. In 1983, a Special Plan for television expansion was approved. The plan was historic because beginning July 1, 1984, one transmitter was commissioned everyday for a period of almost four months. During 1984, India's first soap opera *Hum Log* was introduced with the object of promoting women's welfare, family planning and reinforcing positive social values. The programme became very popular and made headway for other serials.

The Gulf War coverage by CNN in 1991 was a defining moment in the beginning of a new era in television broadcasting in India which ushered in far-reaching changes at a dizzy place. This was also the beginning of multi-channel TV in the country. The Special Edition of *India Today*, caught the spirit of the moment when it heralded the arrival of CNN in January and of STAR TV in April 1991, as "easily the most dramatic revolution took place on the TV screen. 1991 was the year when India ended decades of isolation from the rest of the world". Subsequently also the fortnightly newsmagazine wrote : The mundane television set has suddenly turned into an incredible technicolour dream boat.... and like a lost tribe discovering an oasis in the desert, lakhs of Indians are hot wired into this superbazaar of soaps, sports, news, music, sex and much more....Hungry for any kind of news or entertainment, lakhs of people in cities and towns across the nation are now only too familiar with the names of the new electronic media companies, an alphabet soup of initials promising round the clock entertainment—MTV, CNN, BBC, ATN, Zee TV.

If anything, the number of satellite channels has increased rapidly. The Sengupta Committee, while referring to Satellite channel universe, lists 52 channels operating in the country. The number of satellite channels available at present may be around one hundred.

Today TV is no longer an urban phenomenon. Its penetration, in the suburban and mofussil areas, and even in villages, is not considered a big deal any longer. There has, in fact, been a virtual paradigm shift from state monopoly of electronic media to virtual *laissez faire*; from the position of monopoly national broadcaster to one of the players is indeed a metamorphosis in the media landscape in the country. What does this metamorphosis augur for channelising communication media for development purposes?

Television was started in India for the purpose of development communication as a vehicle of social change and national cohesion by unhesitatingly upholding progressive values and involving the community in a free dialogue, but it has gradually steered away from the enshrined development goals and chartered a course contrary to its development pursuits. Today entertainment has become the primary function of this medium.

The Working Group on Software for Doordarshan, under the chairmanship of P.C. Joshi (1982) indicated : Today development and communication are entirely unrelated. On the one hand, we have a powerful medium like Doordarshan not being used for development task, on the other hand we have developed programme and action without any media or communication support. The two should work hand in hand, reinforce each other if planning has to be effective. The Group also expressed its unhappiness on the VIP orientation of the programmes and said : It is a pity that a television system which is not only publicly funded but is also directly run by the government, on the ground that is necessary to make television serve the purpose of development in the direction of socialism, should show so little orientation towards the common people in its news and current affairs programmes. Doordarshan news should be gathered and presented from perspective not only of the government, the ruling party and the urban well-to-do, but also of the many other social, economic and political groups, who constitute the nation.

The Indian television industry has become completely entertainment oriented; telecast of feature films, *chitrahar*, soaps and other serials has made Indian TV a tool of entertainment with development being relegated to a subordinate slot. Television commenced with the aim of promoting socio-economic development of rural people by disseminating of knowledge, through education and information. During the course of expansion, however, Doordarshan now fulfils the three widely accepted principles : entertainment first, information second, and education last. The entertainment element has gone increasing at the cost of education and information dissemination.

Development programmes are shabbily produced. They lack aesthetics and necessary visuals. Dull production leaves the viewer cold. Development programmes are never telecast on prime time and they fail to attract advertisement revenue. The viewers often consider such programmes as government propaganda and surf channels. TV can be most effective medium of mass communication only if it provides good programmes.

There has been pervasive concern over the impact of advertising on the quality and contents of the television programming at various levels; it has unleashed the forces of consumerism; which is spreading like wildfire, whereas access to the basics of life remains a serious problem for a large number of population. Several studies, seminars and reports of working groups have expressed concern that in order to meet the requirement of sponsors and advertisers, TV channels telecast programmes which threaten family values and usher in a lifestyle out of sync with the Indian traditions. Suggestions have been in place to find solution to this situation which is becoming more and more intractable issue.

Public Service Broadcasting has been one such recommendation which has been put forward in the report of sub-committee of the Consultative Committee for the Ministry of Information and Broadcasting on National Media Policy and the Working Group set-up to review the provision of Prasar Bharati Act; both these reports were submitted in 1996. The Consultative Committee recommended : The national broadcasters should bear the responsibility to offer a high quality public service broadcasting that informs, educates and entertains the people. It also recommended : Adequate care should be taken to enable the setting up of non-commercial broadcasting stations to be run by universities, educational institutions, panchayats/local bodies, state governments, etc. Likewise, the Working Group said : This Group believes that Prasar Bharati as the inheritor of the great tradition should be the quintessential public service broadcaster. This is not to suggest that private broadcasters have no role to play in this sphere. Indeed, the private operators should have an obligation to put out programmes devoted to socially relevant themes and earmark certain slots for the purpose.

The public service broadcasting manifesto, propounded by the first Director General of BBC, John Reith says :

> The service must not be used for entertainment purposes alone. Broadcasting had a responsibility to bring into the greatest possible number of homes in the fullest degree all that was best in every department of human knowledge, endeavour and achievement. The preservation of high moral tone—the avoidance of the vulgar and the hurtful—was of paramount importance. Broadcasting should give a lead to public taste rather than pander to it.

In India, we have to go a long way in putting in place such regulatory measures, and more importantly implementing these meaningfully and sincerely. We will have to ensure media professionals, researchers, civil society, voluntary groups and NGOs—proper initiative, so that new space could be created for public service broadcasting and community media; adequate funding be provided—properly regulated government allocations, a tax on advertising revenue, may be subsidy to production houses for producing educational and developmental programmes.

Multi-media Communication

In the Indian context which has a rich tradition of oral and traditional communication and a vibrant print and electronic media, Internet has emerged as an important factor in the fast developing communication landscape. With internet expanding rapidly the Information Age is well and truly upon us. The worldwide web is a challenge because of the interactive opportunity it offers for instant communication and is racing ahead at a breath taking speed. A large number of newspapers are available on internet. *The Hindu* was the first Indian newspaper to go on the net in 1995. Soon, other newspapers, both in English and Indian languages followed suit as also magazines. As is the predominant practice, the world over, access to Indian newspapers is also free. A major newspaper group chain operating from the capital has sites for all its publications, as well as for classifieds, jobs and careers, property, education, computing, etc. All these sites are easily available.

Internet access in India has not reached a critical mass yet in view of the limitations of the infrastructure and bandwidth. Ever since the internet space was deregulated by the government, the number of internet subscribers is growing. Till date there are more than 2.5 lakh internet subscribers in India and according to a report there will be a quantum leap in the next twenty-four months.

This technology is impacting print media as well. More and more online editions of newspapers will be available. Colour and graphics will play an increasingly important role in newspaper publishing. The newspapers will become increasingly digital in its production processes.

Another India? The other face of India, far different from the wandering monks depending upon oral communication in hoary days of distant past.

Internet and Civil Society—The communication landscape in the country has been undergoing major changes largely due to technological developments during the last two decades. Use of computers has revolutionised the process of collection and dissemination of information. Convergence is yet another technological revolution profoundly impacting the communication scenario. Internet is being widely used by corporate houses, educational institutions, inter-governmental organisations, non-governmental organisations and voluntary bodies. The new technology, in fact is being increasingly used for networking and reaching out to the people in distress and during emergencies. It was indeed surprising to observe that new media particularly telecommunication and digital cameras proved to be the key to communication in India's relief operations during the Gujarat's earthquake in 2001.

With a team of around 150 delegates working on the Red Cross relief operation in Bhuj, devastated by January's earthquake, how can people all communicate with each other? How does a doctor find one of his colleagues in a hurry when a patient turns up needing emergency surgery amid a crowd who don't speak English? How can the field delegates talk to their colleagues in Delhi and at the Federation's Secretariat in Geneva? Good telecommunications are a vital need for humanitarian agencies like the Federation to be able to respond properly to such disasters as this Indian earthquake. The Federation reacted by mobilising a telecommunications emergency response unit, comprising telecom specialists and equipment. The telecom team flew into Bhuj bringing with them one tonne of equipment. After setting up satellite phones, the team set-up a network of radios, giving many delegates their own handset, so they can stay in touch.

At the field hospital, expatriate doctors are surrounded by people who only speak the local Indian language. Much of the efficiency of the hospital can largely be accounted for by the excellent communication among those participating in the operation. The hospital staff remain in constant touch with each other through the radio handsets. The telecom team installed a VHF radio network linking all the different units of the relief operation. This involved 80 handsets for delegates, several vehicle-mounted radios, two base stations and solar-powered repeater, giving altogether a local range of about 50 kms for Bhuj and surrounding area.

Setting up the radio network was not so simple. The team had to negotiate with the government to install the radio communication stations. Climb the only high-rise water tank in the quake-ravaged town to install the repeater and its solar power panels for these radio system.

"Establishing a telecommunication infrastructure is the first job at hand in any disaster situation once the Federation decides its relief operation," says Neil Dewar, the International Federation's telecommunication officer who arrived in Bhuj as soon as the relief programme got under way. Neil was followed by tele-communications colleagues from the Austrian, Spanish and German Red Cross societies.

In addition, the telecom specialists helped install e-mail addresses for the diferent units of the Federation's relief operation, linked to satellite phones. This has made it easier for the delegates to communicate with colleagues elsewhere in the world to discuss everyday administrative matters and solutions to problems on the field. This was particularly crucial in the period immediately following the earthquake when local communications were damaged and destroyed. Normal telephones were out of order for several days and the cellular network was down or congested for more than 2 weeks.

Japanese Red Cross doctors, for example, had been e-mailing digital images of the condition of their patients for a second opinion from specialists in Japan, after a Japanese telecommunication officer established satellite communication links between Bhuj and the Red Cross hospitals back home. The team also helped to update the computer and telecommunication capacities of the Indian Red Cross Society.

The team brought with them a digital camera, a computer and

a satellite phone, which they can use to communicate with experts halfway round the world. After taking the pictures, the doctors then e-mail them to the Kumamoto Red Cross hospital back in Japan for a second opinion. "Our colleagues examine the state of the injury at the Kumamoto prefecture hospital and give us their opinion over the phone. We get specific advice and this is invaluable. It makes it so much easier for us to arrive at the right decision," explains Dr. Akira Miyata, the team leader.

The Red Cross had also earlier used the internet to reunite families dismantled by war, just as it was doing now in the midst of ruins and devastation. Modern technology has once again come to the service of humanity.

In this context two other prominent initiatives worth mentioning are : Voice and Gyandoot. The Andhra Pradesh Government has launched the Vijaywada Online Information Centre (Voice), a state-wide information network where the government information is available right down to the village level via intranets and the World Wide Web.

Likewise the Madhya Pradesh Government has established Gyandoot in Dhar district whereby all revenue and land related papers and certificates of all kinds required by a common citizen from any government office could be down loaded from a computer. The state government is utilising IT for several other purposes to afford more facilities to people in rural areas (Sharad Chandra Behar, *Vidura,* Jan.–March 2001, pp. 51-53).

It, therefore, makes sense for CSOs, large and small, to get around their traditional access constraints by using the internet. It is some what elitist medium at the moment, it is going down social ladder fast. E-mail is not the preserve of the chattering classes any more, nor are web pages. If one doesn't own a computer, one can surely visit a cyber centre, of which there is now no dearth. Internet has been so useful in times of emergency only because there is no administrator, no coordinating authority. Starting from a small network by the US Defence Department, the Internet has grown into a truly international supermarket.

In today's global politics, there is fierce competition in information generation and dissemination. The government and political, economic, social and cultural activities all function in the ever-renewing information medium, which in turn interacts with all these activities. Information generation, absorption, and reaction are integral parts of our existence and our activity today. If the government does not take the lead in providing the correct picture, the information highway gets crowded by news generated by various other parties, not all of them having the best motives. It is essential that our politicians and bureaucrats appreciate the way information be used as a tool of governance, politics and for other nation building objectives.

Non-dominant Communication*

Non-dominant communication processes are media forms, which run contrary to dominant values, ideological propositions and organisational norms. Dominant communication consists of those media processes which have been marginalised by the homogenizing zeal of an industrial economy, and which are largely sustained through an intrinsic local ethos in addressing social issues of the moment.

These forms, amorphous and scattered as they are, may include street theatre based on folk songs and puppetry to convey messages of social importance, write ups and feature stories on important contemporary issues which the mainstream media may not take up (or would take up only when the issue has been articulated through non-dominant processes) and has already become important enough to receive attention at a regional or national level. The way the issues concerning Narmada dam were articulated through the vernacular press at the local level before these found space in the national press, cyclostyled bulletins, leaflets and later on video films, were all instances and forms of non-dominant communication used for serving an important purpose. These processes have provided several feminist groups and voluntary organisations means to express their point of view and represent the ideology these stand for. The noted free lance journalist, Bharat Dogra, who

---

* Based on the papers included in *Seminar* (455).

publishes *News from Fields and Slums*, has found a novel method to articulate his views on poverty, environmental problems and concerns of the common person. He finds that small booklets, 16-32 pages, economically priced helps him focus on an issue and create the necessary impact. The production costs are low; he has managed to carry on the *News* with financial support from his wife, who later on joined him after giving up her government job. He has been, on principle, opposed to foreign funds, and hopes the feature service will motivate the next generation to create necessary climate wherein issues concerning the poor and slum dwellers could be properly focused.

This is in fact the spirit behind non-dominant communication processes.

Changing Trends in Contemporary Media

For the past several years the mainstream media—leading newspapers, newsmagazines and television— has shown disturbing trends: predominance of kitsch, reducing even serious subjects to frivolity and entertainment of a kind which goes against the Indian social and cultural milieu.

It was, of course, premised that with the ongoing trends of globalization and opening of the economy; the market forces would be a major determining factor in shaping the contours of media. However, a closer study of the recent trends in the media shows that the flippant attitude to matters of serious national importance has become all too pervasive.

Now the question is: Has superficiality and triviality taken over even the substantial issues of national import? Let us consider the way the personality of the President Abdul Kalam during his election discussed in the two leading national dailies. The articles, of course carried some interesting information from his autobiography, *Wings of Fire*, but it is pertinent to ask: Is it essential to build a feature on a serious subject or a national personality around an absolutely superficial basis like personal mannerisms or hairstyle. That certainly distracts the issue from serious discussion and degenerates it into the realm of frivolity.

Is journalism not being reduced to kitsch? In the name of good-natured humour, would it be proper to treat the subject lightly only because the television does so? Should the entertainment culture of TV be transformed to serious subjects as "Reflections"?

Unfortunately this trend—of trivializing even serious subjects, of pandering to style over substance, of presenting designers, models, showmen and women, and entertainers as the representatives of society; seems to have taken a stranglehold on media— and particularly so in metropolitan areas so much so that one is startled at the developments.

Beauty Queens and Bandit Queens—In this context, let me refer to the observations of Mr. K.R. Narayanan, who in his inaugural address to the National Seminar on *Press as Leader of Society,* in March 1996, said:

> I have been astounded by the enormous obsession that the Indian media have shown with phenomenon like beauty queens and bandit queens and glamorous criminals. The amount of space that is given to them is really astonishing and the manner in which the reporting takes place tends often to be a sneaky admiration for the qualities of these personalities. The subject of the treatment of women in the Press and in the media has occupied attention a great deal and I am afraid that the Press has not given what one might call a moral and ethical leadership of society in the depiction of women in their columns.

During the intervening six-year period, if anything, the situation has indeed deteriorated quite fast. Let us take a few examples.

An increasing number of newspapers have started special sections on what is happening in the capital city of the country on the P3P circuit to the exclusion of news in other important areas. All these newspapers have, of course, extensive reporting on the political, social and economic issues in the inside pages (6-8 pages), which is looked after by a strong city reporting team.

What do these sections contain? A sample of contents and language:

Sex and the City; a detailed life sketch of a designer; an interview with an actor on his films, family and future, news on the fashion week being organized by Lakme India, let your body say it (making or breaking a date or romantic interest), looking for love, and a number of photographs of women half clad, barely clad and provocative (*Delhi Times, The Times of India*, June 30, 2002. The whole treatment is openly sex oriented. Difficult to assess as to which sections of the society stand benefited and what are the values which such type of journalism tends to impart.

Another newspaper, which also runs a separate city section, may be marginally better. A box headline on the opening page: Erotic chic rules the ramp; New Babe on the block (a bare bodied photograph)—both in 28 June. Models, fashion designers, actors and actresses, society persons and socialites: fixers and the cocktail circuit. It appears all that is happening in the capital city is wining, dining, dancing and dating—hardly one per cent of the people are interested in this kind of stuff. The rest 99 per cent can take care of themselves.

As if that was not enough. An evening tabloid newspaper launched recently from the capital city has gone further. Its opening issue romanticized the suave manners of a "gentleman robber", a thief, in a way that anybody would develop strong empathy with the character of the person. The news feature legitimizes thieving as a perfectly legitimate profession. Inside—how to be a sex goddess, masala max, and P3P — a complete page everyday. The letter from the Editor-in-chief says: One of the objectives of the newspaper would be to provide you information about the choices on how to earn money and *how to spend it even faster*. Perhaps that is the message, which we wish to convey to the upcoming readership of generation next. The newspaper truly illustrates at least the second part of the editor-in-chief's phrase that it will be full of news "from the state of the nation to *the state of fashion*."

At least the metropolitan media seems to be totally encircled by the celebrity and glitterati syndrome.

These trends in the contemporary media are not new. What is new is the virulence and no-quarters-given syndrome gripping the media.

NOTES

1. B.G. Verghese, Seven Deadly Sins (1996), in *Beyond Those Headlines : Insiders on the Indian Press.* The Media Foundation, New Delhi.
2. *Press in India 2001,* (2001) Ministry of Infor*mation and Braodcasting*, Govt. of India, New Delhi.
3. Crispin C. Maslog (1985), Five Successful A*sian Community Newspapers,* Asian Mass Communication Research and Information Centre (AMIC), Singapore.
4. Vincent D'Souza (2000), Community Newspapers for Human Development, *Voices,* Bangalore.
5. S.C. Bhatt (1997), *Indian Press Since 1955,* Publications Division, Ministry of Information and Broadcasting, Govt. of India, New Delhi.
6. Learner and Schramm (1967), *Communication and Change in Developing Countries,* East-West Center Press, University of Hawai, Honolulu.
7. Suneet Vir Singh, India Speaks (1996), in *Beyond Those Headlines : Insiders on the Indian Press.* The Media Foundation, New Delhi.

REFERENCES

Beyond Those Headlines : Insiders on the Indian Press, (1996) The Media Foundation, New Delhi.

Bhatt, S.C. *Indian Press Since 1955 (1997)*—Publications Division, Ministry of Information and Broadcasting, New Delhi.

Crispin C. Maslog, (1985) *Five Successful Asian Community Newspapers,* Asian Mass Communication Research and Information Centre, Singapore.

Gupta, Rahul (1994) *A Profile of Local Newspapers of Hisar,* Indian Institute of Mass Communication, New Delhi.

Lerner and Schramm (1967). *Communication and Change in Developing Countries.* East-West Center Press, University of Hawaii, Honolulu.

Malik, Madhu. *Traditional Forms of Communication and Mass Media in India,* Documents on Communication and Society-13, UNESCO.

McQueen, David (1998). *Television : A Media Students Guide,* Arnold, London.

Melkote, Srinivas, R. (1991). *Communication for Development in the Third World—Theory and Practice,* Sage Publications, New Delhi.

Press in India 2001, Ministry of Information and Broadcasting, Government of India, New Delhi.

Seminar (455). (1997) Alternatives in Communication, July.

Vilanilam, John V. (1987). *Religious Communications in India,* Vol. I, Kairali Books International, Trivandrum.

5

RURAL DEVELOPMENT, POVERTY ALLEVIATION AND WELFARE PROGRAMMES

India is predominantly a rural country—a land of villages. Notwithstanding the rapid industrial and technological progress made by India since independence, the Indian economy is basically agricultural. Agriculture provides employment to 65 per cent of the workforce. Despite a declining share in GDP from 52 per cent in the 1950s to 26 per cent at present, agriculture is the single largest contributor to GDP. Agriculture is the most crucial sector of the economy, for it provides food security, generates employment, helps to alleviate poverty and contributes significantly to the country's exports. India's agrarian economy is a mammoth enterprise with over 20 million farmers and farm workers who constitute backbone for national progress.

The cultural ethos and milieu of India is, by and large, rural. The Indian fairs and festivals are organized to celebrate the bountiful gift of nature—coinciding with the two crop cycles—*rabi* and *kharif*. An average Indian farmer is a hard working, honest and sincere person deeply attached to his fields. The rural areas are repositories of rich cultural heritage.

Rural Development

Rural development, in the broad sense of the term, holds the key to all economic progress, industrial or agrarian, urban or rural. The World Bank Rural Development Policy Sector Study of 1975 defines rural development as : Rural development is a strategy designed to improve the economic and social life of a specific group of people—the rural poor— and involves extending the benefits of development to the poorest among those who seek a livelihood in rural areas.

According to Saha *et al.* (1978), it involves:

(i) ***Physical development***—communication, transport, sewage, irrigation, energy, forestry, animal conservation, environment;-

(ii) ***Economic development***—agriculture, business, industry;

(iii) ***Social development***—education, culture, sports, political activities; and

(iv) ***Health development***—nutrition, sanitation, community health, prevention of water and air-pollution.

A large number of schemes and programmes, notable amongst them being IRDP, TRYSEM, DPAP and DDP were launched primarily to improve the living standards of the mass of low income population. Rural development has been the sheet anchor of all the programmes launched in furtherance of the objectives of planned economic development ever since the beginning of the planning process in 1951. However, according to Dutt (1990): Rural development, has had the effect of increasing income disparities, even though by a process of trickling down it improves somewhat the standard of living of the poor, has dangerous potentials. The discontent caused thereby, and by the lack of social security which often accompanies income disparities, frequently manifests itself in undesirable channels.

According to Kamta Prasad (1990), the approach to rural development followed so far has been essentially bureaucratic rather that participatory. Rural development plans have been prepared at the national and state headquarters and passed on to local level offices of the government for execution. Involvement of the local people has been rather limited. Consequently, there has often been a mismatch between what the people wanted and what they got from the government. Whether it is IRDP, DPAP or any other programme, the dead uniformity which has occurred in the name of national planning has proved highly unproductive. As Sardar Tarkok Singh has pointed out, the interest at the higher level has been increasingly to get at quick numerical results which are easy to report, add up and publicise in one form or another with too little attention to the true impact on the conditions of the people.

Bongartz (1993) analysed as to what went wrong with the rural development approaches: Actually, the community development approach did not provide much support to self-help activities at the village level. Decisions were still made in the centralized planning apparatus. The bulk of the input provided to the villages was absorbed by the better off sections of the rural communities. Existing power structures were accepted and not much was done to set up local self-help organisations of the poor. Therefore, in terms of poverty alleviation or eradication of problems not much progress could be reported.

There is also increasing recognition that past development efforts had not fully taken into account social and community needs, cultural values and capabilities as key elements in rural development programmes. However, now there is belated realization that the needs of the people should be at the core of the development process which should be driven by social and environmental concerns rather than economic considerations alone.

There is also renewed emphasis on people's participation in development programmes. Involvement of the local people in schemes of rural development is expected to result in better planning and decision-making because the local people have a better awareness of their needs and preferences and fuller information on the conditions and possibilities of their areas. The local communities, with a more intimate knowledge of the inter-dependence of activities at the micro level, would be in a better position to develop integrated programmes which would avoid duplication and produce the maximum impact with minimum cost.

Many development thinkers and agencies are becoming increasingly determined that people's needs and demands are more fully understood, and wherever appropriate, integrated into wider development context.

Media and Planned Development

Ever since the beginning of the era of planned development in

1951, the role of the media came to be emphasized in greater measure. The media was enjoined to provide communication support and inform the general masses about the objectives, targets and benefits of the plans.

The Second Five Year Plan document stressed that the Plan to be carried into every home in the language and the symbol of the people and expressed in terms of their common needs and problems. The Plan also outlined the measures for expansion of plan publicity through the mass-media.

The Third Plan (1961-66) observed: As part of the programme for strengthening public co-operation and participation during the Third Plan, it is proposed to intensify the existing arrangements for bringing home the implications of rapid development and carrying the message of the Plan to the masses throughout the country.

Similarly, the observations of two study teams appointed to make proper recommendations: the Study Team on Mass Communication sponsored by the Ford Foundation and the Team for the Study of Plan Publicity appointed in 1963, popularly known as the Vidyalankar Committee, are quite valid even today.

The Ford Foundation Team observed: India's development task is so great and her population so large that only by the most efficient possible programme of public information—necessarily emphasizing mass communication—can communicators hope to reach people often enough and effectively enough to activate, on the needed scale, discussion process and subsequent actions in the cities, towns and villages.

Media strategies for rural development will have to be essentially geared to the ethos and the relevance to the people whom development plans are intended to benefit. The basis of media strategies should highlight the localness of approach and dissemination of culturally appropriate and user-friendly technology. The media strategies would succeed in creating the right kind of climate and environment of development only, within the parameters and constraints, which are associated with the rural population. These strategies, would have to be innovative, realistic, chiseled and shaped to fine tune the aspirations of the people; and should preferably be operated by the local resource persons in tune with the sensibilities of the clientele. The media strategies for rural development would, therefore, essentially include the rural press, local radio stations, rural programmes on television and reinforcement through extension agencies, so as to facilitate and reinforce the adoption process through interpersonal and face to face communication process.

Our Agriculture Future—The observations made while delivering the Sardar Patel Memorial Lecture, 1973, on Our Agriculture Future, by Dr. M.S. Swaminathan are as relevant today as when these were made almost thirty years ago.

The technology is now becoming available but the mechanism for transferring it to the illiterate and small users in an effective manner does not exist. Ironically, there is a global communication network which makes the latest findings of science available almost immediately to research workers in any corner of the world; but what is urgently needed is such a communication network at the service of the poor farmer in our country. It is not only knowledge that is needed, but an approach which will be able to supply the right knowledge and tools to the right people at the right time and place. The worker on the spot, whether he is an agricultural officer, a teacher, a *gram sevak* or a social worker, must be able to identify the local problem or need which will act as a catalyst for promoting cooperative endeavour in that area—it may be lift irrigation in one place, dairying in another, pest control in a third, supply of farm machinery or fish fingerlings in a fourth and marketing in a fifth. In this network, the mass communication media, particularly, the radio, television, cinema and the language press, have a very important role to play; so have the research and the extension worker, the education system and the drive for technical literacy.

Rural Press—The rural press, as a link between the policy makers, development bureaucracy and farmers; as a second line of conversion of scientific knowledge into information for utilization in the field situation, imparting adult education; as a vehicle for reinforcing the literacy habit, is being increasingly recognized as a viable means of the promotion of social awareness and development. The rural press is a promising medium for disseminating information and knowledge about nutrition, health and hygiene, improved farm practices, family planning measures and development plans to those sections of society where the information is needed most.

Wilbur Schramm, in his book, *Mass Media and National Development*, considered rural newspapers as one of the great movers of national development. Such a newspaper gives the neo-literate reason to learn to read better and makes public participation in governmental policies more informed, relevant and meaningful. Apart from broadening the actual educational base of its readers, the rural papers break down the barriers of isolation and provide written material to the villagers who have learnt to read so that they can apply their reading ability to increase their production.

The printed word, particularly in the rural areas, has a fascination of its own. It is a catalyst of change and growth. To improve the recognition, understanding and appreciation of the printed word, specially for those for whom it is not a routine matter, to interact with books and newspapers, is a worthwhile task. Aldous Huxley has said: Everyman who knows how to read has the capacity to magnify himself, to multiply the way in which he exists, to make his life full, significant and interesting.

The rural newspaper, with its simple language and contents closest to the interest of its readers, reinforces this reading habit, day in and day out. Since reading is basic to the understanding of the working of a host of social, economic and political institutions, the rural press by cultivating and reinforcing the reading habit, performs an important role in enhancing social and political consciousness.

The extensive reach, effectiveness, popularity and acceptability of the radio programmes for rural development are evident from the fact that many of the crop varieties are known in villages at some places as "Radio Varieties", since information on the new strains reached the illiterate cultivators through the radio.

In his study on, *Television for Rural Development*, Rao (1992) points out that as regards reach and utilization of the media and villagers exposure to other information channels, it was observed that exposure to radio was found to be significantly high, with as many as 80 per cent having access to the medium and getting the benefit of exposure to the broadcasts. Rao also noted that rural/ agriculture programmes were high on the priority of listeners. It is encouraging to note that the villagers attach high importance to the listening of rural programmes.

A rural newspaper has been defined as one that "is primarily published from a rural area, devoting at least 50 per cent of its contents to the problems relating to the rural community, in a language akin to the idiom of the rural readers." When we refer to the rural press, we mean small newspapers with small circulations, serving small communities and catering to their special needs and interests that cannot be met by the urban press.

A rural newspaper provides a forum to articulate the urges of the common man. It takes up local issues and immediate requirements, affecting the people. It gives greater importance to the problems agitating the ordinary people: unemployment, scarcity of agricultural inputs, the law and order situation at the village level, etc. It is best suited to act as the second level of conversion of scientific knowledge into information in a usable form for the benefit of the ultimate clientele—the farmers.

It is well recognized that, by and large, the first conversion of scientific knowledge into information takes place at the level of research institutions. Literature produced at this stage for common consumption can be utilized by the educated and high level functionaries having access to such literature. Such information is further converted, for the second time, in the form of newspaper articles, pamphlets, newsletters and magazines, and transferred through the government extension agencies to the lower level government functionaries like the VLWs or the ADOs. It is here that the rural press plays perhaps its most important role. This is the primary role that most of the rural extension papers and magazines brought out by the agricultural universities and state departments of agriculture are performing. In the absence of the rural press, the knowledge generated in the experimental fields and laboratories of research institutions and universities would have remained confined to the files of the researchers and scientists.

Source of Development Information—It is not only with

respect to the scientific knowledge that the rural press works as the second level of conversion. It also plays an important role as conveyor of information about development plans and programmes of the government such as availability of seeds and fertilizers and loans through the banks and cooperative societies, market rates of agricultural produce, etc. It establishes a link between government functionaries and the village population and fills the much-needed gap in the information process. It has been widely accepted that so long as the rural population does not possess information processing capacity to use opportunities made available by the government, the massive economic inputs notwithstanding, the fruits of planned development will not reach the poor, those living below the poverty line and whose economic status the government plans profess to improve. The rural press is remarkably suited to fill in this missing link between the development functions and the users and consumers of development information.

A significant feature of the rural press is its closer identity with the people on account of emotional and linguistic affinity. The English language newspapers are more analytical in their approach and are interested in broader subjects like functioning of international institutions, legislative reforms, separation of judiciary from the executive, economic reforms, etc. They do not articulate the urges of the common man; whereas the editors of rural or district newspapers give greater importance to the problems concerning the common man—unemployment, rising prices, law and order difficulties at the local level, etc. The rural newspapers, which are in contact with the grassroots levels, and are aware of local problems, will be able to communicate in the language and idiom that the people understand.

It would be interesting to refer to the Chinese media environment in which the rural press has carved a special significance for itself. It has developed a unique culture of its own suited to serve the rural community effectively.

In China, the *Peasants Daily*, the biggest national agricultural four-page newspaper has a circulation of 10 lakhs. It began publication as a weekly in 1980 with a circulation of 2,00,000. Each copy costs about 60 paise, a price most rural families can afford. It sells in all Chinese provinces and ten foreign countries. *It is indeed remarkable to find that, as a rule, every reporter and editor must spend at least two months in the countryside every year during which time they are expected to familiarize themselves with the local peasants, their aspirations and difficulties.* The paper engages 300 peasants as stringers and about 700 as part-time correspondents. The paper chooses the most typical letters for publication while referring the rest to relevant organisations. Very often, investigation groups are sent to the countryside if the letters touch upon matters of significance.

Local Radio Station for Rural Broadcasting—One of the most disquieting features of the contemporary media scenario in India is the steady neglect of radio broadcasting. It is because of the unbridled, misplaced enthusiasm, skewed policies and wrong priorities, that in their zeal to promote television during the past decade, radio has been neglected by default.

Nikhil Chakravarty (1988) said: *The neglect of AIR is based on a popular misconception that radio in the age of television has no future. This has been disproved by the experience in the West, where television could not dislodge radio as a major means of communication. In America for instance, a 10-year old census showed that the number of radio sets was more than double that of the population: it must be many more now. A radio in the car, kitchen, bedroom and the children's room is a common feature even in lower middle class home in the USA.*

The Working Group on Autonomy for Akashvani and Doordarshan (Verghese Committee), had more than 20 years earlier recommended that India should give first priority to the development and densification of radio for at least the next 10-15 years.

Farm and Home Programmes—The establishment of the farm and home units to provide relevant, timely and local specific information areas has proved to be very useful. The emphasis in these farm and home programmes is on a direct method of presentation, dictated by the need to convey hard core scientific and technical information and quick timely guidance. In the broadcast of rural programmes AIR can derive great satisfaction at having gradually won the confidence of the traditionally conservative farmers and helping them through the use of new and improved techniques, to diversify crops, achieve higher production with obvious economic advantage to themselves and the country.

Radio—Extensive Reach—India has a rich tradition of the use of the radio for non-formal education, and rural development programmes and also for providing various types of learning opportunities and information to their people. A large number of countries including China, Australia, Canada, Italy, Nigeria, Pakistan, have reported using radio successfully in reaching "hard-to-reach" rural audiences quickly and quite inexpensively. The relevance of the radio as the most effective way of establishing continuous contact with the rural population has been well-established because of the enormous size of the country and lack of roads. Radio is still the cheapest, fastest and the farthest reaching technique for beginning a communication process.

As part of the process of bringing the media closer to the heads and hearts of the people, and to ensure their greater involvement in the media programmes, the concept of local radio stations has proved most effective. The local radio stations are ideally suited to the dissemination of farm technology according to agro-climatic regions, farming essentially being a regional industry. It draws talent rooted in the genius of the area and produces programmes suiting their socio-cultural environments. This local institution involves strong empathy in the progress and development of which they have their personal stakes and to that extent their personal involvement. The programmes produced at these radio stations are mainly in the areas of agricultural extension, nutrition, home and family improvement including food storage, fruit and vegetable preservation and rural women, etc.

TV and the Rural Development Programmes—When television was introduced in India in 1959, the official policy stressed that television was to be used as a medium for social education as well as an instrument to support programmes of social and economic development. Specifically, it was stated that TV would be used as a weapon against illiteracy and ignorance; it would bring about awareness among the people of sociological problems and make them conscious of national goals; it would create a sense of participation in India's efforts to usher in a new social order; it would play a vital role in cultivating civic consciousness and respect for law and order, public morality and so forth and, in the field of entertainment, it would mould public taste to higher aesthetic levels.

Krishi Darshan—Krishi Darshan is the oldest, well-established and the best known programme for the rural areas and farmers. The foresight and the pioneering spirit of the visionary space scientist, Dr. Vikram Sarabhai and the initiative of Dr. M.S. Swaminathan crystallized into this innovative programme.

The basic objective of the programme is to familiarize the rural audience with the latest technical and scientific know-how about farming practices, agricultural implements, animal husbandry, and rural development programmes; to acquaint the viewers with the importance of health, family planning, personal hygiene, sanitation, etc. as also to provide healthy entertainment.

In order to evaluate the effectiveness of the programme, a survey in three villages of Hisar district, the hinterland of Haryana, was conducted by two faculty members of the Haryana Agricultural University including the author of this book. The objectives of the survey were: to study the TV viewing pattern of rural audience, to ascertain the usefulness of Krishi Darshan programme by the rural community, to identify constraints in viewing Krishi Darshan programme and to undertake content analysis of the programme.

Regarding programme presentation, the respondents mentioned that it was not very appealing as most programmes were studio based monologues with low visual content and appeal. In their view, interviews with farmers in their fields along with their opinions and experiences on various practices would be more useful. The respondents expressed the view that the recommendations of specialists on TV were more related to particular areas of specialization whereas they were more interested to learn about "packages" that could be adopted. Moreover, they stated that the majority of the recommendations could be adopted by big rather than small farmers. As a large majority of the respondents listened to radio programmes related to farming, they felt that they were being apprised about recent practices, more through the radio than TV. Radio was noted to be a more credible source of agricultural information even in those households which had a TV set, primarily because the programmes were scheduled at more convenient timings, were regular and most of them were directly concerned with field operations.

Extension Agency Reinforcement—Interpersonal media which in the context of rural development would include extension works in the agriculture and community development departments of the State governments, personnel of agricultural agencies like MAFAL and Agro-industries centres and extension set-up of agricultural universities and research institutes would provide necessary reinforcement and supplement the media programmes. Co-ordination between extension agencies and rural broadcasting will make those programmes more purposive and meaningful. These agencies can, in fact, help disseminate information about media programmes including topics and subjects for discussion through numerous magazines, leaflets, folders they bring out regularly and on special occasions like farmers' fairs and field days, as part of their extension activities. They can also involve programme producers and planners in programme formulation and modifying programmes to suit the requirement of the target audience.

Training programmes for workers in rural development project like village level workers in communication methods and those of communication practitioners in rural development would go a long way in creating the much needed mutual appreciation of both the aspects.

Demystifying the Media Profession—Knowledge, understanding and expertise in communication practice and profession should not be exclusive prerogative of the media professionals.

This needs to be extended through a basic training course to all the experts and workers at various levels working in the areas of rural development, health, sanitation and other nation buiding activities. A basic appreciation of the elements of communication needs to be imparted through appropriate short-term courses. Media specialists, sociologists and development planners should work out an interdisciplinary mechanism for identifying the audience requirements, establishing proper feedback systems and extend guidance in the evaluation of effectiveness of communication programmes.

Linkages, or co-ordination between different agencies, as has been pointed out earlier would go a long way in providing the remedy which Dube (1988) has stated in his book, *Modernization and Development— The Search for Alternative Paradigms*:

> Communication links are often found to be weak and wide gaps persist between the planner, the implementation agencies and the people. There is a distortion of messages as they descend from the highest levels to the people at the bottom. The feedback is not properly organized; even when it is received its impact is minimal, unless the situation assumes critical proportions. Refashioning and reorganisation of the communication network from top-down to bottom-up is necessary.

CASE STUDIES OF COMMUNICATION SUPPORT TO AGRICULTURE

The premier organisation conducting research in agriculture, Indian Agricultural Research Institute (IARI), had emphasised that agricultural universities and extension departments organise short term courses for agricultural scientists to train them in writing technical articles in simple language by using local equivalents for technical terms. To gear the scientists to the task of writing for farmers is a difficult proposition, mainly because of their preference for research paper writing. In pursuance of the above recommendations, the author in 1996 conceived and directed a Post-Graduate Diploma Course in Agricultural Journalism at Haryana Agricultural University. The programme had been developed to achieve the following objectives : To acquaint the participants with the role and principles of agricultural journalism and development communication; familiarise them with the process involved in print and electronic media; expose them to practical skills in writing for farmers and farm families, research publications, feature writing for newspapers and preparing radio and television programmes; and to sensitise them to various tasks and skills in public relations and public service campaigns.

Since 1996, agricultural scientists and development workers from all over the country including Karnataka, Andaman and Nicobar Islands, Tamil Nadu and Rajasthan, have undergone training. As an essential part of the programme, the trainees had taken up a research project on one of the information/communication aspects of agriculture. Some of the subjects have been : Effectiveness of Farm and Home Units Programmes of All India Radio; TV Viewing behaviour, Critical analysis of agricultural news reporting in leading newspapers, and many more on allied subjects. Research studies undertaken by the participants have been summarised. These studies analyse the effectiveness of sources of farm information and provide useful insight into the communication experiences.

1. Effectiveness of Farm and Home Unit's Programme of All India Radio, Delhi

Jai Parkash Singh Dabas (1998)

In order to achieve the target of increased food production so as to meet the needs of ever increasing population, the scientists need to develop appropriate technologies, which are environment friendly, within the reach of the farmers and contribute to sustainable agricultural production. The generation of technology alone will not help achieve the target, but we have to devise effective strategy for regular and quick transfer of these technologies to the ultimate users—the farmers for adoption. In a country like ours, majority of the farmers are resource poor, illiterate having diversified needs, speaking different dialects, with poor telecommunication and electricity facilities in the villages. In such a situation radio is the cheapest, most convenient and important medium for educating the rural folk about latest agricultural technologies through quick communication, regardless of the distance and literacy level. The present national coverage of All India Radio is 90.6 per cent by area and 97.3 per cent by population (*Manorama Year Book*, 1996).

The country has a network of about 185 radio stations, broadcasting rural programmes on different topics, in different languages and as per the agro-eco-requirement of their range. In order to ensure effective transfer of technical know-how in its intended form to the farmers, coverage alone is not important, but the content of programme should be relevant and informative in terms of farmer's need, and timing and mode of presentation should be effective.

The Delhi station of All India Radio caters to the needs of the farmers of Delhi villages, Faridabad and Gurgaon districts of Haryana, Ghaziabad, Meerut, Saharanpur, Muzaffarnagar, Bulandshahar and Aligarh districts of western Uttar Pradesh. Farmers from Rohtak, Sonepat, Panipat and Karnal districts also listen to the AIR Delhi programmes. The Farm and Home Unit of AIR, Delhi has three important programmes exclusively for agricultural development : *Krishi Charcha* at 6.55 a.m. (5 minutes), *Unnat Krishi* at 2.10 p.m. (10 minutes) and *Krishi Jagat* at 7.05 p.m. (25 minutes).

The objectives of the study were : To study the effectiveness of the content and timeliness of the programmes, and also the mode of presentation adopted in these programmes. The study was conducted for the programmes broadcast by Farm and Home Unit of All India Radio, Delhi station during June 1998. The broadcasts were categorised under 15 sub-heads for making quantitative evaluation of the programmes. Response from 30 farmers from two villages (15 from each village) Palla and Akbarpur Majra was received; information so collected was tabulated and analysed for drawing logical conclusions.

The *Krishi Charcha* programme is prepared and broadcast by the staff of Farm and Home Unit, and the mode of presentation is talk. *Unnat Krishi* programme is broadcast by recording it in advance and is presented by experts, the mode of presentation is talk. *Krishi Jagat*, which is the oldest programme broadcasts information under five sub-heads : News from agricultural commodity markets, scientific information on any topic of agriculture, *lok geet*, weather forecast and news, next day's programmes.

The study is confined to the second component, i.e. scientific information on any topic from agriculture which is selected as per farmers need during that period. Time devoted to this part is 10 minutes. The information is presented by following interview mode of presentation or discussion. The interview is between expert invited from Agricultural Research system or administration and staff of AIR. Sometimes a farmer is also invited and then mode of presentation is discussion between these three.

Under the *Krishi Charcha* programme the broadcast topics have been categorised into 15 major groups for analysis purposes. The data revealed that 23.1 per cent time was devoted to agronomy, followed by plant protection (19.8%), soil and fertilizer management (16.5%), vegetables (13.2%) and orchards (9.9%). Animal Husbandry ranked at sixth place having 6.6 per cent of the total time share.

Broadcast data for *Unnat Krishi* programme indicate that maximum broadcast time was devoted to agronomy (19.8%) followed by orchards (13.2%). About one-third time was devoted to these two topics. Vegetables and plant protection were given 10 per cent time of each of the total broadcast; other categories covered in the broadcast were rainfed agriculture (6.6%), weed management (3.3%), animal husbandry (3.3%), poultry (3.3%), fisheries (3.3%), piggery and goatry (3.3%), agricultural engineering (3.3%) but their share was quite poor. Mushroom cultivation and floriculture were again completely ignored, although these are two important emerging aspects on which no information was provided to the farmers.

Krishi Jagat is the oldest and popular programme broadcast in the evening. In this programme also agronomy got the major share of the broadcast (23.3%), followed by soil and fertilizer management (16.6%). Agronomy along with soil and fertilizer management constitutes the major portion of the broadcast, i.e. about 40 per cent. Plant protection got 10 per cent share and ranks third in broadcast priority. Vegetables and animal husbandry were devoted 6.6 per cent time each. Some important aspects like weed control, poultry and rainfed agriculture did not find place in the broadcast. Little less than one-fourth time was devoted to other aspects like budget, policy planning, forestry, environment and ecology and market management, etc.

Table 5.1 provides a holistic view of programmes broadcast

during June 1993. The data shows that agronomy share was a major one; little less than one-fourth of all the topics broadcast. It has first place in all the three programmes, it was followed by plant protection with 13 per cent share; collectively both these subjects enjoyed more than one-third share in the broadcast programme. Ten per cent time of the broadcast was devoted to vegetable cultivation, soil and fertilizer management and orchard component of agriculture got 9.4 per cent time each.

Table 5.1 : Programme Categories and Time Devoted to Agricultural Programmes

S. No.	*Programme category*	*Programme*			*Total*	*Rank*
		Krishi Charcha	*Unnat Krishi*	*Krishi Jagat*		
1.	Agronomy	35	60	70	165 (23.9)	I
2.	Soil and fertilizer management	25	10	30	65 (9.4)	IV
3.	Plant protection	30	30	30	90 (13.0)	II
4.	Mushroom cultivation	—	—	—	—	
5.	Vegetables	20	30	20	70 (10.1)	III
6.	Orchards	15	40	10	65 (9.4)	V
7.	Weed management	5	10	—	15 (2.1)	XIII
8.	Animal husbandry	10	10	20	40 (5.7)	V
9.	Floriculture	—	—	10	10 (1.4)	X
10.	Poultry	5	10	—	15 (2.1)	VIII
11.	Fisheries	5	10	10	25 (3.6)	VI
12.	Rainfed agriculture	—	20	—	20 (2.9)	VII
13.	Piggery and goatry	—	10	10	20 (2.9)	VIII
14.	Agricultural engineering	—	10	—	10 (1.4)	IX
15.	Miscellaneous	—	10	70	80 (11.5)	

Note : Figures in parentheses indicate percentage share of the total.

Mushroom cultivation was totally neglected and could not find place in the broadcast, though it is very important area and finds favour with the farmers in the urban areas of Delhi, Gurgaon, Faridabad and Ghaziabad.

The farmers were of the view that the discussion mode of presentation, which also involves the farmer, is the best, followed by interview mode of presentation. Farmers also felt that topics like market news, weather forecast, *lok geet* in *Krishi Jagat* make it more interesting and attractive.

Regarding appropriateness of the broadcast timing during the day farmers were of the view that the *Krishi Jagat* programme is best suited to the audience as it is broadcast in the evening, when farmers are free from field operations and are generally available at their homes. The morning programme *Krishi Charcha*, and the afternoon programme, *Unnat Krishi*, are quite often missed, as during these timings farmers are preoccupied with their field and home activities.

In the changing agricultural scenario when need for information is increasing day by day and farmers are information hungry, radio can play a crucial role in providing them the desired information effectively and easily. To meet the farmers' requirement, programmes on agro-enterprises like poultry, piggery, mushroom cultivation, post-harvest magagement, value addition, bee keeping, protected vegetable cultivation, floriculture, etc. need to be given more and more emphasis in terms of quality and coverage.

To make the programmes more interesting and listener-friendly, appropriate mode of presentation, discussion or dramatic presentation may be adopted for effective transfer of technology for less articulate farmers.

2. A Critical Study of Farm Broadcasting at All India Radio, Chennai, Tamil Nadu

I. Dorairajan (1998)

Radio is one of the most important means of reaching the farmers. It is one of the fastest media and is becoming a powerful force for mobilising public opinion and for educating people in all spheres of life. The ultimate object of agricultural communication is that technology and agricultural news should reach the farmers. The message should be clear to the farmers; it should be properly processed so that it is comprehensible, acceptable and motivate the farmers for adoption.

There are certain special advantages that radio has as a medium of communication. It reaches more people, moves more quickly than any other means of mass communication. It is relatively cheap and also reaches illiterate audiences. It builds enthusiasm and maintains interest. The medium has its limitations also—broadcasting facilities are available only in limited places, time assigned for radio talks is generally limited and it is difficult to check on results. The influence of radio is limited only to those who can listen intelligently. The programmes for rural people frequently lose out in competition with entertainment.

All the rural listeners may or may not be educated in the formal sense. Farmers do strenuous work throughout the day and like everyone else, would rather be entertained than educated after a day's hard work. Most of them do not take notes while listening to a programme. They value the radio as a source of news and other information, as a source of entertainment and company. They may not like to follow lengthy programmes unless the programmes hold exceptional interest. The rural listeners do not constitute a uniform type of audience. There are differences in education, age, income, experience, etc. The receptivity of the listeners to the programme depends upon their background and thus varies with the individuals. They have more interest in items of direct, timely and local interest to them. Many of them are faced with several problems and always in a mood to look forward to solutions for problems such as lack of food, clothing, housing, employment, health, etc. They try to stick to their traditions, customs and culture.

The objectives of the study were : to critically study strategies adopted on the programming aspects of farm broadcast to identify constraints, if any, to suggest suitable measures for effective dissemination and to identify the needs of rural farmers.

The study was taken to cover the farm broadcast from AIR

Chennai. Pre-tested questionnaires were used to collect data from AIR, extension workers and the farmers. The respondents were from four major districts of Tamil Nadu apart from minor representations from other districts. The farmers, extension officers and AIR officials were personally contacted and interviewed with the help of questionnaire prepared for this purpose.

The results of the present study showed that despite the availability of highly sophisticated and fast media like Video technology, Computer, Micro Computer technology and Internet, radio still reigns over the rural masses as a source of mass communication, be it for agro-technology or entertainment, regular news, etc. This fact is revealed in the present study as 87.6 per cent of the respondents possessed radio. Further the interest evinced in radio message by the rural people is reflected in the awareness of time of broadcast (94%) among the respondents.

Another interesting feature among the rural farmers is that they like to participate in programmes on radio and more so on television, for the personal appeal. In the present investigation nearly 60 per cent of the respondents had participated in the farm home programme.

As for the listening aspect, more than 55 per cent of the respondents listen to the programme, daily. The impact of radio messages can be evaluated the way the medium has motivated the farmers in adoption of the messages. By way of motivation, it is interesting to note from the study that nearly 92 per cent of the respondents discussed the messages with their colleagues. To add up to this, it is surprising to learn that 93.8 per cent of the farmers have adopted what they hear from the radio.

Further it was observed that the illiterate radio listener is either equal to or higher than the literate one in communities without radios in terms of the level of general awareness. This observation clearly demonstrates the impact of radio even among the illiterate rural communities.

The present study also revealed the need for a sort of orientation training for the participants in radio talks. One skilled radio professional with a good tape recorder can produce high quality material for radio.

The economic well-being of the nation largely depends on agriculture and radio has attained the status of indispensable extension medium.

Generally, it is understood that the farmers are aware and interested in participating in the radio programmes. Many of the farmers discuss the technology with their fellow farmers and it is encouraging to note that majority of the farmers are adopting the message they listen. From this study it is clear that farmers are interested in discussions and interviews rather than just talking along.

The study concludes that radio has been doing a marvellous job in uplifting the rural masses. By following the suggested correctional measures, the efficiency can be further improved in the interest of national development.

3. A Study on the Sources of Information Used by Farmers in Mahendergarh District

Dr. R.S. Kanwar

Agricultural technology is transmitted to the farmers through various media, personal localite or informal media, and personal cosmopolite or formal media. This project was planned to ascertain the sources of agricultural information used by the farmers in Mahendergarh district of Haryana with the following objectives : To explore the sources of agricultural information used by farmers, to compare the role of mass media with other sources used in dissemination of agricultural information, and to suggest suitable information strategy for the farmers of Mahendergarh district.

Mahendergarh is one of the oldest districts of Haryana; its landscape varies from flat to undulating, marked by sand dunes and small dry Aravali hills of varying heights. Fields suffer from water and wind erosion. Soils of the district are sandy to sandy loam with low organic matter. Water table is generally very deep with only 36 per cent of cultivable area under assured irrigation. It is considered to be an agriculturally backward district of Haryana. Small land holdings, poor irrigation facilities, poor economic conditions and lower literacy rate (44% as compared to 56% of

Haryana) are some of the factors responsible for agricultural backwardness. These factors also directly affect the adoption of new farm technology by farmers. In general, lack of awareness, technical know-how and knowledge regarding resource factors such as credit, storage and marketing, etc. are the major reasons for non-adoption of technology by the farmers. A well-developed communication system can help to improve the existing condition of lack of information.

A questionnaire was developed for the study and the data were collected by personally interviewing the farmers, both on soico-economic characters and use of media sources. The sources of information were categorised as under :

1. Mass media included television, radio, newspaper, agriculture literature, trainings, exhibitions, Kisan Melas (farmers' fairs) and demonstrations.
2. Interpersonal, external or formal sources included university and KGK scientists, personnel of agriculture department, cooperative society, HSDC, NSC, HAFED, NEL, IFFCO, KRIBHCO, etc.
3. Interpersonal, local or information sources included neighbours, friends, progressive farmers, private dealers, relatives and family members.

The study revealed that whereas 42 per cent respondents had television sets and 24 per cent watched agriculture programme (*Krishi Darshan*), an earlier survey in five villages of this district showed use of TV by 11 per cent farmers. Radio was a more frequently used medium (58%). Majority of the respondents listen to evening programme (*Krishi Jagat*) from Rohtak station. Lack of time, interest and need-based programmes are some of the important reasons for not using television and radio, as mentioned by the farmers. Most of the farmers cannot adopt the information gained from these media sources because (i) they do not write down the information and hence forget them, and (ii) the questions arising in their minds remain unanswered for which they have to use interpersonal sources.

The other important sources of information used by the farmers to a great extent are demonstrations/trainings/Kisan Melas and exhibitions. Field demonstrations, agricultural trainings, Kisan Melas, tours and exhibitions were used by 24, 20, 14 and 4 per cent respondents, respectively. Among interpersonal local sources, private dealers were used by maximum (92%) farmers followed by neighbours (80%), friends (56%) and progressive farmers (52%). Neighbours, friends and progressive farmers collectively serve as the most important localite source of agricultural information as 96 per cent respondents use these sources. To some extent, relatives (12%) and family members (8%) are also used as information sources.

Table 5.2 : Sources of Agricultural Information Used by Farmers in Order of Preference

Source	*Order of preference/utilization*					
	First		*Second*		*Third*	
	Number	*%*	*Number*	*%*	*Number*	*%*
1. N/F/PF	27	54	13	26	12	24
2. Private dealer	8	16	21	42	15	30
3. Family member	2	4	2	4	0	0
4. Univ./Krishi Gyan Kendra	5	10	8	16	5	10
5. Agriculture Department	1	2	2	4	3	6
6. Haryana Seed Development Corporation/ Cooperative Societies	0	0	1	2	5	10
7. Radio	4	8	3	6	10	20
8. Agriculture literature	3	6	0	0	0	0
Total	50	100	50	100	50	100

N=Neighbours, F=Friends, PF=Progressive farmers.

Education has a marked effect on the use of media. About 93 per cent illiterate farmers used local sources, for agricultural information, whereas educated farmers used all the three types of communication sources, i.e. formal, informal and mass media sources. With the increase in education level dependence on local sources decreased. All the three categories of farmers (small, medium and big) used all types of sources, viz., formal, informal and mass media; but big farmers used local sources less and mass media more than small or medium farmers.

On the basis of the study it was suggested that since farmers depend more on local sources, particularly neighbours, friends, progressive farmers and private dealers so the group leaders among these localites should be identified and made information rich so that agricultural technology can be effectively transmitted to 'information deficient' clientele. This can be done by training these progressive farmers and group leaders, and providing them with literature on agriculture.

Local relay stations of TV and radio, and local newspapers can be very useful for meeting the requirements of farmers by providing them with local and need-based programmes/material.

Agricultural literature should be made available in villages at some common places like Panchayat Bhawan, Farmers' Clubs, etc. so that interested readers can make use of it.

Demonstrations, trainings, exhibitions, etc. are quite effective and reliable sources of information. So, these methods should be used to the maximum extent.

4. Study of Influence of Doordarshan and Cable Network on Socio-Economic Parameters of Rural Households of Karnataka

P.V. Rama Gowda (1998)

The present study is an attempt to ascertain the socio-economic impact of TV viewing rural households in the Kolar district of Karnataka. The objectives of the study were : To analyse the association between the socio-economic parameters of TV owners of rural households, and to assess the influence of TV viewing on agriculture as well as on health and nutrition.

Sixty respondents were randomly selected from the TV owners of the two villages in Kolar district. A well structured pre-tested questionnaire was used to collect information from the sample respondents, and data obtained by contacting each of these respondents by personal interviews. The entire analysis was worked out separately for those two groups of respondents; first group comprising those who watch only Doordarshan and second group comprising those who watch both Doordarshan and cable network programmes. Simple tabular analysis with percentages was used to analyse the data.

The study revealed that TV viewing timings in rural areas ranged from 2-4 hours in case of those who watch Doordarshan programmes and ranged from 3-6 hours per day in case of those who watch both TV and cable programmes with an average time of 4.34 hours/day.

Regarding the viewing behaviour of the respondents, 68 per cent of the total respondents have indicated that they watch TV/cable for entertainment programme. This percentage is high in case of those who watch only Doordarshan programmes at 75 per cent (compared to 61% in cable network). About 55 per cent of all the respondents have indicated that they watch TV/cable in order to pastime and this percentage is high in case of those who watch cable network (64% against 47% in case of Doordarshan viewers).

The entire sample of households who had TV are literate indicating that most of literate households like to have TV in their homes. About 40 per cent of the total respondents in the rural households have collegiate education and more. The distribution of level of education in both groups of respondents was almost similar excepting higher education in case of those respondents who watch both TV and cable wherein all the respondents were from this category.

About 53 per cent of rural respondents have opined that watching TV/cable has influenced the 'good living practice' and nearly equal number of respondents (52%) have also felt that the mass media has influenced positively regarding their knowledge of 'health awareness'. A moderate per cent of respondents (ranging from 35-41 per cent) in their opinion on the other health parameters under study such as 'tackling health problem', 'child nutrition' and 'child upkeep', have indicated that watching TV/cable has positive effect on their attitude towards health and nutrition.

Majority of rural respondents have opined after watching TV/ cable network that there is an influence on the use of technologies in agriculture (65% of the respondents) and crops they are planning/ growing (60%) and managing the diseases and pests (40%). Again about 43 per cent of the farmers indicated that watching TV provided information on markets as well as on price. On price forecasting, only about 12 per cent respondents positively opined that they were getting information on future prices of the commodities.

TECHNOLOGY

References and definitions of technology represent the diverse and many faceted nuances of the phenomenon. It has been understood as a process, a set of mind, and instrument for national development. The way technology is understood and defined covers a really vast canvas of human experience and understanding.

Technology, in a limited aspect, has been understood as applying scientific knowledge to industrial process. In a broader sense, technology means application of science to practical arm of life. It refers to the transformation of scientific laws into machines, tools, mechanical devices, instruments, innovations, procedures and techniques to attain tangible ends or manipulate environment for practical purposes. It has also been defined as a design for instrumental action that reduces uncertainty in the cause effect relationships involved in achieving a desired outcome.

Likewise technology has also been classified as :

1. *High technologies* : Capital and energy intensive, require heavy use of non-renewable resources, and generate large volume of toxic wastes.
2. *Appropriate technology* : Low cost technology using mainly local or easily available materials and skills.
3. *Intermediate technology* : Small scale technologies emerging out of a gradual process of technological innovations sustainable in the communities. Avoids pitfalls of high technologies especially exploitation of natural and human resources.

In the context of technology for rural areas the concepts of technological determinism and transfer of technology are equally important. Technological determinism, according to Rogers, is the degree to which technology is main cause of social change in the society. The adherents to this concept consider technology as a prime mover which help shape a society. In a country as vast as India, with varying levels of educational standards and academic excellence to absorb and adopt technologies, it will be a tall order to presume that technological determinism would be so strong as to factor as a cause of social change. It could at the most be one of the factors for such a change and that too not always beneficial.

Transfer of technology—Technology transfer is a process by which innovations are exchanged between individuals and organizations that are involved in research and development, on the one hand and in putting technological innovations into use on the other. Transfer of technology does not mean merely taking a new idea or procedure or product just by transferring it physically. Mere physical shift will not ensure its use. The people, so affected will not be passive recipient to apply a particular technology. Since people have their attitudes, opinions and values new technology has to work within the social environment. It cannot be a push button shifting of technology. The technology must be compatible with social and cultural systems. Communication of technologies alone is not enough. Several other aspects including infrastructure, availability of support services, marketing etc. must be in place for its effective utilization.

For reaching out benefits of technology transfer to rural areas, the Government of India in 1987 put five key technological missions in place so as to employ suitable technology to promote development. These missions were on telecommunications, immunization, drinking water, literacy and oilseeds development. In 1989, the oilseeds mission achieved its target a year ahead of schedule, and the drinking water mission covered 70,000 villages out of 1,00,000 it was projected to cover by 1990. The telecom mission was established during 1989 to direct India's telecommunication revolution.

New agricultural technologies bring many ecological problems such as salinity, soil erosion, surface and ground water pollution. The undesirable effects of new agricultural technology on natural resources have raised the issue of sustainability—whether agriculture in its present form has capacity to remain productive while maintaining the resource base. Development of technology in isolation from users creates more problems. Agricultural technologies generated at well-endowed research farms are input intensive and expensive. Several studies and seminars have pointed out to the undesirable consequences of introduction of agricultural technologies in terms of environmental pollution, ecological imbalance and degradation of natural resources.

Women and adoption of technology—It has been heartening to observe that several innovative experiments have been successful in making women to adopt technologies. The East Asian experience has demonstrated that women excel at new technologies, as they are more disciplined, less unionized, and, can easily master new skills useful in such key industries as computers, electronics and value-added fashion garments.

The success story of the Grammeen Bank in Bangladesh, its approach which emphasizes the creation of enabling conditions in which every human being may have the opportunity to carve out dignified ways of living for herself/himself, has been an inspiring illustration for the developing countries. Grameen Bank has not only expanded its credit operations which are targeted at the poorest of the poor in rural Bangladesh, it has also rapidly diversified its activities. Grameen Bank today is the focal point of a global network of institutions and individuals who provide micro-credit to fight poverty. Within Bangladesh, the Bank has undertaken major investment initiatives in those sectors where the poor have the comparative advantage in terms of their skills, enterprise and productive capacity. It has recently begun a scheme to provide mobile phones to women in every village. This shows that women can easily adapt themselves to the new communication technologies and use them for their family and economic survival.

The Self-Employed Women Association (SEWA) has shown the way by the using video technology for articulating grievances of women construction workers, vegetable sellers and other such self-employed women who had no forum for collective social action. It has gone a long way in innovating several self-help programmes like opening bank accounts for the illiterate women etc. These women workers also learnt to operate and handle video camera and other audio-visual equipments.

Caution in Approach—The lessons learnt in the process of adopting technological innovations should not be lost sight of. Technological innovations open up vast new possibilities. However, they are not instant miracles, but tools to be introduced and used only after careful consideration is given to all possible resulting ramifications. Each has particular potential, yet none is isolated. They are parts of a total system, which should be planned and shaped keeping in mind the impact such a technology is likely to create on society. Technological innovations can often have negative effects, both economic and social, and may distort directions and priorities for overall developmental activities. We have also seen as to how certain communication technologies (particularly television, video and cable television), which were presented as technologies for rural development offering choices of programmes have proved to be technologies largely for the entertainment. The Report of the International Commission for the Study of Communication Problems, had in 1978, agreed that "*The promise of cable television (multiple channels, multiple choices for the viewers) may have been oversold in the early development period.* Similarly, the communication planners and scholars are once again revisiting the benefits of satellite and new communication technologies.

Therefore, let a caveat be entered : Introduction of new technologies, particularly in rural areas, need to be planned with abundant caution, not only with respect to the economic and social costs involved but also keeping in mind long term impact such a step is likely to create in the village society.

POVERTY ALLEVIATION PROGRAMMES

From all accounts faster economic growth has helped us to reduce poverty. The progress on this score was low during the 1970s when growth was slow. In the 1980s and 1990s growth-accelerated poverty had also come down. However, there is widespread concern that resources used for poverty alleviation schemes and for various types of subsidies in the name of the poor may not have been effective in alleviating poverty. The Approach Paper points out:

> Today Rs. 60 out of Rs. 100 in wage schemes is reserved for wages, but it has been reported that in some states only Rs. 10 to 15 actually goes to the poor worker, the rest is illegal income for bureaucracy, contractors and politicians. An issue repeatedly highlighted in public hearing on these schemes is that of payment of lower wages to women workers. Norms for reservation for women under-employment schemes are also not followed consistently. The absence of sex-disaggregated data on beneficiaries in non-targeted schemes makes it difficult the monitor and control such violations.*

The Approach Paper has, therefore, come out with several suggestions for effective implementation of poverty alleviation programmes. Some of the suggestions are:

1. ***Swaranjayanti Gram Swarozgar Yojna (SGSY)***—should be transformed into a micro finance programme to be run by the banks and other financial institutions, with no subsidy.
2. ***Contribution from Gram Sabhas***—Funds to gram sabhas should be extended only when the people contribute, either in cash or in kind, say 15% in normal blocks and 5% in tribal/poor blocks. This will instill a sense of ownership in the community.
3. ***Undertaking Productive Works***—There should be a single wage employment programme to be run only in areas of distress. The focus should be on undertaking productive works and their maintenance, such as rural roads, watershed development, and rejuvenation of tanks, afforestation, irrigation and drainage. The payment of wages should be

* See "Approach Paper to the Tenth Five Year Plan (2002-2007)", Sept. 2001.

mainly in the form of foodgrains with some cash component. This will improve self-targeting.

4. ***Grassroots Women's Groups***—Grassroots women's groups should be empowered and encouraged to implement selected poverty alleviation schemes, particularly food-for-work schemes in areas affected by natural disasters.
5. ***Marginal and Small Farmers***—Special efforts should be made to strengthen the economy of the marginal and small farmers, forest produce gatherers, artisans, unskilled workers etc. The poor should not merely benefit from growth generated elsewhere, they should contribute to growth.

WELFARE PROGRAMMES

India is a welfare state, committed to the welfare and development of its people in general and of vulnerable sections in particular. The Preamble, Directive Principles of State Policy, Fundamental Rights and specific sections, namely, Articles 38, 39 and 46, in the Constitution of India, stand testimony to the commitment of the State to its people.

Welfare programmes are oriented towards empowering the disadvantaged and marginalized sections of the society, viz., Scheduled Castes, Scheduled Tribes, other backward classes, minorities, disabled, aged persons, street children and drug addicts.

In keeping with the thrust of the majority of welfare programmes to empower the weaker and socially and economically deprived sections of the society the Ministry of Welfare was constituted on 25 May 1998. The Department of Tribal Affairs, was created on 13 October 1999.

The areas which are of concern to the Ministry of Social Justice and Empowerment are also those where a major role is played by the State governments. Thus the responsibility for implementation of the schemes is shared between the Central and State governments. The Central Government is responsible for formulating the related policies and programmes besides coordinating and promoting implementation of services by states.

The Scheduled Castes (SC) are specified in accordance with Article 34 of the Constitution. While the Constitution has prescribed certain protective measures and safeguards for these classes, successive Five Year Plans have regarded their progress as major objective of national policy.

The Constitution prescribes protection and safeguards for Scheduled Castes, Scheduled Tribes and weaker sections either specially or by way of insisting on their general rights as citizens with the objective of promoting their educational and economic interests and removing social disabilities. Main safeguards are : (i) Abolition of untouchability and forbidding its practice in any form [Article17]; (ii) Promotion of their education and economic interest and their protection from social injustice and all forms of exploitation [Article 46]; (iii) Throwing open by law of Hindu religious institutions of public character to all classes and sections of Hindus [Article 25 (b)]; (iv) Removal of any disability, liability, restriction or conditions with regard to access to shops, public restaurants, hotels and places of public entertainment or use of wells, tanks, bathing ghats, roads and places of public resort maintained wholly or partially out of state funds or dedicated to the use of general public [Article 15 (2)]; (v) Curtailment by law in the interest of any Scheduled Tribes of general rights of all citizens to move freely, settle in and acquire property [Article 19 (A)]; (vi) Forbidding of any denial of admission to educational institutions maintained by the state or receiving grants out of state funds [Article 29 (2)]; (vii) Permitting the state to make reservation for backward classes in public services in case of inadequate representations and requiring the state to consider claims of the Scheduled Castes and Scheduled Tribes in the making of appointments to public services [Articles 16 and 335]; (viii) Special representation in the Lok Sabha and State Legislative Assemblies to Scheduled Castes and Scheduled Tribes till 25 January 2000 [Articles 330, 332 and 335]; (ix) Setting up of tribal advisory councils and separate departments in states and appointment of a special officer at the Centre to promote their welfare and safeguard their interests [Articles 164 and 338 and Fifth Schedule]; (x) Special provision for administration and control of Scheduled Tribal areas

[Articles 244 and Fifth and Sixth Schedules]; and (xi) Prohibition of traffic in human beings and forced labour [Article 23].

By virtue of the Constitution (Sixty-fifth Amendment) Act, 1990, the Special Officer's post under Article 338 of the Constitution has been created by the National Commission of Scheduled Castes and Scheduled Tribes. The Commission has a Chairperson, a vice-chairperson and a five other members to be appointed by the President. It shall be the duty of the Commission: to investigate and monitor all matters relating to the safeguards provided for the Scheduled Castes and Scheduled Tribes under the Constitution or under any other law; to enquire into specific complaints with respect to the deprivation of rights and safeguards of the Scheduled Castes and Tribes; to participate and advise on the planning process of socio-economic development of the Scheduled Castes and Scheduled Tribes; and to evaluate the progress of their development under the Union and any state; to present to the President annually, and at such other times as the Commission may deem fit, reports upon the working of these safeguards; to make in such reports/recommendations as to the measures that should be taken by the Union or any state for the effective implementation of those safeguards and other measures for the protection, welfare and socio-economic development of the Scheduled Castes and Scheduled Tribes; and to discharge such other functions in relation to the protection, welfare and development and advancement of the Scheduled Castes and Scheduled Tribes as the President may, subject to the provisions of any law made by Parliament, by rule, specify.

The Government had set up three Parliamentary Committees, first in 1966, second in 1971 and third in 1973 to examine the implementation of the constitutional safeguards for welfare of Scheduled Castes and Scheduled Tribes. The Committee has since been constituted as a Standing Committee of Parliament on Labour Welfare.

The states and Union Territories have separate departments to look after the welfare of Scheduled Castes and Scheduled Tribes and other backward classes. Administrative set-up varies from state to state. In Bihar, Madhya Pradesh and Orissa separate ministers have been appointed to look after tribal welfare as prescribed in Article 164 of the Constitution. Some other states have set up committees of members of state legislatures on the pattern of the Parliamentary Committee at the Centre. All the states having scheduled areas including Tamil Nadu and West Bengal have constituted Tribal Advisory Councils as per the provisions in the Fifth Schedule to the Constitution to advise on matters pertaining to the welfare and advancement of Scheduled Tribes.

A number of voluntary organisations also promote welfare of Scheduled Castes and Scheduled Tribes. Among them, the important organisations of all India character are : *Harijan Sevak Sangh*, Delhi; *Indian Red Cross Society*, New Delhi; *Ramakrishna Mission,* Narendrapur; *Bhartiya Adimjati Sevak Sangh*, New Delhi; *Ramakrishna Mission*, Puri, Silchar and Purulia and *Bhartiya Samaj Unnati Mandal*, Bhivandi. The Government also provides grants-in-aid to voluntary organisations of local character working among Scheduled Castes. During 2000-01, 340 voluntary organisations were given grant-in-aid to the tune of Rs. 22.50 crore.

For enlarging the scope and making penal provisions more stringent, the Untouchability (Offences) Act, 1955 has been comprehensively amended and renamed as the Protection of Civil Rights Act, 1955 which came into force with effect from 19 November, 1976. This Act provides for penalties for preventing any person on ground of untouchability, from enjoying the rights accruing on account of abolition of untouchability. Enhanced penalties/punishments have been provided for subsequent offences. The Scheduled Castes and Scheduled Tribes (Prevention of Atrocities) Act, 1989 which came into force on 30 January 1990, specifies offences which are considered as atrocities and provides for deterrent punishments for commission of the same. Comprehensive Rules were also framed under the SCs & the STs Act in 1995, which among other things provide for relief and rehabilitation of the affected persons. It also envisages preventive measures, and states have to evolve schemes, among others, for economic and social rehabilitation of such victims. All states and Union Territories except Arunachal Pradesh and Nagaland have specified special courts for trial of offences under this Act.

Exclusive special courts have been set up in Andhra Pradesh, Madhya Pradesh, Rajasthan, Gujarat, Karnataka, Tamil Nadu and Uttar Pradesh.

The National Overseas Scholarships for Higher Education Scheme provides financial assistance to meritorious selected students for pursuing higher studies abroad in specified fields of Masters level courses, Ph.D. and Post Doctoral research programmes in Engineering, Technology and Science only.

The Constitution of India guarantees various socio-economic and political rights to the Scheduled Tribes as enshrined in various Articles to ensure effective participation of the tribals in the process of planning and decision-making. In order to give more focused attention to the development of Scheduled Tribes, a separate ministry known as the Ministry of Tribal Affairs was constituted in October 1999. The new ministry carved out of the Ministry of Social Justice and Empowerment, is the nodal ministry for overall policy, planning and coordination of programmes and schemes for the development of Scheduled Tribes. It also supports and supplements the efforts of other Central Ministries/Departments as well as States/Union Territories for the development of these communities.

Fourteen Tribal Research Institutes (TRIs) have been set up by the Andhra Pradesh, Assam, Bihar, Gujarat, Kerala, Madhya Pradesh, Maharashtra, Orissa, Rajasthan, Tamil Nadu, West Bengal, Uttar Pradesh, Manipur and Tripura. These institutes are engaged in providing planning inputs to the State Governments, conducting research and evaluation studies, collection of data, codification of customary law and conduct of training, seminars and workshops. Some of these institutes are also having museums exhibiting tribal artifacts.

The Ministry gives grant-in-aid to voluntary organisations working for the welfare of the Scheduled Tribes for projects like residential schools, hostels, medical units, computer training units, shorthand and typing training units, balwadis/creches (in areas not covered by ICDS programmes), libraries and audio-visual units. The grant is generally restricted to 90 per cent of the approved total cost of the project and the balance 10 per cent is borne by the grantee organisations. During 2000-01 an amount of Rs. 21.88 crore was released to 228 NGOs.

Article 15(4) of the Constitution enjoins upon the state the creation of special provisions for the advancement of any socially and educationally backward classes of citizens or for the Scheduled Castes and Scheduled Tribes. Another Article 16 (4) further enables the state for making provisions for the reservation of appointments or posts in favour of any backward class of citizens, which in the opinion of the state is not adequately represented in the services under the state. The other provisions of the Constitution make it obligatory for the state of "strive to promote the welfare of the people by securing and protecting as effectively as it may, a social order, in which Justice, Social, Economic and Political shall inform all the institutions of the National Life." Article 46 further contains a very significant directive regarding promotion of educational and economic interests of other weaker sections and protects them from social injustice and all forms of exploitation. Part XVI of the Constitution contains "special provisions relating to certain classes" and under this part Article 340 envisages the appointment of a Commission to investigate the conditions of Backward Classes.

The Government considered seriously the objectives of Articles 15 and 16 of the Constitution and the Second Backward Classes Commission (Mandal Commission) was appointed in 1979. The terms of reference of the Commission included (i) determination of the criteria for defining the socially and educationally backward classes, (ii) steps to be taken for the advancement of socially and educationally backward classes, (iii) desirability or otherwise of making provision for the reservation of appointments in favour of backward classes which are not adequately represented in public service and (iv) presenting a report setting out the facts as found by the Commission making such recommendations. The Commission submitted its Report on 31st December 1980.

After long deliberations on the recommendations of the Mandal Commission, it was decided by the then Government to implement the same and an Office Memorandum on 13 August 1990 was issued providing 27 per cent reservation for Other Backward Classes (OBCs) in civil posts and services under the Government of India. As a consequence of this Memo, there was widespread protest against the reservation for Other Backward Classes and several Writ Petitions were filed in Supreme Court questioning the said reservations. All the Writ Petitions were disposed of by the Hon'ble Supreme Court by its judgement dated 16 November 1992. By a majority judgement, the Supreme Court held that the implementation of the Office Memorandum dated 13 August 1990 shall be subject to the exclusion of socially advanced persons (Creamy Layer) amongst the Other Backward Classes.

The following Schemes were launched in 1998-99 for the welfare of OBCs by the Government of India :

- **(a)** ***Pre-Examination Coaching***—The objective of the scheme is to coach candidates belonging to Other Backward Classes (OBCs) to enable them to compete in various competitive/ entrance examinations. The candidates whose parents'/ guardians' total income including the income of the candidates is below Rs. one lakh annually are eligible for admission to the pre-examination coaching centre.
- **(b)** ***Hostels for OBC Boys and Girls***—The hostels under the scheme will be constructed in States/UTs having a large OBC population but inadequate hostel facilities. The hostels will be constructed for middle, secondary, college and university level students. At least one-third of the hostels to be set up will be exclusively for girls. Five per cent of the total seats will be reserved for disabled students.
- **(c)** ***Pre-matric Scholarship for OBCs***—Scholarship awards will be sanctioned to students whose parents'/guardians' income does not exceed Rs. 44,500 per annum. The scholarships are given to the students in class-I or any subsequent class of pre-matric stage to day-scholars and class-II or any subsequent class of pre-matric stage to hostellers.
- **(d)** ***Post-Matric Scholarships to the OBCs***—The scheme provides financial assistance to the OBC students at post matriculation/post-secondary stage to enable them to complete their education. Hundred per cent Central

assistance for the scholarship will be provided to the State governments/UTs to which the applicant belongs.

(e) ***Assistance to Voluntary Organisations for Welfare of OBCs***—The scheme involves the voluntary sector to improve educational and socio-economic conditions of the OBCs to get them gainfully employed. Assistance will be given to establish centres and develop services which equip the OBCs to start income generating activities.

The Government has notified five communities, namely, Muslims, Sikhs, Christians, Buddhists and Zoroastrians as Minorities at the national level. As per census of 1991, population of minority groups constitutes 17.17 per cent of the total population of the country. The Constitution of India protects the interests of minorities and recognizes their rights to conserve their languages, scripts or culture and establish and administer educational institutions of their choice.

REFERENCES

Gupta, V.S., (1996). Media Strategies for Rural Development, *Kurukeshtra* XLIV (4-5) Publications Division, New Delhi.

Gupta, V.S., (1995). *Third Revolution in Indian Perspective–Contemporay Issues and Themes in Communication,* Concept Publishing Company, New Delhi.

India 2002 (A Reference Annual). Publications Division. Ministry of Information and Broadcasting, Government of India, New Delhi.

Planning Commission (2002). *National Human Development Report 2001* Government of India, New Delhi.

Planning Commission (2001). *Approach Paper to the Tenth Five Year Plan (2002-2007),* Government of India, New Delhi.

Phadnis, Umashamkar (ed.), (1998). *Exploring the Heartland–An Agenda for Media,* Gyan Publishing House, New Delhi.

6

LITERACY, EDUCATION AND NEW INFORMATION AND COMMUNICATION TECHNOLOGIES

As the country moves towards a higher level of economic and social development, the contribution of literacy and education to nation building becomes crucial. In developing countries the emphasis is on basic education including literacy. Since this is vital to their progress, it is not only an important input for economic growth but also a necessary element in participatory democracy. In developed countries, the infrastructure and systems to assume basic education are already in place. Their focus is, therefore, on higher and continuing education. In both categories of countries, there is growing recognition about the critical role of education. The contemporary thinking is largely based on the realization that economies are built not merely through accumulation of physical capital, human resources and skills, but on a foundation of information, education and continuous process of learning.

During recent years, major national and international agencies have accorded priority and due recognition to the contribution that literacy and education can make to various aspects of nation building, particularly so the UNDP through its *Human Development Reports*. Trained manpower throughout the world, and more so in developing societies, is becoming a precious resource. With the growing criticism of the centres of training and education, the universities—unless they undertake major restructuring and revision of their academic programmes— in most of the countries are in danger of becoming redundant and insignificant, as they cater to the privileged few. The recent trend towards free market economy has also made more and more countries realize the need for providing an easy access to affordable higher education to the masses.

One cannot enter the contemporary social and communication order if one is not literate, "An illiterate person has hundreds of enemies : epidemics, hunger, disorder and humiliation", said the Soviet Government's statement on elimination of illiteracy in 1920. Illiteracy also makes one victim of false information and false consciousness. Therefore, the key to progress is education which alone can uplift a society. This is by now universally accepted that a year's schooling can increase a woman's future earnings by about 15 per cent. Hence, the role of education in nation building. Therefore the key to progress is education which alone can uplift a society.

Knowledge is critical for development, because everything we do depends upon knowledge. Simply to live, we must transform the resources we have into the things we need, and that takes knowledge. And if we want to live better tomorrow than today, if we want to raise our living standards as a household or as a country and preserve our common environment we must do more than simply transform more resources in ways that generate ever-higher returns on our efforts and investments. That too takes knowledge, and in ever greater proportion to our resources.

The need for developing countries to increase their capacity to use knowledge cannot be over-stressed. It will be long time before literacy and education status in the country presents a satisfactory situation. However, what can still be taken up with certain amount of satisfaction is the belated realization that unless radical changes are initiated in redesigning social policies, including those in basic education and elementary health care, the prospects of raising the general living standards of the population in the country would continue to be none too bright. The contemporary society is characterised by swift pace of change which affects our lives in diverse ways : rapid technological development, faster evolution and aggregation of knowledge, rising aspirations of the people towards a more fulfilling quality of life, and increasing demand for qualified and trained manpower. Therefore, it is imperative that potential of communication technologies for educational purposes, not in the restricted sense of structured formal academic system, but by way of opportunities for distance education and life long learning available throughout the life span of an individual be further strengthened.

The rapid obsolescence of knowledge requires individuals to make special efforts to stay up-date. This means that one can collect, process and disseminate information very quickly. Television and radio satisfactorily meet this criterion. Also, learning has to be at the pace and knowledge level of the viewer. This implies the use of viewer controlled technologies so that the viewer may learn at a time convenient to him. Apart from other reasons, this clearly indicates that continuing education has necessarily to be based on distance learning modes. The need for earning while learning is another factor that is bound to make distance education the preferred form of the future.

Literacy not only imbues a person with a sense of self-worth and confidence, it opens for him vistas of opportunities outside the confines of his limited environment. In this context Wilbur Schramm observes: Print, when one learns to read, is not only a source of much pleasure, but also a source of understanding of many problems in the world. Even beyond that, literacy is not just learning how to read but is concerned with comprehending a form of reality beyond immediate experience. Print, therefore, is a liberating revolutionary experience; it helps free an individual from his group, his social customs, his routine.

LITERACY AS KEY FACTOR IN CAPABILITY BUILDING

Literacy has continued to be a dominant theme in endeavours of the international community and the national governments. Literacy has great potential to make life significant, interesting and full. It is one of the cultural areas considered essential for human development. Illiteracy and poverty are considered to be the two sides of the same coin.

The importance of literacy as a key factor in capability building, and in enhancing the quality of life of an individual has been long accepted. It would be pertinent to refer to what Aldous Huxley had said in this context: *"Every man who knows how to read has to magnify himself, to multiply the way in which he exists, to make his life full, significant and interesting."* Since literacy is basic to the understanding of the working of a host of social, economic and political institutions, even primary level education performs an important part, particularly in rural areas.

The lack of reading and writing skills drastically limits the expansion of a person's overall capacities and abilites. The Learning Project Report to the Club of Rome, *The Human Gap*, 1979 says :

> "Most people think of waste in physical terms, such as waste of resources, energy, or money. Indeed, the global problematique has focused attention on the wasteful misuse of non-renewable physical resources. But another kind of waste has an even more serious impact on a number of global problems : the waste of human learning potential. In this context, waste can result not only from the misuse that relegates people to marginal positions, but also from the lack of use or neglect of human capacities. Unacceptably large numbers of people find themselves excluded from all but the most rudimentary, informal opportunities to develop their learning processes. Illiteracy, both a symptom and a cause of the downward spiral of ignorance and poverty, epitomizes the waste of human learning potential."

A number of eminent economists, development thinkers and policy makers worldwide have emphasized the role of literacy and education as being pivotal for progress of the society. Nobel Laureate Amartya Sen *et al.* in *India : Economic Development and Social Opportunity,* (1995) says :

> Literacy is a basic tool of self-defence in a society where social interaction often involves the written media. An illiterate person is that much less equipped to defend himself in court, to obtain a bank loan, to enforce her inheritance rights, to take advantage of new technology, to compete for secure employment, to get on the right bus, to take part in political acivity, in short to participate successfully in the modern economy and society. Similar things can be said about numeracy and other skills

acquired in the process of basic education. The basic education is also a catalyst of social change.

In a similar context, Amartya Sen in the opening chapter of the book, *Indian Development—Selected Regional Perspectives* (1996) says : The persistence of endemic illiteracy and educational backwardness in India has many adverse effects. It limits, in general, the freedom and well-being of the Indian masses, and has a direct role in the relative deprivation of women in particular. It sustains high levels of mortality and fertility rates. It contributes to the comparative lack of pressure for social change, and to the moderateness of political demand and pressure for effective public attention in such fields as health care. But in addition the lack of elementary education also makes the goals of economic expansion very much harder to realize. We have to face here two quite distinct but inter-related problems that limit the attainment and use of economic growth. First, elementary education is extremely important for successful integration with the world market. The nature and range of commodities sold by, say, South Korea since the seventies or China from the eighties bring out clearly how crucial basic education is for catering to the world market, with production to specification and reliable quality control. Secondly, the wider the coverage of the population that takes part in the integration with the world market, the more 'participatory' the process of growth would tend to be, raising the income earning power of the large parts of the nation. Even if India were to grow very fast with its highly technical industries (making use of special skills that India has cultivated and drawing on the trained middle class labour force), such as modern computer software or engineering products, the bulk of the Indians may still receive little reward from it.

In India the responsibility for the spread of literacy and educational development rests largely with state governments. The Central Government has also been taking initiatives under constitutional obligations to supplement the efforts of state governments by meeting some of the critical gaps in the programme for literacy improvement.

According to the 2001 census the literacry rates among the population of seven years and above in the country stands at 65.38 per cent. The corresponding figures for males and females are 75.85 and 54.16 per cent. In other words three-fourths of male population and more than half of female population in the country is literate today. The gap in male and female literacy rates has decreased from 28.84 in 1991 Census to 21.70 percentage point in 2001.

For the first time since independence absolute numbers of illiterates has shown a decline. The decline is as large as 31.96 million during 1991-2001. Kerala continues to lead the literacy rates followed by Mizoram 88.49 and Lakshadweep 87.52 per cent respectively. Bihar has recorded the lowest literacy rate of 47.53 per cent in the country.

The nodal agency for strengthening the literacy movement in the country, National Literacy Mission (NLM) has been working in this area since 1988. Ever since the programme was launched 166 districts in the country were declared as totally literate.

The Earnakulam District Total Literacy Campaign (TLC) was the first district level movement of its kind in India. It established a method for literacy campaigns in the districts of the state and proved to be a trend setter for such programmes in the country. The programme was spearheaded by Kerala Sastra Sahitya Parishad (KSSP) in the field of literacy from 1977 onwards. The KSSP mastered the technique of mobilising people in a very large way through *Kalajathas* and other media and itself grew into a mass organisation. It was only because of sustained and consistent efforts of organisations like KSSP and people's mobilisation that Kerala was declared fully literate on 18 April 1991. In a pamphlet *Make Literacy Work : A People's Movement*, it was argued : No programme will succeed without people's support... In all the countries which have achieved universal literacy one can see the support of the entire people for the movement. It is the failure to attract the attention of the mass of people that is the cause of the lack of success of literacy programmes in our country. If they degenerate into ordinary official activity carried out for the sake of a government job, nothing can save them. It should be possible to convert literacy-work into a big people's movement.... The literates and the illiterates, individuals and organizations, school students and vice-chancellors...all can participate in this...

The work and contribution of KSSP has attracted worldwide attention because the KSSP activists have been important organizers of total literacy campaigns in different parts of the country.

EDUCATION

In terms of human development objectives, education is an end in itself, not just a means to an end. Education which is a basic human right, is critical for economic and social development. It is crucial for building human capabilities and for opening opportunities.

The report of the Brundtland Commission, *Our Common Future* added urgency to the concept of sustainable development, which is generally understood to be used only in terms of environmental protection. According to contemporary thinking sustainable improvement in the quality of life becomes the central focus for policy making in all countries; and therefore, highest priority should be accorded to meeting the basic minimal survival needs of the population. It has also been stressed that the capital invested in people's health and education becomes an important economic factor. This sort of capital as against the earlier definition of capital (as investment in economic goods for increasing production) can be sustained by raising the level of investment in education, health and other social services. The Jomtien Declaration on *Education for All (1990)* introduced an additional element calling for right to life long education and training. Rethinking on all aspects of education—along with other important facets of development—has broadened our understanding of the vast dimensions of education as a process, as a factor encouraging an individual to participate in the political and social life of the community and the country, as well as an instrument for the empowerment of the women and disadvantaged sections of the population. One such dimension : Education is no longer seen as a fixed stage in life, beginning at about five years of age and continuing through primary, secondary and possibly tertiary level and ends once employment begins. In case we wish to achieve the full potential of education to solve the social and economic problems, and also that of an individual to rise up to his full capability and genius. We will have to give up this limited view. That is why learning is becoming a life long process and age is considered no bar to improve one's academic, technical and professional prospects and attainments. Information technology, innovations and improvements have also made it feasible to study at one's own pace—Open Learning Systems which would include Open Schools and Open Universities and now virtual classroom and virtual universities have made the pursuit of life long learning a real possibility.

In the context of economic development and employment, education has to equip the pupils with competence, in terms of knowledge and skills, in various combinations at different levels of understanding, relating to the opportunities of employment in the context of a particular pattern and rate of development. Education has to play an important role in integrating the individual into the social system. It is also meant to indicate suitable habits for health care, mental application, management of time and conservation of physical, mental and emotional energy.

The World Bank study on *The East Asian Miracle* shows that the single most important factor in launching the miracle countries on a path of rapid, sustained economic growth was universal or near-universal primary school enrolment.... In 1960 Pakistan and Korea had similar levels of income, but by 1985 Korea's GDP per capita was nearly three times of Pakistan's... In 1960 fewer than a third of the children of primary school age were enrolled in Pakistan while all were enrolled in Korea. [Jan Nederveen Pieterse, (2001), *Development Theory : Deconstructions/Reconstructions*].

Today, besides the integration of the individual into the social system, it is equally essential that he equips himself with knowledge and skills imperative for a globalised economy in the 21st century. It is because of the foresight and vision of Prime Minister Jawaharlal Nehru that apex institutes of higher learning and research in engineering and business management were established—Indian Institutes of Technology (IITs) and the Indian Institutes of Management (IIMs). These institutes—which are sometimes criticised for their elitist orientation are in the forefront of providing brain power for the corporate and information technology sectors in the country. True, quite a number of their students migrate to USA for better opportunities, but some of them do return to India and provide leadership to Indian enterprises. Those who criticise the misplaced emphasis of the Indian planning on expansion and strengthening of the tertiary education in the beginning, and consider higher education as 'non-merit good' (the current thinking in the UGC) tend to ignore the fact that in the absence of government investment in these institutions, the Indian students would not have been able to avail of the opportunities of upward mobility and excellence presently available to them. The infrastructure of higher education that India has been able to put in place in areas like biotechnology, information technology and applied sciences needs to be strengthened and improved.

India has a vast infrastructure of formal systems of education right from the primary and secondary level schools to colleges and universities at the tertiary levels. However, mention may be made of Navodaya Vidyalayas started in 1985-86 to provide good quality modern education to the talented children predominantly from the rural areas, and Kendriya Vidyalayas for the children of the employees of public sector undertakings, central and state governments and those working in defence forces. The National Council of Educational Research and Training was established in 1961 with a view to ensuring qualitative improvement and excellence in school education as well as teachers education. It designs courses and generates software systems and also sets up resource centres for computer literacy in school projects.

The number of institutions imparting higher education numerically is impressive—259 universities including 16 central universities and 38 institutions declared deemed universities under the University Grants Commission Act, 1956. In terms of infrastructure and capability in the fields of teaching in medicine and research in agriculture, science and technology, the country has developed apex bodies including Indian Council of Medical Research (ICMR), Indian Council of Agricultural Research (ICAR) and Council of Scientific and Industrial Research (CSIR). The

ICMR is entrusted with the responsibility to stop mushroom growth of medical colleges, besides maintenance of uniform standards of medical education; the ICAR promotes science and technology programmes in the areas of agricultural research, education and extension education. The ICAR research set up includes 47 central institutes, five national bureaux, nine project directorates, 30 national research centres, 80 All India Coordinated Research Projects and four deemed Universities. The ICAR also promotes research, education and extension education through 33 State Agricultural Universities (SAUs). The ICAR system is one of the largest such systems of highly trained and competent scientific manpower in the world. The CSIR, with its all-encompassing character has played crucial role in the transformation of several industrial sectors in the country and made wide ranging important contribution in the fields of drug and pharmaceuticals manufacture, agrochemicals, petroleum and petrochemicals and rural industries through its extensive network of 41 laboratories and 80 extension centres throughout the country.

India undoubtedly has an extensive—almost unwieldy set up of institutions of higher learning and research in most of the important disciplines; in some areas notable strides have indeed been made. It is a cliche to say that India has the third largest scientific manpower in the world. At the same time there is an utter dissatisfaction, by and large, at the quality of research and academic work being done. These institutions have become, in most of the cases large bureaucracies performing day-to-day maintenance functions.

The number of research papers published or abstracted by the Indian scientists in the international journals is not commensurate with the contribution expected of huge investment being made over the years. The academic and scientific institutions are fast becoming a pale shadow of huge government bureaucracies with senior scientists more interested in administrative work and responsibilities. In a leading agricultural university, a research editor—a senior scientist—entrusted with the task of editing scientific journals has been more interested in bringing out telephone and faculty directories, his own work remains in backlog for years, work which needs expertise of a scientist and a trained mind gets neglected and sidelined. A drastic improvement in the work culture of institutions of higher learning and research is generally called for but hardly implemented in actual practice.

The Report of International Commission on the Development of Education, 1972, *Learning to Be, The world of education—today and tomorrow*, articulated the concept of lifelong education as covering the entire educational process, from the point of view of the individual and of society. It first concerns the education of children and, while helping the child to live his own life as he deserves to do, its essential mission is to prepare the future adult for various forms of autonomy and self-learning. This later learning requires many wide-ranging educational structures and cultural activities to be developed for adults. These, while existing for their own purpose, are also a pre-condition for reforming initial education. Another International Commission on Education for the Twenty-first Century, appointed by UNESCO in 1993, reaffirmed the concept of lifelong education. The title of the report, *Learning : The Treasure Within,* reminds us of the importance of learning throughout life, as also the need to develop an initiative and practice of education that goes beyond schooling. The treasure is learning itself—the remarkable asset possessed by every individual that needs to be harnessed and used wisely. Learning, knowledge and minds are not commodities to be developed and exploited, but treasures to be nurtured and cultivated to improve the quality of life—of the individuals as well as of the society. Learning throughout life will in due course become the heart beat of society.

As technology advances, the ideal of learning, "what you want, when you want, where you want, and at your own pace", becomes possible and lifelong learning is no longer just a slogan. A series of exciting new technological developments have significantly expanded and enhanced the instructional potential of television. Likewise computer technology has advanced at a remarkable pace, and should play a key role in the future educational expansion. The electronic media offers new dimensions to expand educational opportunities, to improve the quality of instruction, and to increase the cost effectiveness of the present educational system.

It is therefore essential that potential of NICTs be properly harnessed to reach the dispersed learning groups. As Kiran Karnik suggests (1995) continuing education and refresher courses be organised for para medical staff, agricultural extension workers, and school teachers, dispersed in rural areas and often cut off from means of updating their knowledge, NICTs can help such dispersed groups as also other such groups of farmers, craftsmen and entrepreneurs in rural areas. Today's technologies havae enormous potential to increase access to education and reduce its unit costs.

Notwithstanding the contribution of literacy and education to the economic and social development, as also to nation building, the fact remains that even after 50 years of planned effort in the education sector, nearly one-third of the population or close to 300 million persons in age-group 7 years and above are illiterate. As the *National Human Development Report*-2001 points out : There are critical gaps in the availability of infrastuctural facilities and qualitative aspects of education including teachers training, educational curricula, equipment and training materials, particularly in the publicly funded schooling system of the country. Likewise the Approach Paper to the Tenth Five Year Plan says : Our performance in the field of education is one of the most disappointing aspects of our developmental strategy. Out of approximately 200 million children in the age group 6-14 years, only 120 million are in schools and the net attendance at the primary level is only 66 per cent of the enrolment. This is completely unacceptable and the Tenth Plan should aim at a radical transformation in this situation. *Education for All* must be one of the primary objectives of the Plan.

Education as a Fundamental Right—The Constitution of India envisages provision for free and compulsory education for children. The Central Government had introduced the 93rd Constitutional Amendment Bill, 2001 for enacting the fundamental right to free and compulsory education for the children in the age group 6-14 years. Till this initiative there was no Central Act on compulsory education. The grant of Presidential assent for the 93rd Constitutional Amendment that makes free and compulsory education a Fundamental Right for all children marks a significant step in the country's aim to achieve "Education for All".

> The amendment holds out a constitutional guarantee for providing free education upto high school to all its 190 million young and growing minds between 6 and 14 years. More significantly, the new law will seek to bring into the educational mainstream 35 million boys and girls who are yet to be covered by formal schooling systems.
>
> The amendement alone is not enough. Every state, specially those with poor literacy and drop out records, needs incentives to frame laws to extend the constitutional guarantee and provide free, compulsory, quality, equitable school and early childhood care and education upto higher secondary level. Gender injustice and adult illiteracy are problems that need legal instrumentalities for lasting solutions.*

In this sense an objective set by the framers of the Constitution—that the State shall endeavour to provide within a period of ten years from the commencement of this Constitution can be achieved at least in a decade from now. Eradicating illiteracy by 1960 (within ten years of the commencement of the Constitution) remained a dream for a number of reasons. Therefore there was no way for a citizen to seek enforcement of this objective as the constitutional provision was only part of the Directive Principles of State Policy and hence it was not enforceable.

It is now incumbent on activists and groups, who have been in the vanguard of the movement for making the Right to Education as a Fundamental Right, by strengthening the movement further and to ensure that the Fundamental Right is not infringed upon by the State Governments by way of reducing schools to mere sheds where children are herded together as has been happening in single teacher schools in several states.

The Chairman of WIPRO Corporation—an Indian IT giant—Azim Premji sometimes back, in a newspaper article, reflected on

* *The Hindu,* 21 December 2002.

the sorry state of education in the country. He thought it inconceivable that in a country like India, which had emerged as a superpower in IT industry in general and global software services in particular, and was yet unable to universalise elementary education in the country. The need to universalise elementary education is critical as a number of studies have revealed that basic education had a direct positive impact on a number of social and economic indicators like population stabilisation, healthcare and sanitation, law and order, GDP and economic growth. He also made an important suggestion that the definition of literacy needs to be changed to education till the 10th standard, and IT literacy be made compulsory.

> Azim Premji said : *There is in every child, unlimited potential to learn and achieve. All the children need an opportunity to discover and develop their full potential. The most important issue is that every child has a right to childhood and right to education.*

Despite some disappointing areas in the over all educational scenario at the national level, several initiatives and innovations undertaken in various states present a happy augury for the future of education in the country.

The PROBE (Public Report on Basic Education) study, conducted in 234 randomly selected villages of Bihar, Madhya Pradesh, Rajasthan, Uttar Pradesh and Himachal Pradesh enumerated several encouraging steps in strengthening basic education in the country.

The study pointed out that the Operation Blackboard (launched in 1987 with the aim of ensuring that every primary school had a minimum quota of facilities and aids) has achieved some positive results in the form of improving infrastructural facilities. An NGO, *Lok Jumbish,* working in Rajasthan rural areas made significant contribution in mobilizing people for education. The schooling revolution in Hamachal Pradesh is one of the most satisfying developments of the post-independence period in the field of elementary education. The PROBE survey found plenty of evidence of the rapid progress of schooling in Himachal Pradesh.*

Knowledge for Development—In one of the excellent World Development Reports 1998-99, *Knowledge for Development,* the World Bank has discussed most persuasively the significance of knowledge in advancing economic and social well-being. In its Foreword to the Report, the President of the World Bank says : The information revolution makes understanding, knowledge and development more urgent than ever before. New communication technologies and plummeting computing costs are shrinking distance and eroding borders and time. The remotest village has the possibility of tapping a global store of knowledge beyond the dreams of anyone living a century ago, and more quickly and cheaply than anyone imagined possible only a few decades ago, And distance education offers the potential to extend learning opportunities to millions who otherwise be denied a good education.

Knowledge is important for individuals and households—knowledge of oral rehydration therapy reduces infant mortality. The knowledge of a parent can raise the living standard of all family members. For instance in Vietnam, people living in households headed by someone with no education have a poverty rate of 68 per cent. Primary education for the poverty household head brings the rate down to 54 per cent, secondary education to 41 per cent, and university education to 12 per cent.

Today most of the technologically advanced economies are truly knowledge-based. And as they generate new wealth from their innovations, they are creating millions of knowledge related jobs-knowledge engineers, knowledge managers and knowledge co-ordinators.

Education—which is key to the adoption and effective use of health knowledge has expanded in almost every country. Many studies reveal that the amount of education attained by girls and women is an important determinant of children's health.

The implications of the above discussion are clear : knowledge

---

* Public Report on Basic Education in India (1999) Oxford University Press, New Delhi.

is essential for reducing poverty; health care and econommic development. As the Report says : Knowledge is the key to development—knowledge is development.

The earliest our policy makers and administrators, get to appreciate and acknowledge the significance of literacy, education and knowledge; and implement the resolve to make education a fundamental right and evolve means to impart quality education, the earliest the country will be on road to development—social, economic and technological. The road to development can be transversed only through the territory of literacy, education and knowledge.

New Information and Communication Technologies and Distance Education

The closing decade of the 20th century has witnessed the exponential growth in the ambit and application of communication technologies which have far reaching relevance to education, its expansion and quality. The implications of the growth in communication technologies impacting the very nature of learning process and education system, are equally far reaching, necessitating a continuous reassessment with respect to its effectiveness and scope. The traditional roles assigned to school, classroom and teacher and the expectation of the society in terms of quality of education are changing at a very fast pace. Concepts like the Learning Society, Interactive Technologies, Collaborative Learning, Knowledge Industries and Virtual University are not only transforming the way education is being imparted but is also changing the transmission of education itself.

New Information and Communication Technologies (NICTs) have brought human kind face-to-face with fundamental changes : by abolishing distances they are instrumental in shaping the societies of tomorrow; the most accurate, up-to-date information (in fact information as the events are developing) is now available to anyone, anywhere in the world, often in real time and reaches the remotest regions.

The dramatic emergence of information societies has led to a revolution in communications in the shape of multimedia systems and the spectacular expansion of information technology networks, including internet. Eventhough the impact of the expansion of internet is still limited in developing countries, owing to the relatively small number of people with the necessary technology know-how; everything suggests that an unstoppable revolution is in progress which will make it possible to transmit an ever-increasing mass of information in shorter span of time. At the same time, thanks to the falling cost of equipment, the new technologies are steadily finding their way into every aspect of work.

As the world moves towards a knowledge-based, post-industrial information society, the crucial importance of education becomes self-evident. In the Indian situation stress would not only be to ensure basic education to every child, prevent dropouts and ensure relevance of education, but to also provide opportunities to those outside the conventional education system, and to the workforce for continuing education. In developing countries there is growing awareness about the critical role of education : as also the conviction that since the traditional means of education suffer from several major deficiencies, these would not be able to cope with the challenges of emerging situation in the twenty-first century.

In his book, *The Death of Distance*, Frances Cairncross points out : The death of the distance as a determinant of the cost of communicating will probably be the single most important force shaping society in the first-half of the next century. Technological change has the power to revolutionize the way people live, and this one will be no exception. It will alter, in ways that are only dimly imaginable, decisions about where people work and what kind of work they do, concepts of national borders and sovereignty, and patterns of international trade. The death of distance will also give rise to proliferation of ideas. New ideas and information will travel faster to the remotest corner of the world. The Third World countries will have access to knowledge that the industrial world has long enjoyed.

At a time when knowledge industries are taking off at top speed, education has to be seen as a factor of crucial importance even as a part of economic policy. France has announced a new television channel known as 'knowledge channel'. This knowledge channel will work like the information highway—by extending its range and scope to benefit both the children and the adults.

Lifelong Learning : A vast responsibility rests with the educational planners in formulating workable strategies towards providing educational opportunities for those who missed out in the first instance and also to reorient education to meet the demands of industry and economy. Since human knowledge is rapidly expanding in many fields, degrees gained years ago are no longer adequate qualifications. The introduction of new technologies, production methods and techniques advance more rapidly than the setting up of new specializations and new curricula at colleges, universities, and other academic and vocational education establishments. At the same time the rising aspirations for better quality of life have also induced several sections of society to pursue higher education.

It is obvious that the distance education and open learning institutes, which have come up in a big way, not only in the developed countries, but more so in the Third World countries could not have fulfilled the task of imparting education but for the use of communication technologies on a large scale. The role of the teacher—the key to the success of the educational system—also has to be changed; instead of dispensing information and knowledge he has to guide the students in the acquisition of knowledge from the ever-expanding learning resources. The rapid development of communication in most countries, the expansion of various forms of mass communication and in particular of audio-visual communication, combined with the spread of informatics, open up new horizons and multiply the linkages between education and communication. There is an evident increase of the educational potential of communication. *While the education system loses the monopoly of education, communication becomes itself a vehicle and subject for education.*

Tele-education, by all means, has been considered to be a

landmark development. The extensive use of television for educational purposes in Asia in the two most populous countries of the region—China and India, the limitations of being oneway medium notwithstanding, is indicated by two important developments : The largest distance teaching institution of the world, the national multimedia distance learning institution in China, is called the Central Radio and Television University (CRTVU). One of the largest communications experiments in which television programmes were received by local viewers directly from space—Satellite Instructional Television Experiment (SITE) was conducted in India for a period of one year from 1 August 1975.

While the SITE has been extensively documented in the communication literature, the contribution of CRTVU needs to be highlighted in the context of the role of open learning system. The CRTVU employs broadcast as the main delivery vehicle and supplements it with print, audio-visual media, tutorials and computerized instruction. Programmes are broadcast directly to learners at home, in the workplace or the study centres located throughout the country. The CRTVU courses follow a multi-media approach. The input of non-print media varies according to the subject area—science and engineering courses have greater proportion of TV programmes, whereas radio is the chief medium for social science courses. TV programmes are transmitted by the Central China Television (CCTV) nationally through the microwave network.

The remarkable aspect of the working of CRTVU is the expansion of its operations in rural areas to meet the shortages of technically trained manpower. The university has been able to create a vast network to meet the shortage of educated persons in various fields and also meet the demands of fresh graduates from high schools, since it is not possible for the provincial universities to meet these demands.

The rapid expansion of television in India during 1984, facilitated the launching of the countrywide classroom (CWCR) project by the University Grants Commission. The programme is aimed primarily at the undergraduate students of colleges located at different places. The contents of CWCR programmes are not linked to any examination, these are neither based on a particular syllabus. Instead these telecasts seek to provide new insights, bring new findings and take the students to various places and laboratories they would rarely see. The project aims at the widest possible utilisation of television's potential to improve the quality of university level education.

Teleconferencing **:** Another important form of technology being widely used in distance education is teleconferencing. Teleconferencing is an interactive electronic communication among two or more locations. The attraction for adopting teleconferencing is said to be the savings it results in minimizing physical travel. The time saving involved in this process is also a significant factor and the experience of advanced countries in which teleconferencing is in wide usage shows that apart from economy and time saving, this technology improves corporate efficiency and enables participatory management.

The World Bank, in its World Development Report, 1998-99, *Knowledge for Development* points out as to how expanding telecommunications hold the promise to improve every developing country's capacity to absorb knowledge by providing opportunities for high quality, low cost adult learning. The Virtual University of the Monterrey Institute of Technology in Mexico is a consortium of collaborating universities including 13 outside the country. It enrolls 9,000 degree and 35,000 non-degree students each year in Mexico and other Latin American countries. It delivers courses through printed texts and live and pre-recorded television broadcasts, with communication between students and faculty aided by computers and the Internet.

The African Virtual University, headquartered in Nairobi, seeks to increase University enrolments and improve the quality and relevance of instruction in business, science, and engineering throughout Africa. In each participating country, a local institution is competitively selected to oversee operations. This institution provides hardware and software for interactive courses, registers students, supervises study programmes, offers a structured study environment, and awards local course credit. The University has installed 27 satellite receiver terminals throughout Africa and developed a digital library, to compensate for the dearth of scientific journals in African Universities. Although it is too early to assess results, such initiatives give reason to hope that new technology can make a big contribution to narrowing knowledge gaps.

Virtual Classroom **:** A virtual classroom comprises electronic classroom from which the class is taught, a network of specially equipped electronic classrooms at which the students are present, and the satellite, microwave or cable linkages between them. For teaching purposes, virtual classrooms can either be two-way video with two-way audio, often called video conferencing or more accurately video teaching or one-way video and two-way audio.

The learning technologies offer valuable opportunities to expand educational infrastructure to improve the quality of instruction, and to increase the cost-effectiveness of present education systems. However, they also can become educational "white elephants" that consume a nation's financial resources without effectively delivering the much needed instruction that was originally hoped for. Media projects, with their heavy initial start-up costs, represent an especially unnerving, educational gamble for developing nations. While their potential to reach large numbers of students may be tremendous, if that potential is not realized, the financial losses can be staggering, especially for an already impoverished country. The implementation of large educational media projects is generally very complicated, and the possibility exists for major difficulties arising in different ways. (*Educational Media in Retrospect, Discussion Paper—Education and Training Series, the World Bank, 1987.*)

The unique potential of electronic media to transcend barriers create logistical challenges. The modern electronic media are seen as a means to overcome vast distances, overcoming topography, and underdeveloped communications infrastructures. So, educational media projects are designed for some of the least accessible regions. It is no wonder that some of these projects fall short of expectations, when they are carried out in the hope that they may transcend adverse circumstances that cannot be overcome in any other way. Another managerial challenge is the difficulty of overseeing such a complex range of projects, which include procuring equipment, hiring personnel, producing programmes, distributing written material, dealing with international agencies, etc. To further complicate matters, many of these activities involve a high degree of technical expertise, so that various specialists must be brought into the project. Administrators sometimes do not fully understand the needs of these technicians.

In most of the Asian countries access to personal computers, modem, and domestic TV, telephone and VCR for the learners may not be feasible for several years. Therefore, creating a Virtual University in the Asian context would continue to be a vision for a large number of Asian countries. Technologies such as audio cassette players, television and VCR, even though familiar to the students, constitute essentially leisure and entertainment media and till such time as sustained efforts are made to reorient these technologies for instructional purposes their potential may not be fully utilised.

A caveat needs to be entered regarding over-optimism of the effectiveness of the educational technologies in certain situations. Educational television, for instance suffers from certain limitations, the most serious being the element of anonymity inherent in its very operation. It is strictly a one-way communication. The teacher-taught contact, considered vital all over the world, is almost missing in the case of television—no physical contact, no physical identification, no scope for repetition, clarification or elaboration.

Distance Education : India has made rapid headway in imparting education through distance education mode and open learning system both at the school and tertiary level. The open learning system has brought about a virtual revolution in education—in terms of the number of institutions offering education through the above mode, the number of students who join courses offered by these institutions, the new programmes of study introduced and multi-media usage employed in this mode of education. Heralding the revolution are two institutions at the national level—Indira Gandhi National Open University (IGNOU) established in 1985 and the National Open School (NOS) set up in 1989. There are of course eight other open universities in the country; numerous universities also offer a number of courses through their directorates of distance education.

The IGNOU which provides higher education in the country through multi-media distance education mode is patterned on the British Open University. Compared to traditional Indian Universities, IGNOU's admission procedures and academic programmes are more flexible. The major objectives of the University include widening access to higher education to larger segments of population, organising programmes of continuing education and initiating programmes of higher education for specific target groups like women, people living in backward regions, hilly areas, etc. The University has innovated multi-media instructional strategy comprising printed material, audio-visual aids, supported by counselling sessions at a network of study centres throughout the country. Since 1998 the University has made phenomenal progress in introducing latest information technologies—teleconferencing, phone-in radio programmes, etc. It has also widened the base of its programmes by introducing computer education in a large number of centres throughout the country.

Technological innovations open up vast new possibilities. However, a world of caution is necessary: they are not instant miracles, but tools to be introduced and used only after careful consideration is given to all possible resulting ramifications. Each has particular potential, yet none is an isolated means; they are parts of a total system, which should be planned and shaped bearing in mind the integration of all its parts. Technological innovations can often have negative effects, both economic and social, and may distort directions and priorities for overall development activities. Inviting introduction of some new technologies is often easier than subsequent provision of software required for their optimum utilization. This has been repeatedly brought home to the educational planners and administrators in developing countries; but implementation of this advice is always tardy.

In a paper, *Application of Interactive Technologies in Open and Distance Learning : An overview*, A.W. Khan and Patricia McWillams, detail comprehensively barriers to the use and expansion of educational technology in a significant way. The authors have articulated the dilemma, frequently mentioned in the context of the limitations to the applications of educational technology in distance education programmes : It would be remiss not to recognise the present lack of available technical infrastructure of sufficient quality to support distance education on a wide spread basis in many countries and regions of the world. Although here too one can be optimistic given the speed of growth and penetration in this sector we are still, in many instances, dealing with 'dirt roads, in the age of the 'information highway' and we are driving on that road with tractors, not high performance sports cars of the 90s. In practical terms, it is extremely difficult to effectively deliver quality education using an audio-conferencing system when half of the receive sites are off-line due to technical difficulties at the local telco! A further important component to an efficient technical infrastructure is experienced and trained human resources, a commodity which often requires several years to develop adequately.

NOTE

Since NICTs are being extensively used for educational and learning purposes; in several countries technology based education in developing into online instruction; and the terms being used are not only Learning Technologies but also New Learning Technologies (see Mirza, J.S., IJOL, 7 (1), 98 : pp. 89) these terms are being used interchangeably.

REFERENCES

Dreze, Jean and Sen, Amartya, (1995) *India : Economic Development and Social Opportunity*, Oxford University Press, Delhi.

Dreze Jean and Sen, Amartya, (1996) *Indian Development—Selected Regional Perspectives*, Oxford University Press, New Delhi.

Frances Cairncross, (1997) *The Death of Distance,* Harvard Business School Press, Boston Massachusetts.

Haq, Mahbub ul, (1998) *Human Development in South Asia, 1998,* Oxford University Press, Karachi.

Human Development Report, (1996) UNDP, Oxford University Press, Oxford.

India, A Reference Annual, (2002) Publications Division, New Delhi.

Indian Journal of Adult Education, (1985) New Delhi.

Kiran Karnik, (1995) New Information/Communication Technologies : Their Role in Education, in *Media Asia* (22 : 2), AMIC, Singapore.

National Human Develepoment Report 2001, (March, 2002) Planning Commission, Government of India, New Delhi.

Report of International Commission on Education for 21st Century (1996). *Learning, The Treasure Within,* UNESCO, Paris.

Schramm, Wilbur, (1964) *Mass Media and National Development,* The Role of Information in the Developing Countries, Stanford University Press and UNESCO, Paris.

UNESCO, (1972) *Learning to Be the World of Education,* Today and Tomorrow, Paris.

The World Bank, World Development Report, (1998-99) *Knowledge for Development,* Washington, D.C., U.S.A.

7

HEALTH, POPULATION AND COMMUNICATION STRATEGY

The following excerpt from the memorable speech of Jawaharlal Nehru in the Constituent Assembly on 14-15 August 1947 gives us a glimpse of what the founding fathers of the Indian independence movement had envisioned for the country:

> Long ago we made a tryst with destiny, and now the time comes when we shall redeem our pledge... The achievement we celebrate today is but a step, an opening of opportunity, to the great triumphs and achievements that await us... the ending of poverty and ignorance and disease and inequality of opportunity.

Article 47 of the Indian Constitution says: The state shall regard the raising of the level of nutrition and the improvement of public health as among its primary duties.

However, facts collated from the two documents* published by the Government of India depict a sorry picture of progress made in the health sector in the country. Some of the concerns in this respect are:

1. More than half of the children 1-5 years old in rural areas are undernourished, with girl children suffering even more severe malnutrition.
2. The infant mortality rate has stagnated at 72 for the last several years.
3. Only 60 per cent of urban households have taps within their homes, and far fewer have latrines in their houses.

---

* (1) Approach paper to the Tenth-Five Year Plan (Sept. 2001) and (2) National Human Development Report 2001 (March 2002).

4. Deterioration in urban environment, increase in slum population, and in air, river and water pollution has vastly affected the quality of life of the urban poor.
5. Over half of the children under the age of five years in India are moderately or severely malnourished, 30 per cent of new born children are significantly underweight and nearly 60 per cent of women are anemic.
6. The decline in the juvenile sex ratio over the last decade indicates that constitutional assurance of freedom and equality for women is still for from being fulfilled. A reduction in this ratio implies higher female mortality in comparison to men indicating discrimination against girl child.

In the opening chapter of the World Development Report 2000-2001, *Attacking Poverty,* it has been pointed out : Inproving health outcomes not only improves well-being but also increases income-earning potential. Increasing education not only improves well-being—it also leads to better health outcomes and to higher incomes. Providing protection to poor people not only makes them feel less vulnerable—it also allows them to take advantage of higher-risk, higher-return opportunities. Increasing poor people's voice and participation not only addresses their sense of exclusion—it also leads to better targeting of health and education services to their needs.

Despite concerted efforts India continues to record high levels of morbidity, especially among infants, children, the elderly and women. The burden of short duration and major morbidity fall on the vulnerable sections of the population, including wage labourers, minorities and the low-income groups.

In his Convocation Address at the All India Institute of Medical Sciences in July 1998, Prime Minister Atal Bihari Vajpayee said that our record in health care was far from edifying. He called for radical reforms in both health care and medical education systems to ensure that the advances in medicine and the vast infrastructure for health care created over the past five decades were made accessible to the masses at affordable cost.

In this context, the Approach Paper to the Tenth Five Year

Plan says: Improvement in the health status of the population has been one of the major thrust areas in social development programmes of the country. This was to be achieved through improving access to the utilization of Health, Family Welfare and Nutrition Services with special focus on under-served and under-privileged segments of population. There will have to be a continued commitment to provide essential primary health care, emergency life-saving services, services under the National Diseases Control Programmes and the National Family Welfare Programme free of cost to individuals based on their needs and not on their ability to pay. At the same time, suitable strategies will have to be evolved, tested and implemented for levying and collecting user charges from people above poverty line and utilizing funds obtained for improving the quality of health care services.

The Tenth Plan stresses the reorganisation and restructuring of existing health care infrastructure, at primary, secondary and tertiary levels, so that they have the responsibility of serving population residing in a well-defined geographical area and have appropriate referral linkages with each other. At the same time it is essential that there is appropriate delegation of powers to PRIs so that there is local accountability of the public health care providers. The problems relating to poor performance need to be sorted out locally.

It is equally important to invite the willing acceptance and participation of the people for the successful implementation of the health and population programmes, enhancing reproductive facilities for women—an aspect, which had been generally ignored for years; and the effective contribution which the civil society organisations can make to this sector of nation building. The situation in the health and population sector continues to pose formidable challenge to the government and the policy planners in the country, also because public spending on health has been declining over the years. In terms of health infrastructure, countries like China and Sri Lanka are way ahead of India.

After the International Conference on Population and Development (1994), the Government of India made a provision for the reproductive health needs of the women. The poor reproductive health situation in India and particularly that of the

Indian women calls for a women-centred orientation including strategies to empower women in terms of control of economic resource, information and education, and enhancement of their rights.

One of the major challenges in the 21st century is to enhance the outlay for health, ensure its equitable distribution between states, narrow the rural urban gap and remove the lacunae impeding effective delivery of health care services at the community level, both in rural and urban areas. A sizeable population living in slums has no access to affordable medicare despite proliferation of private practitioners, nursing homes and corporate hospitals.

This record of national health achievement has, however, certain extenuating features. The brightest of the achievements is dramatic improvement in life expectancy, before independence the average life expectancy was less than thirty years; today a baby born in India can hope to live twice as long. Likewise the rate of infant mortality has been reduced to less than half of what it was in 1945, just before independence. Smallpox has been eradicated and epidemics such as cholera have been controlled. The overall picture, by and large, remains highly unsatisfactory.

Health is an indicator of well-being that has direct implications not only for the quality of life but also indirect implications for the production of economic goods and services. '*Health for All by the Year 2000*' was a national goal set by Indian policy-makers over 20 years ago in Alma Ata.* Since then a lot of planning, effort and public expenditure have gone into improving human health both in rural and urban India. The spread of accessibility to modern medicine has improved substantially across the country. Despite concerted efforts, however, India continues to be among the many developing countries of the world with high levels of morbidity, especially among infants, children, women, and the elderly.

There is also a high incidence of communicable diseases normally associated with low levels of sanitation and public hygiene, poor quality of drinking water and under-nutrition.

* A global initiative towards health-related research and action was taken at an international conference on Primary Health Care held in Alma Ata (in the erstwhile USSR) in 1978. In its Declaration, the conference spelt out the goal of the signatory nations which was to ensure 'Health for All by the Year 2000' with primary health care as its top priority.

In this context the Nobel Laureate Indian economist Amartya Sen has noted the thorough going *underactivity of the government* in the health sector and has supported effective government intervention in this sector. Sen says : "There are many failures, particularly in the development of public educational facilities, health care provisions, social security arrangements, local democracy, environmental protection, and so on, and the stifling of market incentives is only one part of that larger picture. The failures can, thus, be scarcely seen simply as the result of an 'overactive' government. That can be justifiably seen as overactivity in some fields has been inseparably accompanied by thorough going *underactivity* in others."

Role of Health Care : Among the different forms of interventions that can contribute to the provision of social security, the role of health care deserves forceful emphasis. Illness is, obviously enough, one of the most widespread causes of human deprivation and economic insecurity in India. It affects not only the actual patients and those who depend on them for their subsistence, but also other members of the society, in so far as the *threat* of disease arising from widespread morbidity reduces the quality of life. Further, the limitations of private provision in the domain of health care are well known. A well-developed system of public health is an essential contribution to the fulfilment of social security objectives.*

This is one field where there is an overwhelming need for bold initiatives and comprehensive reform. Compared with many other developing countries, India has poor health achievements despite spending a comparatively large part of its GNP on health (if one adds up public and private spending). Much of this mismatch between resources and achievements is due to the poor functioning of the public health care system, especially in rural areas. In some states, this system is little more than a collection of deserted primary health centres, filthy dispensaries, unmotivated doctors, and chaotic hospitals.

Paradoxically despite the improvement in health infrastructure, many citizens, mostly in rural areas are deprived of basic health

---

* *India : Econmic Development and Social Opportunity* (1995).

care. A chunk of health budget goes to urban hospitals at the expense of primary health care or services in rural areas.

Through these various inter-connections, education and health can be variables of great strategic importance in the process of economic development. India's failure to have an adequate public policy in educational and health matters can be, thus, of profound significance in assessing the limited success of Indian development efforts over the last half a century.

Reproductive Health Rights as Human Rights

Ever since the inception of family planning programme, one of the serious deficiencies has been that reproductive health component of health service was completely ignored. It was only as a result of Programme of Action of the International Conference on Population and Development (ICPD), 1994 that the Reproductive and Child Health (RCH) programme was launched in October 1997. Under this programme a comprehensive package of services for family planning, maternal and child health plan has been envisaged. Large scale assistance from the World Bank and other donor agencies has been committed for its successful implementation.

The idea of reproductive rights is not new. The rights result from the integration of several universally accepted rights emerging from fundamental liberties and other guarantees and from 'social rights'. Many national constitutions clearly provide and include right to :—

- Protection of family, e.g. family planning;
- Constitution of a family;
- Education and support of children;
- Special protection during and after pregnancy;
- Parenthood as an eminent social value;
- Health; and
- Integrity of all persons.

The Convention on the Elimination of All Forms of Discrimination Aganinst Women (1979) recognized the right to choose family size, 'freely and responsibly', the right to family planning education, information and counselling services, and the right to safe pregnancy, delivery and post-natal care. The right to health, accepted in all international treaties on social rights, implies all other rights.

The current focus on reproductive health marks a global recognition that reproductive health needs have been largely neglected. Consequently this neglect has had profound adverse impact particularly for women.

Reproductive health encompasses a range of health concerns, yet there remains some confusion about what really constitutes reproductive health, how it differs from ongoing MCH/FP programmes and why there is a need for a broad reproductive health orientation to the family planning policies in India.

The International Conference on Population and Development, defined reproductive health as "a state of complete physical, mental and social well-being and not merely the absence of disease or infirmity, in all matters relating to the reproductive system and to its functions and processes." In short, a reproductive health orientation, drawn from this and other sources, includes :

1. A satisfying and safe sex life free from the fear of disease and free from coercion and violence,
2. The capability to reproduce, and the freedom to decide if, when and how often, to do so, that is, access to both infertility services on the one hand and contraceptive services on the other,
3. Access to safe and affordable abortion facilities,
4. Reproductive choice for women and men; that people have the right to be informed and have access to safe, effective, affordable and acceptable methods of family planning of their choice,
5. Safe child-bearing: access to appropriate health care services that will enable women to go safely through pregnancy and child birth and provide for a healthy infant,
6. Access to services for the prevention and care of reproductive health problems, both gynaecological and obstetric, in a culturally sensitive manner,
7. Special attention to adolescents whose reproductive health

needs have been particularly overlooked. Whatever the criterion, the available evidence points to poor reproductive health among women in India.

Despite the interest in women's reproductive health in India, information on the reproductive health situation continues to be incomplete and patchy. Lot of data are available on one aspect of reproductive health, i.e. contraceptive use patterns but there is almost no information available on the prevalence of reproductive tract infections, abortion related morbidity and infertility. Safe motherhood is still a dream for much of India and particularly for its rural areas. Few women have access to ante-natal care, the recent NFHS study shows that only half of all rural women were immunised against tetanus : only two in five have received an ante-natal check up from a doctor or other health professionals and only 45 per cent received iron supplementation. As a result, high risk cases go undetected, anaemia is widespread, and knowledge of health and nutrition needs during pregnancy and the post-natal period are poorly understood.

Access to safe delivery is equally poor : three in four rural Indian women continue to be delivered by untrained attendants in unhygienic conditions (Kanitkar and others, 1994). It is no surprise, therefore, that maternal deaths account for a large proportion of all deaths of women of reproductive age; more among rural women.

Regarding access to safe and affordable abortion services, it is found that roughly five million abortions continue to be performed annually, of these about 0.6 million abortions are performed under health services network. The growing tendency to misuse sophisticated prenatal diagnostic technique to abort female foetuses, suggests the disturbing possibility of increased abortions and repeat abortions. Safe abortion services are available only in urban areas. There is no information and counselling about legal termination services available to rural women. There is limited publicity about the law and there is widely held perception that abortion is illegal.

Little is known about the levels and patterns or consequences of infertility in India. Factors underlying infertility include women's poor health and nutrition status which can lead to repeated miscarriages and foetal wastages, unhygienic obstetric and abortion procedures, STDs and even tuberculosis. The health services are scarcely comprehensive enough to provide access to reliable information, sympathetic counselling and services to infertile couples. What is required is a sound referral system for infertile couples, along with primary health care which can provide basic information and counselling.

Although more than two in five couples in the reproductive age use a method of contraception, there is little informed choice in the matter of contraception. Programme priorities promote female sterilisation and as a result of the emphasis on terminal contraception, young and low parity women remain unprotected from repeated and closely-spaced pregnancies which enhance chances of reproductive morbidity.

The focus on sterilisation, target fulfilment and incentives has resulted in obscuring the spacing needs of women and their right to exercise an informed choice. Service delivery strategies and quality of care have been largely insensitive to the needs of women, the constraints the average woman faces in seeking services, in voicing fears and side-effects and their right to have complete pre-acceptance counselling, including information on potential side effects and complications and post-acceptance follow-up.

Gender Disparities in Health Care—Adolescent girls are particularly vulnerable and neglected, coming under the purview of government programmes only when they are pregnant. The majority are out of school and are neither serviced by educational or school health programmes nor by child health and nutrition services. At the family level too, girls are highly vulnerable : Son preference is pervasive, resulting in gender disparities in health care, food intake, school attendance and child labour from an early age. Complications of pregnancy, pre-natal and neo-natal mortality and low birth weight are much higher among adolescent women than among older women.

Increasing sexual activity combined with ignorance about safe sex is a particularly alarming combination in the light of the HIV epidemic. It is time that sex education programmes became more realistic in terms of information needs of adolescents and youth both in and out of school.

The health delivery system has been largely insensitive to the reproductive health care needs of women and constraints they face in expressing these— let alone the constraints they face in obtaining services. Doorstep services are essential for secluded women and these are rarely undertaken, and where undertaken, focus more on contraception than on reproductive health in general. A comprehensive focus on adolescent girls mostly out of school to improve their nutritional levels, access to health services, information, vocational skills development and increase their ages at marriage would meet an important health needs at an early stage in the lifecycle.

Health workers themselves are poorly informed about reproductive morbidity, can be insensitive in probing and are preoccupied with achieving contraceptive targets rather than offering a range of reproductive health services. *The poor reproductive health situation in India and particularly that of the Indian women calls for a broad reproductive health programme and a women-centred orientation.* Strategies and programmes to empower women in terms of control of economic resources, information and education, their rights, as well as in terms of self-confidence and ability to recognise, articulate and seek care for health problems are necessary conditions enabling the enhancement of women's health and rights.

POPULATION POLICY

By common consent, the greatest failure since independence has been our inability to prevent the exponential increase in population. With the present alarming growth of population, it is unrealistic to expect the state of nation to improve, poverty to be alleviated and unemployment to be contained. With over one billion population, it is indeed a disturbing thought that we have over 300 million people who live below the poverty line and go hungry to bed every night. The state of deprivation for such a large chunk of population could not have gone further. India has more than 400 million uneducated people, with mounting problems of unemployment, lack of shelter, poverty, malnutrition; this situation in the ultimate analysis is likely to result in a revolt against the present system. When the situation is assessed against the fact that the Government of India was the first in the world to initiate a comprehensive Family Planning programme in the world in 1952, the failure of the programme to control population does raise a question mark as to where and how we had gone wrong.

India's family planning programme provides a glaring example of dissonance between the use and development of the technology for reproductive control and other major variables which constitute the entire system. Decision makers held a strong conviction that an ideal contraceptive is the key to solving the population problem of the country. They ignored the fact that action for demand-generation and the development of an efficient and effective delivery system are the more crucial variables of the system. The privileged classes, who dominate the decision-making process, have been lukewarm towards the developmental programmes which are crucial to demand generation. This resulted in their totally unrealistic expectations about the development of technology for reproduction control.

It is now generally accepted that the target oriented, heavy handed approach, with an element of coercion created an adverse impact; and a mind set which was not conducive to successful implementation of the programme. The programme, instead of becoming a people's movement and people's concern, became a pre-occupation which concerned the government alone. In a study, *From Population to People* (1988), Ashish Bose says : Bulldozing does not make a programme a people's programme. On the contrary, it comes in the way of people's participation....the people are alienated by the family planning programme; they are angry with insensitive officials who are administering this programme; they are critical of unhelpful politicians who make speeches in the name of the people; the doctors feel humiliated at the treatment given to them by the higher bureaucracy, both medical and non-medical; the multipurpose workers feel harassed at the sterilisation quota allotted to them. But the number game in New Delhi goes on.....targets are set and targets are achieved in rows of statistical figures presented in the government reports. How long will this number game go on? For whom will the target toll?

Since the issue of bringing down the birth rate of population continues to be a constant pre-occupation with the government administrators and planners, there has been discussion, as to why China's achievements in bringing down birth rate over a short period through coercive measures may not be adopted in India as well.

The policy planners in India would do well to heed to the note of caution administered by Amartya Sen who says : It is not clear how the acceptability of coercion can be tested except through democratic confrontation. While that testing has not occurred in China, it was indeed attempted in India during the Emergency* period in the seventies when compulsory birth control was tried by Mrs. Gandhi's government, along with suspending various legal rights and civil liberties. The policy of coercion in general—including that in birth control—was overwhelmingly defeated in the general elections that followed. Furthermore, family-planning experts have noted how voluntary birth-control programmes received a severe set-back from that brief programme of compulsory sterilization, as people had become deeply suspicious of the entire movement. The coercive measures of the Emergency period, in fact, aside from having little immediate impact on fertility rates, were followed by a long period of *stagnation* in the birth rate, which only ended in 1985.

There is evidence that some form of compulsion or forceful pressure to accept birth control (especially sterilization) continue to be used in some Indian states, particularly in the north, where fertility rates tend to be high. Even when coercion is not a part of official policy, the government's firm insistence on 'meeting the family planning targets' often leads administrators and health-care personnel at different levels to resort to all kinds of pressure tactics that come close to compulsion. Some of the instances generally reported by the family welfare personnel are : verbal threats, making

---

* The Janta government, which came to power after the Emergency, changed the nomenclature of the Ministry from Family Planning to Family Welfare.

sterilization a condition of eligibility for anti-poverty programmes, depriving mothers with more than two children of maternity benefits, reserving certain kinds of health care services to persons who have more than two children from contesting panchayat elections. The long-run consequences of these practices can be quite disastrous both for health care and for the consensual emergence of social norms favouring smaller families.

NATIONAL POPULATION POLICY 2000

In 1952, India was the first country to launch a national programme, emphasising family planning, to the extent necessary, for reducing birth rates to stabilise the population at a level consistent with the requirement of national economy. But it was only in 2000 that a *National Population Policy 2000* was adopted in the country. The policy has the long term objective of achieving a stable population by 2045, at a level consistent with the requirements of sustainable economic growth, social development and environmental protection. The policy has set the following goals for 2010 :—

1. Universal access to quality contraceptive services in order to lower the Total Fertility Rate to 2.1 and attaining two-child norm.
2. Full coverage of registration of births, deaths and marriage and pregnancy.
3. Universal access to information/counselling services for fertility regulation and contraception with a wide basket of choices.
4. Infant Mortality Rate to decline below 30 per thousand live births and sharp reduction in the incidence of low birth weight (below 2.5 kg) babies.
5. Universal immunisation of children against vaccine preventable diseases, elimination of Polio by 2000 and near elimination of Tetanus and Measles.
6. Promote delayed marriage of girls, not earlier than age 18 and preferably after 20 years of age.
7. Achieve 80 per cent institutional deliveries and increase in

the percentage of deliveries conducted by trained persons to 100 per cent.

8. Containing Sexually Transmitted Diseases.
9. Reducton in Maternal Mortality Ratio to less than 100 per 1,00,000 live births.
10. Universalisation of primary education and reduction in the dropout rates at primary and secondary levels to below 20 per cent both for boys and girls.

The National Commission on Population was constituted under the Chairmanship of the Prime Minister and the Deputy Chairman, Planning Commission, as Vice Chairman on 11 May 2000, to review, monitor and give directions for implementation of the National Population Policy. A Strategic Support Group consisting of Secretaries of concerned sectoral ministries has been constituted as Standing Advisory Group to the Commission. Some working groups have been constituted to look into specific aspects of implementation of the policy. *(National Human Development—Report, 2001.)*

Population and Empowerment of Women

There are, however, certain redeeming features to the intractable problem of increasing birth rate—female literacy, enhanced status of women, and the movement for women empowerment would go a long way in easing India's population problem. The worldover, rising female literacy has been accompanied by lower birth rates and enhanced social and economic indices. The link between female literacy and fertility is particularly evident. This linkage has been widely observed in other countries, and it is not surprising that it should emerge in India too. The unwillingness of educated women to be tied down to continuous child-rearing clearly plays a role in bringing about this attitudinal change. Education also makes the horizon of vision wider, and, at a more mundane level, helps to disseminate the knowledge of family planning. *The Indian policy making will have to consider population problem not so much in terms of population control, but in terms of strong, positive, societal measures which essentially means better education, skill-*

development and, improved health care along with dignity and empowerment for women.

In the ultimate analysis the challenge of increasing population explosion would be met only if it is understood in the proper perspective, particularly by the political leadership. It is essential that the leadership of all the political parties at the national and state level exhibit a firm commitment towards the success of family planning programme, which needs to be linked with sustainable development, environment, empowerment of women and social and gender equity.

The role of voluntary organisations in a mass movement such as population control is critical for generation of momentum and accelerating the pace of progress. There is a need to incorporate family planning as a major objective of all voluntary organisations concerned with health and/or education-related activities. Substantially increased amount of funds need to be channelised through these agencies. The establishment of an apex organisation to develop networking between all such voluntary organisations committed to the promotion of national efforts in this important area of human endeavour need to be considered earnestly.

The population welfare programme will succeed only if the movements for empowerment of women and female literacy are strengthened.

It is impossible to conceive the successful implementation of a vast national programme of family welfare without the cooperation of local bodies, particularly panchayati raj institutions, voluntary and non-governmental organisations. It is generally conceded that no government can build a society, whereas voluntary action can. With greater involvement of the people in the population control and family planning programmes through the Panchayati Raj System as envisaged in the Constitution (Seventy-Second Amendment) Bill, 1991, the programme will become one of "people's operation with government cooperation". The health planners and administrators must not only become sensitive and responsive to the felt needs of the people but must also adapt to the instrumentality of local self-government.

Voluntary Development Organisations — The functions of voluntary development organisations have changed over the years such as (a) relief and welfare, (b) community development, (c) sustainable system, and (d) people's movement. NGO-role changed as doer, mobiliser, catalyst and activist. Managerial approach to development also passed through logistic management and self-management over the years. Organisations are strategic if they contribute directly to long term objectives of the society. NGOs have strategic roles in catalysing transformation, checking abuses of power, facilitating reconciliation and providing essential community services. New roles demand new competencies from NGOs to act as advocates, educators, catalysts, monitors, mediators, etc.*

In the health and population sector several voluntary and non-governmental organisations have made commendable contribution in reaching the unreached areas and sections of population where government efforts could not have accomplished the desired objectives.

The Voluntary Health Association of India (VHAI)—a non-profit federation of over 3000 organisations, has been working in the area of health and community development, strives to make health a reality for all. The VHAI fulfils these objectives primarily through training and by providing information to the target groups. It campaigns on relevant and important health issues to ensure that a people oriented health policy is brought about and effectively implemented.

The Family Planning Association of India (FPAI), an NGO with national status, links 2297 NGOs working in diverse fields to promote reproductive health including family planning and gender equality. Its branch units are also actively involving local NGOs and community groups. The orientation programmes conducted by FPAI include individual and group counselling activities, in-house courses for volunteers and staff at various levels to enhance knowledge and competence levels. Family welfare programme, which needs resurrection, can succeed through an approach which is primarily non-governmental and people oriented. Since the

* *Kurukshetra*, October 1998.

Association has most of its projects in rural areas, it has been able to provide access to health services so as to motivate eligible couples to space out the number of children.

The Kerala Sastra Sahitya Parisad, whose contribution in developing literacy campaigns has already been outlined, is one of the few NGOs which has attempted to demystify medicine. Special campaigns on the drug policy, anti-smoking and amniocentesis have had some limited impact, both at the policy level as well as in educating the consumers. The KSSP emphasises that the greatest health problem is poverty and that the majority of ailments arise from the inadequacy of proper food and an unhealthy living environment. It has organised numerous health camps, published several documents on people's health, and are in constant touch with various organisations like the Voluntary Health Association of India. The KSSP believes that health care is a basic right of every citizen and an effective health care delivery system should work towards keeping the entire population physically and mentally healthy. It warns people against the modern health care systems controlled by multinational drug companies, stressing instead the wealth of knowledge that exists in traditional systems of medicine.

IEC Strategies—A major cause of our failure to achieve fuller and quicker results in our family planning and health programmes lies in the failure of communication. The fact that large sections of our rural population have upto now been almost inaccessible, except to their neighbourhood groups, because of remote location, illiteracy and lack of communication infrastructure, except for radio; has certainly made the success of the programme difficult. It has remained a government programme, the community's active involvement and participation being marginal. Due to inadequacy of Information, Education and Communication (IEC) activities the knowledge of the community about the contraceptives, their availability, safety, etc. are at a low level. Adoption of the small family norm and use of appropriate measures for birth control are matters of personal choice and decision.

Information, Education and Communication, which are critical inputs need to be further strengthened and expanded. Greater use of the mass media need be made to disseminate the message of family planning to the remotest corner of the country and the entire system of pricing the media time *vis-a-vis* its social responsibility has to be given a fresh look, different from the commercial angle. Area specific IEC material can be developed and produced only if efforts are made to pool resources of various social sectors and to provide community TV/radio sets, besides maintaining them. The backbone of the IEC efforts will, however, remain the inter-personal communication for which the grassroots level female worker will have to be trained and effectively utilised.

Family Planning must be projected not in narrow technical terms, but as *an enabling transforming force* which represents the ability of human being to take a conscious decision and control the course of life. The message of family planning cannot be given in isolation— it is an integral part of the effort to better the human condition and therefore must be integrated with other development messages. It is also essential to carry out intensive communication campaign for communities that are lagging behind in family planning acceptance. Such a campaign need to be culture and value specific.

Evolving an effective communication strategy for family welfare programmes is no simple, academic task; for here the communication experts have an extremely challenging responsibility to perform; which involves changing the mind set of the people or as the eminent communication scholar, Kiran Karnik says : *Creating change, change, especially of deeply ingrained values and beliefs, is extremely difficult, and for mass media to create such a change, is indeed a tall order. However, if the effort is dovetailed with other uses of media (especially agenda setting/ambience creation and education/training), it may be possible to initiate or trigger a process of change.*

Let us have a look at the rural segment— with its rigid social structure, belief in early female marriage, preference for son (instances where mother is forced to have repeated pregnancies even after the birth of several daughters continue to proliferate except in literate families), gender discrimination, unwillingness to send girls for education or jobs (particularly in BIMARU*

* Bihar, Madhya Pradesh, Rajasthan and Uttar Pradesh.

states)—all these pose serious impediments for a communication expert to cross over; for him it is not a question of media use—print or broadcast, channel—local, national or global; the question will always be to create a message which is attuned to his mind set, in consonance with his socio-economic profile and which does not make him merely a beneficiary of government programmes; but a stack holder in it.

Fortunately during the Sixth Plan period, communication strategies were redefined bringing in issues such as beyond 'family planning factors' which included programmes for child survival, improving the status of women, literacy and others. The major interventions initiated in the Eighth Five Year Plan were with the objectives of (a) inducing a shift in values, attitudes, and behaviour patterns regarding health and health-related issues. Specific programme indicators such as reduction in infant and maternal mortality, universal immunization, coverage of pregnant mothers and infants, increased number of deliveries by trained hands, better utilization of health services and, lastly, reduction in family size by a healthy mix of spacing and terminal methods; (b) mobilizing people, NGOs, and the government machinery through the process of community participation by instituting women's groups in the villages known as *Mahila Mandals* was also to be undertaken; and (c) involvement of non-governmental organizations in health communication and training.

In the ultimate analysis the challenge of increasing population explosion would be met only if it is understood in the proper perspective, particularly by the political leadership. It is essential that the leadership of all the political parties at the national and state level exhibits a firm commitment towards the success of family planning programme. The programme also needs to be linked with sustainable development, environment, empowerment of women and social and gender equity.

Research Study on the Coverage of Health and Nutrition Issues

In a pioneering study of coverage of health and nutrition issues in print media and the readership behaviour of the respondents, Saroj

Dahiya concludes that the coverage of health and nutrition issues suffers from inadequacy and distortion. Issues like food quality control, and nutrition during life cycle were totally ignored in all the selected dailies, whereas topics like recent health/nutrition care and techniques occupied maximum space followed by cookery/ recipes, advances in food science and technology, epidemiology and management of diseases and nutritional quality of foods in all the newspapers. The important issues, i.e. role of food in health/ nutrition schemes introduced by government received meagre coverage in all the papers. Press correspondents of the papers and freelance journalists were important source of information about health and nutrition topics.

Role of food in health and disease, advances in food science and technology, recent health/nutrition care and techniques, foods in advertisements, cookery/recipes were some other topics preferred by majority of the respondents followed by issues, i.e. health/ nutrition programmes and epidemiology and management of diseases in different newspapers. Sixty per cent respondents made it clear that gender makes no difference in reporting health and nutrition issues (Table 7.1). The majority of the respondents suggested to cover sufficient aspects like food quality control, role of food in health and disease, advances in food science and technology, and nutritional quality of foods; more in number and space to enhance the knowledge regarding these issues. It was further suggested that all the news should be reported timely, objectively, in well summarised form based on actual research in depth in the form of articles, interviews with scientists, news, advertisements and features. Health and nutritional status of people in rural areas may also be adequately covered.

Saroj Dahiya suggests that : (i) The coverage of health and nutrition news should be increased. All newspapers should give one-third part (both in number and space) daily to such reporting. The newspapers should regularly take an active part in covering the process of development; (ii) While covering the news/features about various development programmes, reporter should try to make direct contact with those people who are supposed to be the real beneficiaries of such programmes. Such an attempt would provide true information about various development programmes;

Table 7.1: Space Covered by Different Categories of Health and Nutrition Issues in Selected English Dailies

Sl. No.	*Categories of health and nutrition*	*The Hindustan Times (col. cms)*	*The Times of India (col. cms)*	*The Indian Express (col. cms)*	*The Hindu (col. cms)*	*The Tribune (col. cms)*	*Total space*
1.	Role of food in health and diseases	—	22.15	21.30	16.22	—	59.67
2.	Cookery/recipes	18.22	23.70	30.12	25.30	26.72	124.06
3.	Present food trends	17.22	—	—	—	—	17.22
4.	Recent health/nutrition care and techniques	22.07	33.75	24.25	32.76	30.20	143.03
5.	Health and nutrition programmes	25.15	15.65	16.52	24.19	—	81.51
6.	Advances in food science and technology	24.15	18.85	16.52	35.25	28.15	122.92
7.	Foods in advertisements	18.30	—	18.72	17.12	24.91	79.05
8.	Epidemiology and management of diseases	21.72	—	22.13	32.34	36.72	112.91
9.	Nutritional qualities of foods	33.90	—	20.13	—	26.10	80.13
10.	Food quality, control and malpractices	17.27	—	10.12	18.82	—	46.21
11.	Nutrition during lifecycle	—	—	12.19	—	26.20	38.39
	Total space covered (col. cms)	198	114	192	202	199	905

(iii) Health reporting of rural areas and of various health and nutrition programmes should be increased; and (iv) Latest updated news on health and nutrition should be given in the newspapers. It should be based on research conducted. The newspapers should regularly give editorials about various development programmes/ issues analyses the space covered, and different categories of health and nutrition issues, in selected English dailies.

Ministry of Health and Family Welfare **:** The Government of India has a full-fledged Ministry of Health and Family Welfare that formulates from time to time health policy for the country. The current National Health Policy lays special emphasis on population stabilisation, medical and health education, need for providing primary health care with special emphasis on preventive, promotional and rehabilitative aspects, reorientation of existing health personnel, health education, health insurance, health legislation, medical research and inter-sectoral cooperation.

The Ministry also develops and implements a number of health related programmes and schemes both at the central and state levels which include : National Malaria Eradication Programme, National Leprosy Eradication Programme, National Tuberculosis Control Programme, National AIDS Control Programme, Pilot Project on Control of Cardio-Vascular Diseases and Stroke and several others.

All these efforts are directed towards combating communicable, non-communicable and other major diseases as well as working to reduce mortality and morbidity rates. These programmes reinforce the delivery of health care at various levels throughout the country : primary (local level centres), secondary (district level health facilities) and tertiary (specialised health care hospitals, largely based in metropolitan areas).

As a result of these efforts scourge of small pox has been totally eradicated from the country, while concerted efforts are on to eliminate polio. On the other hand, in recent years, new diseases have emerged. AIDS is posing a far greater challenge than was anticipated even a decade ago.

However, in area of disease eradication and health care system, the country faces several challenges. High percentage of women and children continue to suffer from malnutrition in India. Research has shown that girls with malnutrition develop chronoic anemia, which has a significant impact on their child bearing and rearing capabilities while males are more prone to cardio-vascular diseases in adult life. Among the foremost environmental factors influencing health care are clean drinking water, pollution free air and appropriate sanitation. Experience has shown that water borne diseases such as diarrhoea and gastroenteritis can be greatly restricted with provision of safe drinking water. It is a matter of concern that the country is witnessing the return of diseases like plague due to insanitary conditions. All this calls for concerted efforts to make India a happy and healthy country.

World Health Organisation (WHO) : WHO is the major UN agency working in the area of health and disease control. The functions of the organisation are :—

1. to act as the directing and coordinating authority on international health work;
2. to establish, maintain effective collaboration with the United Nations, specialized agencies, governmental health administrations, professional groups and such other organizations as may be deemed appropriate;
3. to assist governments, upon request, in strengthening health services;
4. to furnish appropriate technical assistance and, in emergencies, necessary aid upon the request or acceptance of governments;
5. to provide or assist in providing, upon the request of the United Nations, health services and facilities to special groups, such as the peoples of trust territories;
6. to establish and maintain such administrative and technical services as may be required, including epidemiological and statistical services;
7. to stimulate and advance work to eradicate epidemic, endemic and other diseases;
8. to promote, in co-operation with other specialized agencies where necessary, the prevention of accidental injuries;
9. to promote, in co-operation with other specialized agencies where necessary, the improvement of nutrition, housing,

sanitation, recreation, economic or working conditions and other aspects of environmental hygiene;

10. to promote maternal and child health and welfare and to foster the ability to live harmoniously in a changing environment; and
11. to foster activities in the field of mental health, especially those affecting the harmony of human relations.

WHO defines health **:** Health is a state of complete physical, mental and social well-being and not merely the absence of disease or infirmity. The enjoyment of the highest attainable standard of health is one of the fundamental rights of every human being without distinction of race, religion, political belief, economic or social condition. The definition has not been amended since 1948.

The health of all peoples is fundamental to the attainment of peace and security and is dependent upon the fullest co-operation of individuals and states. The achievement of any State in the promotion and protection of health is of value to all. Unequal development in different countries in the promotion of health and control of disease, especially communicable disease, is a common danger. Healthy development of the child is of basic importance; the ability to live harmoniously in a changing total environment is essential to such development. The extension to all peoples the benefits of medical, psychological and related knowledge is essential to the fullest attainments of health. Informed opinion and active co-operation on the part of the public are of the utmost importance in the improvement of the health of the people.

Governments have a responsibility for the health of their peoples which can be fulfilled only by the provision of adequate health and social measures.

UNAIDS **:** As the leading advocate for worldwide action against HIV/AIDS, the global mision of UNAIDS is to lead, strengthen and support an expanded response to the epidemic that will :

1. prevent the spread of HIV,
2. provide care and support for those infected and affected by the disease,

3. reduce the vulnerability of individuals and communities to HV/AIDS,
4. alleviate the socio-economic and human impact of the epidemic.

UNAIDS Mission statement—As the main advocate for global action on HIV/AIDS, UNAIDS leads, strengthens and supports an expanded response aimed at preventing the transmission of HIV, providing care and support, reducing the vulnerability of individuals and communities to HIV/AIDS, and alleviating the impact of the epidemic.

From 1986, WHO had the lead responsibility on AIDS in the United Nations, helping countries to set up much-needed national AIDS programmes. But by the mid-1990s, it became clear that the relentless spread of HIV, and the epidemic's devastating impact on all aspects of human lives and on social and economic development, were creating an emergency that would require a greatly expanded United Nations effort. Nor could any single United Nations Organization provide the co-ordinated level of assistance needed to address the many factors driving the HIV epidemic, or help countries deal with the impact of HIV/AIDS on households, communities and local economies. Greater coordination would be needed to maximize the impact of UN efforts.

Addressing these challenges head-on, the United Nations took an innovative approach in 1996, drawing six orgnizations together in a joint and cosponsored programme—the Joint United Nations Programme on HIV/AIDS (UNAIDS). The six original cosponsors of UNAIDS were : UNICEF, UNDP, UNFPA, UNESCO, WHO and the World Bank.

The goal of UNAIDS is to catalyse, strengthen and orchestrate the unique expertise, resources, and networks of influence that each of these organizations offers. Working together through UNAIDS, the cosponsors expand their outreach through strategic alliances with other United Nations agencies and national governments.

Nutrition —The major nutrition-related public health problems currently are : chronic energy deficiency, micronutrient deficiencies, such as anemia due to iron and folic acid deficiency,

Vitamin A deficiency, iodine deficiency disorders and associated health hazards. Nutritional problems need to be tackled across a broad front. There need to be a continued increase in food grain production to meet the needs of the growing population. This increase should be more in the case of coarse grain production to meet the energy requirements of BPL families at lower cost. Efforts have to be made to check the sluggish trend in per capita availability of pulses, and increase pulse production, improve affordability of pulses and increase consumption. Similarly, increased availability of vegetables at affordable cost throughout the year in urban and rural areas is desirable to address nutritional needs of the population.

Poor Healthcare in Public Hospitals : The deaths of a number of children in Kolkata during September 2002 in the sole paediatric referral hospital in the city have once again highlighted the sorry state of health care system in the public sector. The public sector hospitals are termed as virtual death traps. This has led to demands for the privatisation of the government run health care system. In a cogent article on the subject in the *Hindustan Times* (21 September 2002) the eminent journalist Mrinal Pande argues against such a step which will make the availability of the basic of health services to the poor still more inaccessible. It is a fact that private sector in health care has grown in size and importance in the country but it has not taken the responsibility for long term investment in public health, specially of the preventive kind. Therefore it means that while the government complains of lack of funds and withdraws from vital programmes such as preventing the spread of diseases like TB and malaria, the largely unregulated private sector turns away from this non-profit area. Consequently even more virulent forms of malaria and TB keep growing. One of the reasons of sorry state of affairs in the public sector health care system is the meagre allotment of funds for this sector (Gujarat spends only 1.63 per cent of its net state domestic product). Whereas in states like UP and Maharashtra inadequate funding and several other factors have further affected the work of government hospitals and PHCs, in Tamil Nadu the state government has initiated a cost effecive system to supply drugs to PHCs. It has also linked its post-graduate medical education to rural services. The remedy, therefore lies, in improving the quality of services available in rural areas at PHCs rather than privatising the healthcare system.

NOTE

The research study, Health and Nutrition Issues in Print Media— A Study of Some National Dailies, was conducted by Saroj Dahiya as a part of her Post-Graduate Diploma Course in Agricultural Journalism, 1999, at Haryana Agricultural University. The study deals with two major aspects : content analysis of health and nutrition news/issues, and readership behaviour of respondents regarding these issues. Five selected English newspapers; four published from New Delhi and one from Chandigarh were studied for a period of one month, 1-30 June 1999. Food and nutrition issues published in the selected newspapers for the above period comprised the sample of study.

REFERENCES

Approach Paper to the Tenth Five Year Plan (2002-2007). Government of India, Planning Commission.

Bose, Ashish (1988). *From Population to People*. BR Publishing Corporation, New Delhi.

Dreze Jean and Amartya Sen (1996). *India : Economic Development and Social Opportunity*. Oxford University Press, New Delhi.

India—2002. A Reference Annual, Publications Division, New Delhi.

India Human Development Report (1999). Oxford University Press, New Delhi.

Karnik, Kiran (1993). Communicaton Technology and Population in (ed.) Vasant Gowariker, *The Inevitable Billion*. National Book Trust, New Delhi.

Pande, Mrinal (2002) A life and death question, *Hindustan Times*, 21 September, New Delhi.

Planning Commission, (2001) Approach Paper to the Tenth Five Year Plan (2002-2007). Government of India, New Delhi.

Planning Commission, (2002) *National Human Development Report 2001*, Government of India, New Delhi.

Trakroo, P.L. and Gita Bamezai (1996). A Paradigm Shift in Communication Strategies for Health and Family Welfare Programmes in *Media Asia* 23 (3), AMIC, Singapore.

Voices (Vol. III, No. 2) 1995, Banglore.

8

HUMAN RIGHTS AND HUMAN DEVELOPMENT

The concept of human rights evolved over a long period of history. The concept developed as an instrument for limiting the use of autocratic power; as such it applied, to start with, only within states and had no international application. Even within states, the concept tended to be confined to the rights of the upper strata of society, and a long time elapsed before it extended to all human beings without distinction of class or creed. The famous Magna Carta of the thirteenth century represented an agreement between the king and the baronage, and although it contained a few clauses of general application, its main purpose was to protect the rights and privileges of the feudal lords of Britain. A much wider extension of the concept of human rights was brought about by the British revolutionaries who, after deposing and executing their king, laid down in the Bill of Rights of 1689 the minimum liberties to which all citizens were entitled. Nearly a century later, in 1776, the American revolutionaries after throwing off the yoke of the British King embodied in their Declaration of Independence the 'inalienable' human rights, which included the right to "life, liberty and the pursuit of happiness". Shortly thereafter, the French revolutionaries, on deposing and executing their king, made the Declaration "men are born and remain free and equal in rights" and that purpose of any political association was the confirmation of the human rights of "liberty, property, security and resistance to oppression". Thus the concept of human rights has been all along a revolutionary concept.

The Charter of the United Nations which was adopted after the war by the San Francisco Conference gave prominence to the aim of promoting human rights and freedom. In the preamble of the Charter it was proclaimed : "We the peoples of the United

Nations, determined..... to reaffirm faith in fundamental human rights, in the dignity and worth of the human person, in the equal rights of men and women and of nations large and small... have resolved to combine our efforts to accomplish these aims." In the very first article of the Charter, one of the declared purposes of the United Nations was stated to be the achievement of international cooperation in promoting and encouraging respect for human rights, the other purposes being the maintenance of internal peace and the development of friendly relations among nations.

Universal Declaration of Human Rights

The universal declaration of human rights was adopted by the general assembly "as a common standard of achievement for all peoples and all nations." Serious doubts were initially entertained about the practical value of the declaration even by people who appreciated the basic importance of human rights. These doubts must have been resolved by the experience of the last twenty-two years. Time and again the principles laid down in the declaration have been invoked and acted upon by the general assembly and other organs of the United Nations. The rival principle of "domestic jurisdiction" did not prevent the general assembly from interfering or trying to interfere in cases where human rights were blatantly violated. This is well illustrated by the treatment given by the general assembly to the policy of apartheid pursued by the government of South Africa. By now the declaration has acquired a degree of practical authority, which had led some people to believe that it has virtually become a part of international law.

The contemporary international statement of these rights is the Universal Declaration of Human Rights which was adopted on 10 December 1948. The Declaration proclaims economic, social and cultural rights in addition to political and civil rights and freedom for the people of the world. These rights are considered the foundation of freedom, peace and justice in the world. Through this Declaration, the United Nations reaffirmed its faith in the worth of human beings and in the equal rights for men and women, and expressed determination to promote social progress and better standards of living for the large majority of the people.

Human rights, as the term most commonly used, are the rights which every human being is entitled to enjoy and to have protected. The underlying idea of such rights, which are fundamental to human dignity—is that these rights be respected in the treatment of all men, women and children. These rights exist in some form in all cultures and societies. Human rights have been legally granted to the citizens of countries all over the world. These in general terms pertain to a decent life, protection from ill health and unemployment, freedom of expression, right to education and many other rights. The urge to freedom was enshrined first in the American Declaration of Independence, 1776; and the French Declaration of Rights of Man and the Citizen and the American Bill of Rights were among the first historic initiatives to include human rights.

Basic Principles

Some of the important basic principles of the Universal Declaration of Human Rights are :

1. All human beings are born free and equal in dignity and rights. They are endowed with reason and conscience and should act towards one another in a spirit of brotherhood.
2. Everyone is entitled to all the rights and freedoms set forth in this Declaration, without distinction of any kind, such as race, colour, sex, language, religion, political or other opinion, national or social origin.
3. Everyone has the right to life, liberty and security of person.
4. No one shall be held in slavery or servitude; slavery and the slave trade shall be prohibited in all their forms.
5. No one shall be subjected to torture or to cruel, inhuman or degrading treatment or punishment.
6. Everyone has the right to recognition everywhere as a person before the law.
7. All are equal before the law and are entitled without any discrimination to equal protection of the law. All are entitled

to equal protection against any discrimination in violation of this declaration and against any incitement to such discrimination.

The major advances in human rights and human development came after the horrors of the Second World War. The 1945 Charter of the United Nations, followed by the Universal Declaration of Human Rights in 1948, ushered in a new era of international commitment to human freedoms :

1. Emphasizing the universality of rights, centred on the equality of all people.
2. Recognizing the realization of human rights as a collective goal of humanity.
3. Identifying a comprehensive range of all rights—civil, political, economic, social and cultural—for all people.
4. Creating an international system for promoting the realization of human rights with institutions to set standards, establish international laws and monitor performance (but without powers of enforcement).
5. Establishing the state's accountability for its human rights obligations and commitments under international law.

Work on international human rights legislation also continued. But polarized by the cold war, the rhetoric of human rights was reduced to a weapon in the propaganda for geopolitical interests. The west emphasized civil and political rights, pointing the finger at socialist countries for denying these rights. The socialist, and many developing countries, emphasized economic and social rights, criticizing the richest western countries for their failure to secure these rights for all citizens. In the 1960s this led to two separate covenants—one for civil and political rights, and the other for economic, social and cultural rights.

According to a well known analyst of international relations : "No other act of the United Nations has had anything like the same impact on the thinking of our times, the best aspirations of which it incorporates and proclaims. It may well be that it will live in history chiefly as a statement of great moral principle. As such its influence is deeper and more lasting than any political document or legal instrument."

Civil and Political Rights, Economic, Social and Cultural Rights

The Declaration covers two broad sets of rights. One set is known as Civil and Political Rights. The other set of rights is known as Economic, Social and Cultural Rights. In the words of the Declaration, these two sets of rights aim to give all people 'freedom from fear and want'. Both sets of rights must be protected as the 'foundation of freedom, justice and peace in the world'.

It is the responsibility of governments to protect the human rights proclaimed by the Declaration. Under the heading of Civil and Political Rights, all governments are to protect the life, liberty and security of their citizens. They should guarantee that no one is enslaved and that no one is subjected to arbitrary arrest and detention or to torture. Everyone is entitled to a fair trial. The right to freedom of thought, conscience and religion and to freedom of expression is to be protected.

Under the heading of Economic, Social and Cultural Rights, all governments are expected to try progressively to improve the living conditions of their citizens. For example, they should try to guarantee the right to food, clothing, housing and medical care, the protection of the family and the right to social security, education and employment. They are to promote these rights without discrimination of any kind.

Several governments, however, as well as the news media, have come to use the term 'human rights' in a very narrow sense, referring only to the Civil and Political Rights set out in the Declaration. As a result the term 'human rights' is often broadly misused to mean only Civil and Political Rights and to exclude from consideration as a matter of rights, fundamental issues such as the right to food, health, education and social security.

The conventional wisdom had been that human rights were 'indivisible', meaning that respect for Civil and Political Rights could not be divorced from the enjoyment of Economic, Social and Cultural Rights. Expressed the other way round, authentic economic and social development could not exist without the political freedom to participate in the process, including the freedom to dissent.

Right to Development

'The right to development' was elaborated in the 1986 General Assembly Declaration on the Right to Development. It emphasizes the importance of Economic, Social and Cultural Rights and establishes that achieving these is both an individual and a collective effort.

The World Conference on Human Rights held at Vienna in June 1993 in its Final Declaration said : 'The universal nature of these rights is beyond question.' The entire spectrum of human rights was endorsed, without division. 'All human rights are universal, indivisible, and interdependent and interrelated.'

The Way Forward—The World Conference affirmed an affirmative action plan to implement the Declaration. Some of the important goals set for the future are :

- The full range of human rights must be respected as the equal and inalienable birthright of all people. All people, regardless of their characteristics or social situation, must be understood to have the same fundamental rights. No one is to fall, at any time or for any reason, outside the circle of those whose rights are to be universally protected.
- The achievement of development and democracy must be based on universal respect for human rights and fundamental freedoms. This is essential if people are to determine their own political, economic, social and cultural destinies and to participate fully in their societies. This applies to all people and all societies and must be understood to embrace individuals and groups thus far excluded from the free and equal expression of human rights.
- The process of development, which has to include the

eradication of extreme poverty and the alleviation of the debt burden of developing countries, must become one of the highest priorities of the international community. This can only be carried out on the basis of a new pattern of global cooperation that meets the needs of both present and future generations.

- The promotion and protection of economic, social and cultural rights must become subject to the same scrutiny and enforcement which can already be applied to civil and political rights. The first need is for a system of indicators to measure progress in the realization of the rights set forth in the International Covenant on Economic, Social and Cultural Rights.
- Gross and systematic violations of civil and political rights are taking place on a vast scale. Every effort must be made to halt these abuses which include arbitrary detentions, torture, summary executions, and 'disappearances'. Every instance must be condemned and measures taken to end impunity for those responsible.
- The protection of one of the rights must not be invoked as a justification for the denial or violation of other universally recognized rights. The promotion of social justice cannot be used to legitimize political persecution; nor may the rule of law be used as a basis for the perpetuation of economic injustice and social deprivation.
- Discrimination in all its forms must be eliminated, if people are to be able to exercise their inalienable rights and freedoms. Racism and racial discrimination, xenophobia and other forms of intolerance must be the target of major legislative and social programmes to prevent these abuses, protect potential victims and create a global ethos of mutual respect between all members of the human family.
- The rights of women of all ages, which have been denied on a massive scale worldwide, must be accorded full respect. This is a fundamental building block in the protection of the fundamental rights of all people everywhere. Action in a wide range of fields—legislative,

economic, social, and educational—is needed to halt all forms of violence against women and to curtail their exploitation and harassment.

- Children are among the most vulnerable people on the face of the earth and are frequently the defenceless victims of the most appalling violations of human rights. These abuses must stop and be prevented in future. This requires the adoption of the wide ranging measures stipulated in the Convention on the Rights of the Child, in addition to special measures to come to the defence of victims such as street-children, those who suffer from economic and sexual exploitation, those in detention and those who have become refugees.
- Every state must have an effective system for investigating and redressing violations of human rights. A strong and independent administration of justice must be secured in order to sustain human rights, democracy and development. Ratification of international human rights treaties by all governments is also an indispensable part of the process of establishing a universal rule of law in defence of human rights.
- Education in human rights must be treated as an essential contribution to the development of the global human rights culture. This requires the teaching and discussion of human rights in both the formal educational system in each country and informal channel of learning.
- The role of non-governmental organisations in the defence of human rights must be openly recognized and accepted. The harassment and brutal attacks to which human rights workers are often subjected must cease.

Third Generation of Human Rights

Human rights are indivisible, but they are also inseparable from the major aspirations of our time. It is, therefore, vital to foster constantly an awareness of the links uniting human rights, development, peace, disarmament and many other issues. This broad vision ties in with the thinking of those who call for and urge the formulation of "third generation" human rights. If the principles proclaimed by the American revolution (1776) and the French revolution (1789) defined the "first generation" human rights—civil and political rights, the October revolution (1917) gave rise to economic and social rights, which have been confirmed and enlarged by the different revolutionary movements during the twentieth century and which constitute the "second generation" rights. In certain international forums—there has been a strong view that "third generation" rights be enshrined as strongly as the earlier rights and implemented vigorously. These are : the right to development, the right to a healthy environment, the right to peace, the right of access to the common heritage of mankind—rights whose distinctive feature is that they all reflect a certain humane conception of life.

The arbitrary exercise of power has traditionally reinforced the helplessness of the powerless. When governments operated on the principle of the divine right of kings, rulers did not seek legitimacy for their power in any notion of justice. The struggle against such injustice demanded that social institutions be based on legitimacy, consent and rule of law. In the 21st century securing freedom against injustice will require institutions that protect people through transparent rules applied equally to all.

Human Rights and Indian Constitution

The Preamble to the Indian Constitution, Fundamental Rights and Directive Principles, which together have been described as forming the Core of the Constitution reflect the basic principles of the Universal Declaration of Human Rights. The Indian Constitution has been considered to be socio-economic instrument with a revolutionary thrust. The Fundamental Rights guaranteed under the Constitution including the Right to Freedom of Speech and Expression and other rights under Article 19 cannot be appreciated and fully enjoyed unless a citizen is educated and is conscious of his individualistic dignity.

The four basic ideals mentioned in the Preamble are justice, liberty, equality and fraternity, the last three having been taken from the slogan of the French revolution. The Constitution says that the people of India are determined to secure to all its citizens justice, liberty, equality and fraternity. Justice in social, economic and political spheres is to be realized through the Constitution. The Indians are assured of liberty of thought, expression, belief, faith and worship. Equality of status and of opportunity is to be secured through the operation of the Constitutional provisions. Promotion of fraternity in India is to be achieved by ensuring the dignity of the individual and the unity and integrity of the nation.

Preamble

The promise of the Constitution is contained in the Preamble itself, in which the people of India solemnly resolved to secure to all of its citizens :

> "**Justice,** social, economic and political;
> **Liberty** of thought, expression, belief, faith and worship;
> **Equality** of status and of opportunity; and to promote among them all;
> **Fraternity** assuring the dignity of the individual and the unity and integrity of the Nation."

And the heart and soul of the Constitution are contained in its Parts III and IV, which guaranteed to the people of India their fundamental rights and directed their Governments on the principles they were to follow as State Policy.

The rights include right to equality, freedom of speech and personal liberty, protection against arrest and detention in certain cases, freedom to manage religious affairs, prohibition of traffic in human beings and forced labour, rights of minorities to establish and administer educational institutions etc.

The Indian Constitution has been considered to be socio-economic instrument with a revolutionary thrust. The eminent crusader for civil rights, Justice V. R. Krishna Iyer says : Indeed

Table 8.1 : Different Articles of Universal Declaration of Human Rights and the Indian Constitution

S. No. of Article	*Universal Declaration of Human Rights*	*Article No.*	*Indian Constitution*
1	2	3	4
1.	No discrimination on the ground of race, colour, sex, language, religion, birth	15	The State shall not discriminate race, colour, sex language, religion, birth, against any citizen on grounds only of religion, race, caste, sex, place of birth or any of them.
2.	Right to life	21	No person shall be deprived of his life or personal liberty except according to procedure established by law.
3.	Arbitrary arrest and detention	22	1. No person who is arrested shall be detained in custody without being informed, as soon as may be, of the grounds for such arrest nor shall he be denied the right to consult, and to be defended by, a legal practitioner of his choice. 2. Every person who is arrested and detained in custody shall be produced before the nearest magistrate within a period of twenty-four hours of such arrest excluding the time necessary for the journey from the place of arrest to the court of the magistrate and no such person shall be detained in custody beyond the said period without the authority of a magistrate.
4.	Right to religion	25	All persons are equally entitled to freedom of conscience and free profession, practice and propagation of religion.
5.	Freedom of thought and conscience	25(1)	All persons are equally entitled to freedom of conscience and the right freely to profess, practise and propagate religion.
6.	Freedom of information and expression	19(a)	All citizens shall have the right to speech and expression.
7.	Peaceful assembly and association	19(b)	All citizens shall have the right to assemble peaceably and without arms.
		19(c)	To form associations or unions.

we can never forget that the people of India as a whole, not the elite nor the upper strata nor indeed the power brokers, but all the people are the title holders under the Constitution. The Fundamental Rights guaranteed under Part III of the Constitution of India including the Right to Freedom of Speech and Expression and other rights under Article 19 cannot be appreciated and fully enjoyed unless a citizen is educated and is conscious of his individualistic dignity.

National Human Rights Commission

The army and para-military operations to combat insurgency in the north and north-eastern parts of India, a series of custodial deaths during police investigations which occurred towards the end of 1982, elicited strong reactions from human rights advocates. Shocking investigation reports in several newspapers and embarrassing questions in legislatures put the state and central governments on the defensive. The courts entertained several letters as petitions and issued orders and directions against alleged disappearances of people taken in custody.

It was in this backdrop and as a result of persistent efforts by human rights activists over several years that NHRC was constituted in pursuance of the Human Rights Act, 1993. The constitution of NHRC gave rise to expectations that protection of human rights would no longer be ignored. However, concern continued to be expressed as to whether the Commission would have the autonomy and the capacity to meet the ever growing challenge to the human rights.

The Protection of Human Rights Act was enacted in 1993 and NHRC was soon constituted with a former Chief Justice of India as its chairman, two other superior court judges, two persons with practical experience on human rights matters, and the chairpersons of three National Commissions as its members (Minorities, Women and SC/ST). An elaborate procedure involving the opposition parties and presiding officers of both Houses of Parliament has been provided for selection and appointment of chairman and members to the Commission.

The functions of the NHRC are different from other national level commissions inasmuch as its powers of investigation are wider and the resources available to it in this regard are much greater. Section 12 of the Act stipulates the functions which include :

(a) Enquire *suo motu* or on a petition presented to it into complaints of violation of human rights or negligence in the prevention of such violation by a public servant;
(b) intervene in any proceeding involving allegation of violation of human rights pending before a court;
(c) visit jails and detention places to study living conditions of the inmates and make recommendations thereon;
(d) recommend legislative changes for better enforcement of human rights;
(e) recommend better implementation of international human rights instruments; and
(f) spread human rights literacy and mobilize voluntary action for human rights observance.

The Act further stipulates in section 30, the establishment of Human Rights Courts for each district for the speedy trial of human rights violation cases, and for this purpose, to appoint special public prosecutors for conducting cases.

Ever since its inception, the Commission has certainly made a difference to the human rights situation in the country. The Commission has accorded priority to issues : protection of human rights in areas of terrorism and insurgency, systemic reforms in police administration and criminal justice, custodial deaths, rape and torture, condition of the jails and the jail inmates etc. Through a series of visits to some of the notorious prisons of the country, the Commission is now trying to focus attention on essential reforms for custodial justice. Custodial deaths, custodial rapes and custodial torture seem to have decreased because of the public exposure and outcry and the transparent procedures being followed at the instance of the Human Rights Commission.

The Act envisages constitution of state-level Human Rights Commissions so that the redressal of grievances could be swift and inexpensive and the message of human rights reaches the grass-roots level in the languages of the people of the country. The need for state-level commissions has been felt acute because of rapid increase in the number of complaints. So far only ten states have set up these commissions and most appalling is that the two states—Uttar Pradesh and Bihar—which account for 65 per cent of the 50,000 complaints received, have not set up the state level HRCs.

NHRC and Socio-economic Policies—The Commission has, with increasing stridency, been urging policies in the economic and social sector that are truly responsive to the needs of the most vulnerable in our society : primary health facilities to provide the potable drinking water and levels of maternal and child welfare essential to a life in dignity; food and nutritional standards essential to fulfilling the potential of a human being. There is a greater realisation among the major political parties that there is no easy road to national salvation that avoids these issues. The Commission has felt the need to be increasingly pro-active in respect of issues that raise fundamental questions of equity and justice in our country : the rights of Dalits and the atrocities perpetrated against them, the displacement of populations, especially tribals, by mega-projects; issues of food scarcity and allegations of deaths by starvation; the unconscionable cruelty of child-labour, especially in hazardous industries and child prostitution; the rights of women subjected to violence and discrimination; the rights of minorities and issues of religious tolerance, to mention but a few of its principal concerns.

It is also evident that the right to development, in all of its ramifications, is becoming central to its concerns, for it is this right that provides the integral link between civil and political rights, on the one hand, and economic, social and cultural rights, on the other, between the Universal Declaration of Human Rights of 1948 and the Vienna Declaration of 1993.

There is a correlation between the Human Development Index and respect for human rights, there is also an infallible correlation between the quality of governance and the promotion and protection of such rights. Keep the institutions of governance in good repair. It is also essential to press for systemic reform : of the police, of the custodial justice system; and, indeed, of the criminal justice system itself. All elements of civil society need to be brought into the fold : the bench and the bar, administrators and defence personnel, doctors and scholars, politicians and trade unionists, public and private sector employees and members of the fourth estate.

The adoption of the Protection of Human Rights Act, 1993 gave rise to considerable expectations that the nation would act with renewed vigour to promote and protect the rights relating to life, liberty, equality and dignity guaranteed by our Constitution or embodied in the International Covenants to which our country is a party. These expectations were tempered by a concern as to whether the instrument created by the Act, namely, the National Human Rights Commission, would indeed have the autonomy, the will and the capacity to meet the expectations that had arisen.

In a democracy, good governance requires that each of its three pillars, the Legislature, the Executive and the Judiciary function with competence and integrity, watched over by a free and independent press. When any of the pillars shows weakness, or a loss of integrity, a disproportionate burden falls on the others, leading to excesses that negatively affect the fine balance of the Constitution and the equilibrium of democracy itself, including the manner in which the rights of its citizens are respected.

In recent years, there has been a growing concern in the country that the processes of governance have, on occasion, been corroded by a nexus between criminals, less than scrupulous political elements and members of the executive lacking in integrity. The deleterious effects on human rights resulting from such a nexus can be gauged from the nature of the petitions received by the Commission, many of which complain of violations because the supposed protectors of rights have themselves turned predators. It is because of such complaints that the Commission has been calling for systemic reforms in the police, designed to insulate its investigative work from extraneous influences that would otherwise destroy its integrity.

The promotion and protection of human rights—the expansion of essential freedoms—must be the central purpose of governance.

And this can only be assured by probity and honesty, by diligence and a sense of direction that places the concerns of the disadvantaged and vulnerable foremost in the considerations of policy and action.

Human Rights and Human Development

Human rights and human development share a common vision and a common purpose to secure the freedom, well-being and dignity of all people everywhere. Prof. Amartya Sen in the first chapter of UNDP's Human Development Report 2000, titled *Human Rights and Human Development* charts out seven key features needed for a better approach to securing human rights. These are listed as under :

(i) Every country needs to strengthen its social arrangements for securing human freedoms—with norms, institutions, legal frameworks and an enabling economic environment. Legislation alone is not enough.

(ii) The fulfilment of all human rights requires democracy that is inclusive—protecting the rights of minorities, providing separation of powers and ensuring public accountability. Elections alone are not enough.

(iii) Poverty eradication is not only a development goal. It is a central challenge for human rights in the 21st century.

(iv) Human rights—in an integrated world—require global justice. The state-centred model of accountability must be extended to the obligations of non-state actors and to the state's obligations beyond national borders.

(v) Information and statistics is a powerful tool for creating a culture of accountability and for realizing human rights. Activists, lawyers, statisticians and development specialists need to work together with communities. The goal : to generate information and evidence that can breakdown barriers of disbelief and mobilize changes in policy and behaviour.

(vi) Achieving all rights for all people in all countries in the

21st century will require action and commitment from the major groups in every society—NGOs, media and businesses, local as well as national government, parliamentarians and other opinion leaders.

(vii) Human rights and human development cannot be realized universally without stronger international action especially to support disadvantaged people and countries and to offset growing global inequalities and marginalization.

REFERENCES

Human Rights, the New Consensus, (1994) Regency Press in association with United Nations High Commissions for Refugees, New York.

Planning Commission, (2002) *National Human Development Report 2001,* Government of India, New Delhi.

UNDP, (2000) Human Development Report, *Human Rights and Human Development,* Oxford University Press.

Voices for Change, (1998) Vol. 2, No. 3, Understanding Human Rights, Benson Town, Bangalore.

9

ENVIRONMENTAL PROTECTION
From Rio to Johannesburg

Environment has been defined as the complex of physical, chemical and biotic factors (as climate, soil, and living things) that act upon an organism or an ecological community and ultimately determine its form and survival. Life on earth has been a history of interaction between living things and their surroundings.

To a large extent, the physical form and the habits of earth, vegetation and animal life have been moulded by environment. However, only within the present century has one species—man—acquired significant power to alter nature. This power to change has resulted in pollution—of the air, water and land. There is a severe scarcity of clean air and water. Man's haphazard planning and scant regard for nature has resulted in accumulation of garbage and hazardous wastes, which can cause disease and deformities.

Development has led to environmental problems like global warming, rising sea levels and unpredictable climate patterns. Pressure on land for housing and agriculture has resulted in extinction of plant and animal species. These are the major challenges that man faces today. If environmental protection is not taken up earnestly, all the progress and development that man has seen will be negated. The ambience aspect of environment—quality of water, air and noise pollution—has a direct impact on an individual's health and sense of well-being.

It is not that governments and individuals are unaware of man's meddling with nature, which can result in a severe backlash. To address such concerns, several conferences have been held on sustainable development and protection of environment. One such global summit—Earth Summit—was held in 1992 in Rio, where important decisions were taken to address the man-nature conflict.

Despite rising awareness, neither has there been an appreciable change in the lifestyles, nor significant steps taken by governments to protect the environment.

INDIA AND ENVIRONMENT

An Overview

The *Sanctuary* magazine says, "with a mere 2.5% of the world's land, India is groaning under the pressure of supporting half of the world's buffaloes, 1/6 of the world population of people and 1/7 of the cattle and sheep in the world.

Out of a total land area of 328.73 million hectares (mha), 142.21 mha are under cultivation. In a bid to increase food production both grazing lands and wastelands have been brought under the plough, depriving the cattle and further degrading the land."

Similarly, rivers are under severe pressure because of increase in the drinking water requirement, irrigation purposes and use of water in industries. Even the ground water is falling steadily because of excessive usage for drinking and irrigation. Another threat to the ground water is from contamination because of seepage of toxins and chemicals from industries.

Likewise, the quality of air in most Indian cities and towns has gone down because of increased vehicles and a large number of industries. A study by the Centre for Science and Environment in 1996—The Deadly Story of Vehicular Pollution in India—exposes the dreadful conditions of Indian metros, caused by the ever-growing craze for vehicles, poor-fuel quality and non-existent traffic planning.

Another study a few years later found that it is not only the metro cities which have a high load of pollutants in the air, but even the smaller cities suffer from high levels of air pollution.

The National Human Development Report 2001, shows the vast degradation of environmental resources in the country. About river pollution, the report says: While the level of water quality parameters vary across States, studies have found that sewage waste pollution is predominant in the States of Uttar Pradesh, Gujarat,

Tamil Nadu, Assam and even Delhi. Gujarat followed by Maharashtra, Andhra Pradesh, Tamil Nadu, Uttar Pradesh and Punjab has high levels of chemical pollution in their water resources.

Pollution in Yamuna— About the Yamuna, the report says Yamuna is the most polluted river in the country with high BOD coliform levels in the 500 km stretch between Delhi and Etawah. The main cause of pollution is industrial discharge, irrigation run-off and untreated sewage. The sewage system in Delhi has lost 80 per cent of its carrying capacity on account of age, silage and poor maintenance—a fact that has come to light only after setting up of sewage treatment plants for the city.

As a result, only 20 per cent of the domestic waste water is being treated, the rest flows through storm water drains into the river. The treated effluent is being put back into filthy drains as cent per cent interception of sewage at the treatment point has not been achieved.

The treated waste water is carried along with the untreated into the Yamuna. In addition, the over extraction of water for irrigation brings down the water flow below the minimum required for maintaining ecology of the river and for diluting pollutants that flow into it. A number of slums and shanties, unserviced by sewage system also add to the pollution in the river. There is ample evidence that establishes domestic sewage to be the primary source of water pollution in India, especially, in and around large urban centres. The sewage treatment facilities are inadequate and often under-utilised in most cities and almost absent in rural areas.

At the national level, 90 per cent of the urban population has access to safe drinking water but only 49 per cent have access to sanitation services. The latter poses a threat to the continued availability and improvement in the supply of safe water to households.

Only 25 per cent of Class-I cities have base water collection, treatment and disposal facilities. Fewer than 10 per cent of 201 smaller towns have waste water collection systems. As a result, not more than 20 per cent of all waste water generated in Class-I cities and 2 per cent in Class-II towns is treated. Access to safe drinking water, therefore, continues to be a challenge for a large part of the country and its inhabitants.

The *Sanctuary* says, "The World Commission for dams has estimated that there are 4291 dams in India, second only to China with 22,000 dams. Bhakhra, Tehri and Sardar Sarovar are amongst the ten largest dams in the world. The huge lake formed by restraining a river behind a wall submerges thousands of villages, forests and fields, causing immense damage to cropland, livelihoods and bio-diversity."

Air Pollution—Deterioration in air quality is globally one of the major and the more widespread environmental problems in urban areas. The ambient air quality has deteriorated all over the country, especially, in semi-urban and urban areas.

Anthropogenic activities result in air pollution on account of three broad sources, viz., stationary sources (use of fossil fuels in industries and thermal power plants), mobile sources (vehicles) and in-door sources (burning of bio-mass). The relative contribution of these sources varies across cities depending upon vehicle ownership, type of industry and dependence on commercial *vis-à-vis* bio-mass sources for cooking and heating as well as the enforcement of pollution control norms for some of these sources.

The air pollutants are generally categorised into Suspended Particulate Matter (SPM) and gaseous pollutants. A study on the ambient air quality recorded for 23 cities in the country reveals that SPM levels remains critical in many cities. More importantly, small to medium towns such as, Indore, Ahmedabad, Patna and Ludhiana have higher SPM levels than those prevailing in metro cities. Though, sulphur dioxide and oxides of nitrogen levels have registered an upward trend, they remain well within the National Ambient Air Quality Standards in all the cities. In addition to these common air pollutants, some of the toxic and carcinogenic chemicals are being detected in urban air. Very little monitoring, if any, of these pollutants is currently being done.

Pollution in Rural Areas—A major source of air pollution, particularly, in rural areas is caused by burning of unprocessed cooking fuels in homes. Rural households mostly rely on bio-fuels such as cowdung, fuel wood, crop residues and in some cases mineral coal for meeting their fuel and energy requirements. The indoor pollution on account of the pollutants released in closed and unventilated places is, perhaps, more dangerous than the air pollution outdoors.

It is estimated that indoor pollution in India's rural areas is responsible for five hundred thousand premature deaths annually, mostly of women and children under 5. This accounts for 6-9 per cent of the national total measured in terms of Disease Adjusted Life Years. These estimates make the health impact of indoor exposure larger than the burden from all but two of the other major preventable risk factors that have been quantified, malnutrition (15 per cent) and lack of clean water and sanitation (7 per cent).

Much of the air pollution is a result of faulty planning of civic amenities, inappropriate technology and, above all, indifferent enforcement of pollution control norms. An integrated approach involving each of these elements has become imperative for public policy and administration in most of the urban and rural areas in the country. An additional requirement, especially for the rural areas is the urgent need to make it possible for the people to move up the energy ladder with a view to address the adverse health impact of indoor pollution on account of the use of unprocessed cooking fuels.

Urban Solid Waste and Noise Pollution—The levels of urban solid wastes being generated in different cities poses a serious threat to environmental quality and human health. Many cities generate more solid wastes than they can dispose of. Even when there are adequate resources available by way of public provisions to the municipal authorities, the safe disposal of solid waste often remains a problem. Open dumping and uncontrolled land filling are in most cases the main disposal methods.

The organic material (garbage) is a fertile breeding ground for bacteria and viruses that cause disease. Due to inadequate collection, improper disposal and lack of proper storage facilities, solid waste gets into open drains and obstruct free flow of water. This in turn becomes an ideal breeding ground for diseases. The municipal solid waste sites often receive industrial and hazardous waste including those from hospitals and laboratories adding to the problem of disposal and serious consequences for environment and health of individuals. The system for disposing non-biodegradable urban solid waste is practically non-existent. There is a tremendous scope for improving technological input and institutionalization of responsible social practices such as the practice/requirement of segregating household solid waste into distinct categories for facilitating an efficient and environmentally safe disposal. A major problem in urban solid waste management relates to sewage disposal. With inadequate and often inappropriate and malfunctioning systems of sewage disposal, the threat to the availability of safe drinking water is quite serious in most urban areas in the country. There is an urgent need for revamping and maintaining the sewage system in almost all cities and more importantly increasing its coverage to slums and the shanties that are entrenched in most metro cities.

Noise Pollution—It is perhaps, the most underrated and underemphasized aspect of urban environmental hazard to human well-being. The noise pollution refers to presence of sound in the environment at levels that are injurious to human health, especially, when exposed on a sustained basis. Persons regularly exposed to loud sounds are likely to suffer more from hearing impairment, sleep disturbance and general stress than those who live in more salubrious environment.

Vehicular traffic is the most widespread source of noise pollution. In most Indian cities, the average noise level in residential, commercial and sensitive areas (silence zones including, hospitals, educational institutions and courts) exceeded the prescribed standards of CPCB during the day as well as the night-time. Only in industrial areas and that too in the night, the noise levels were within the prescribed limits in case of most cities. In some places, the noise levels in residential areas and in silence zones exceed even those prevailing in industrial areas. This is one area of environmental concern that has practically been unaddressed, where existing legal provisions have largely remained unenforced and adequate social awareness is yet to surface.

GLOBAL ENVIRONMENTAL PROBLEMS

Global warming, ozone depletion, smog and acid rain, industries, agriculture, combustion of fossil fuels like petroleum, coal and natural gas, cooling systems, chemicals from explosives, paints and cleaning agents, etc., disperse vapours or fine solid particles in the air. These then cause changes either by their presence in the atmosphere itself or on drifting down to earth. The heat is on water vapour, carbon dioxide, ozone, methane, nitrous oxide, and the chlorofluorocarbons (CFCs) are known as Greenhouse Gases. Their accumulation in the air traps heat and raises the temperature. There has been a slow and steady rise in global temperatures amounting to an increase of $0.5^{\circ}C$ since 1600. Starting with the melting of the polar ice cap, it is also going to cause rising sea levels, reduced agricultural yields, reduced water flows, increased health hazards, uncertain weather, more ecological refugees and a lot of yet to be noticed problems.

In the last century, the sea-level rose by 20 to 30 centimetres and is expected to rise by 1 metre in this century. There will be a spate of migration from the coast to the interior, placing a strain on the resources available over there. China, India, Bangladesh, Indonesia, Vietnam and the Philippines will in particular be affected.

A hole in the protective curtains the use of chlorofluorocarbons in refrigerating and air-conditioning units and also in aerosols has precipitated the issue of ozone depletion. A hole has been torn in the thin veil of ozone just above the Antarctic. Ultraviolet radiation which used to be filtered by the ozone layer is now streaming in and we are all exposed to its harsh effects, viz. skin cancer and cataract in humans and blindness in rabbits and salmon have been noted.

During the closing decades of the 20th century environmental issues have emerged as a major concern for the survival and welfare of mankind throughout the world. Modern civilization, armed with rapidly advancing technology and fast growing economic system is under increasing threat from its own activities causing pollution of air, water and soul. The fast eroding life support system of our bio-sphere not only endangers the future of human race as such but is a major threat to life itself.

The UN Conference on Human Environment at Stockholm in June 1972 heralded the first serious effort to take note of the environmental issues at the global level. Ever since then concepts like environmental sustainability and carrying capacity of earth have become central themes for policy making around the world. Environmental problems remain acute in most countries and continue to escalate in many parts of the world. There has been a quantum increase in awareness of the magnitude of the problem and of the need for action during the last few years. The Conference proved to be the high watermark in the history of environmental revolution. It provided a focal point for the gathering in the history of environmental concerns of the present day. It gave birth to the United Nations Environmental Programme (UNEP) to act as a catalyst and as the environmental conscience of the UN system. The UNESCO Programme of Man and Biosphere (MAB) in the seventies, and international conferences on desertification (Nairobi, 1977) were the other important milestones in strengthening the awareness about environmental concerns.

The United Nations Conference on Environment and Development (UNCED) held at Rio in June 1992, and attended by 150 heads of states and governments, was the largest such gathering to deliberate on issues of environmental protection. The Conference adopted an action plan for sustainable development set out in agenda 21. The UNCED clearly recognized the need for environmental education as a means of achieving the goals of sustainable development.

Most people understand environment to be limited to only one aspect, *i.e.* pollution. Pollution is only one facet of environmental problem. Environment is not an abstract concern, nor it is just a matter of aesthetics or personal tastes. Our physical nature, our mental health, culture and institutions, opportunities for fulfilment, our very survival are directly related to, and affected by, the environment in which we live. Environment involves vast range of subjects from resource depletion to the effects of over-grazing. The aesthetic degradation due to demolition of old buildings and their replacement by multi-storeyed blocks, people inadvertently taking action which will deteriorate their immediate surroundings, building huge dams, paving away large stretches of land, boom in tourism—all have bearing on environment-related issues.

The World Development Report 1999-2000, *Entering the 21st Century,* defines Sustainable Development as : Any sustainable development agenda must be concerned with intergenerational equity—that is that future generations have the same capability to develop as the present generation. A development path is sustainable only if it ensuses that the stock of over all capital assets remains constant or increases over time. These assets include manufactured capital (such as machines and roads), human capital (knowledge and skills), social capital (relationship and institutions), and environmental capital (forests and coral reefs). This environment matters not just because of its effect on psychic and non-economic welfare but also because of its impact on production over the long term.

Environmental sustainability is also connected with inter-generational equity. While the wealthy consume more resources over all, the poor tend to rely more heavily on the direct exploitation of natural resources than the rich. If they have no access to environmental resources and so have limited capacity to adopt they may have no choice but to engage in unsustainable use of environmental resouces.

DEFORESTATION AND ITS CONSEQUENCES

India accounts for 10 per cent of world population while land area constitutes only 2.4 per cent. Already India is as densely populated as China, putting heavy pressure on environment, infrastructure and basic services. Providing basic human needs for such a large population will continue to remain a major task. There is a chronic shortage of safe drinking water, both in rural and urban areas. About 20 per cent of urban and 50 per cent of the rural population is still to be provided with safe drinking water.

Excessive exploitation of forests has decimated seriously our forest resources. Deforestation in the Himalayas and other hilly areas has led to soil erosion which has adversely affected river water quality, apart from the rapid siltation of dams and reservoirs. Deforestation leads to the destruction of wild life habitats. Over one hundred species of wild animals need immediate protection as their population has dwindled to dangerously low levels. Deforestation also creates crushing workload for rural communities, particularly for women and children who share the major responsibility for fuel, water and food collection burden.

The overuse of natural resources results not only in resource depletion and ecological degradation that threaten the livelihood of the poor but also result in high environmental health risks, manifested by high infant and child mortality and high morbidity specially among the poor. The principal causes are all environment related-poor quality of drinking water supply and lack of sanitation, indoor and outdoor air pollution and toxic and hazardous agro-industrial waste disposal and discharges.

Deforestation essentially means loss of tropical forests due to collection of fuel wood, commercial logging, shifting cultivation, grazing, road construction, ranching, mining and fire. Leads to solid erosion and flooding and endangers wildlife through habitat destruction.

According to many environmental scientists from around the world, deforestation is one of the most serious environmental problems in Asia. Two-thirds of the world's Tropical Moist Forest (TMF) is rain forest and consists of trees that never lose their leaves. The rest is moist deciduous forest where trees shed leaves annually. Rain forests are wetter, warmer, denser, darker and more diverse than deciduous forests. Deciduous forests are more open to sunlight and have denser undergrowth. They include monsoon forests in Burma, Thailand, Kampuchea, and Indonesia.

Deforetation is a critical problem not only because it depletes a natural resource of critical importance to the people of the region that cannot be replaced overnight, but also because of its far-reaching side effects. It is a major contribution to a variety of other environmental problems, including desertification, soil erosion, flooding, mudslides, siltation and sedimentation, habitat destruction and species extinction, and salt and chemical degradation. It is accompanied by economic, health and social hardships brought about by people trying to live and cope with a drastically changed environment.

Deforestation in Asia is caused mainly by the collection of fuelwood, commercial logging, shifting cultivation and degradation through grazing and fire. Demand for fuelwood is far greater than the resources available to meet that demand. Scientists estimated recently that India, for example, needs 133 million tons of fuelwood, but has only 33 million tons available. Fuelwood consumption in Thailand was 25 million cubic metres, while annual production was estimated to be only 16 million cubic metres. This means that perhaps as much as 9 million cubic metres were removed illegally from Thai forests.

Commercial logging not only depletes the forest resources but affects its ability to regenerate. Selectively cutting an individual commercial grade tree invariably damages several trees surrounding it. White logging roads are cut into tropical forests so that tractors and log-haulers can get in and this causes major erosion problems. Changes in the tree canopy caused by cutting alter the forest micro-climate and affect the diversity and growth of the other trees, low-growing plants and wildlife.

An ever-increasing population puts greater pressure on people to clear forests for cultivation because the demand for land no longer lets them practice shifting cultivation on existing lands. Shifting cultivation is the practice of leaving cultivated land fallow for several years to allow it to recover its fertility before being cultivated again. The same population increase that leads to clearing forests for cultivation also leads to using forests for grazing. This destroys undergrowth and seedlings that replace mature trees cut for fuelwood and other purposes. Accidental fires, common throughout the region, also contribute to the destruction of forest resources.

Deforestation Flow Diagram

The following deforestation flow diagram will help to understand better some of the interactions and interrelationships involved in deforestation.

Deforestation flow diagram

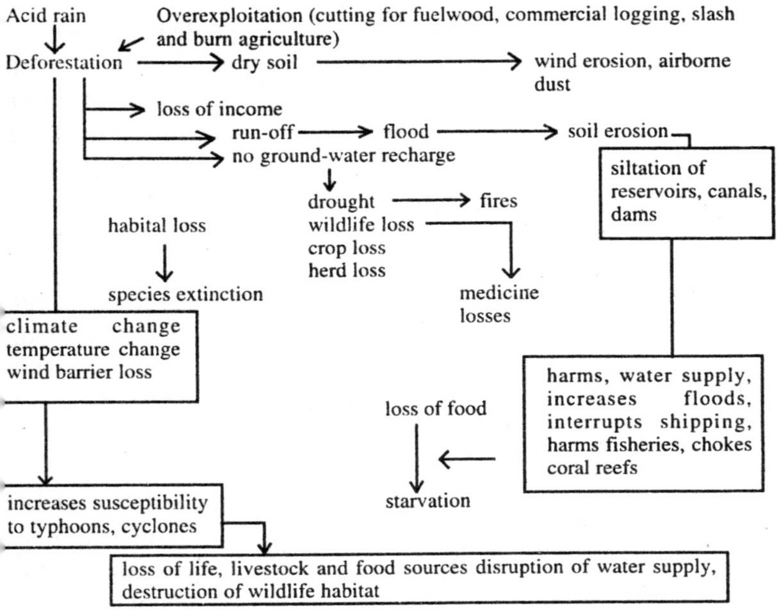

Source : *Reporting on the Environment : A Handbook for Journalists,* UNESCAP (1988).

Forests have a many-faceted ecological role to play which affect human life directly in a variety of ways. They thwart the dangers of cloud drifting, soil erosion, floods, wind erosion, and ground water evaporation. They also protect a wide variety of flora and fauna, provide recreation, and can effectively control air pollution of moderate magnitudes. Thus the importance of forests for the benefit of mankind as well as for other forms of life cannot be overemphasized.

The pressure on the existing forests is quite high in India at present, with high population density and a very low per capita forest area. A wide range of flora and fauna are fast disappearing as their natural habitats are destroyed. This further impoverishes the remaining Indian forests. Though there are some trends in the area on an improvement in the quality of forest, there is still need to have massive reforestation programmes, control over hacking and grazing, and provision of cheap fuel through alternative technologies such as solar power or biogas plants. More kerosene should be made available to save the forest from denudation.

Desertification—It is a process whereby the productivity of the land is reduced through deforestation, waterlogging and salinization, chemical degradation by neutron leaching, rangeland mismanagement such as overgrazing, soil erosion and aridity and semi-aridity.

Some analysts believe desertification is only a phase in a natural climatic process that does not receive attention because it is low and long term. Others believe that "Drought triggers a crisis, but does not cause it. Overcultivation and overgrazing weaken the land, allowing no margin when drough arrives. Thus high human pressure will continue during the drought, leading ultimately to even greater and more visible damage to the land than the deaths of large number of animals."

About 12 per cent of India suffers from the threat of desertification in the arid north-west and in a broad semi-arid zone from the Punjab in the north-west to Tamil Nadu in the south. There are an estimated 1.7 million square kilometres of arid land in India and Pakistan.

Because desertification is a long term process—long in terms of its development and impact—it is difficult to pin-point its cause and effect relationships. It is also a difficult issue for the general public to understand other than as an existing fact of life. The public usually perceives only the consequences of desertification—drought, famine, dying herds and people. Because of its long term nature and association with other more obvious or pressing problems, decision makers have great difficulty addressing it as a problem.

The effect of population growth on the environment can be seen in the desertificaion process. Overcultivation, for example, leads to declining soil fertility and falling crop yields, crusting of exposed topsoil by rain and sun, increased surface run-off and accompanying erosion of soil and gullying, wind erosion, encroachment of sand dunes on arable land and destruction of crops by dust-bearing winds.

Some solutions to desertification include : Improving crop production, irrigation practices, livestock husbandry and range lands, reducing stock numbers and afforestation, which receives great emphasis in many Asian countries. Other practices involve desert reclamation, social forestry (where villagers take responsibility for forests that surround their village), the use of plantations and agro-forestry or forest farming.

It has been estimated that between 1975 and 1995, when the Indian economy doubled, *industrial pollution levels went up four times and vehicular eight times* and we could see what single rupee of economic growth could do. It is already impossible to breathe in most Indian cities and towns and we are still in the early stages of industrialisation.

The battle ranging to protect environment has truly assumed epic proportions—the battle is no less to protect our very survival : our skies, the air we breathe, the water we drink and the food we eat. This is the major challenge that the mankind faces in the 21st century. All our strategies for development would be negated if we do not take up in the right earnest the challenge of environmental protection.

The judicial intervention at the highest level by the Supreme Court has led to the consolidation of environmental movement. The check on the pollution caused by the vehicular traffic in a capital city like Delhi could not have been imposed but for the repeated and forceful intervention of the Supreme Court.

At the same time there has been strengthening of official involvement in environmental management, with increased scientific, technical, administrative and legislative back up at central and state levels. Certain legislative measures have also been taken. Emphasising the critical importance being attached to the protection of environment, the Approach Paper to the Ninth Five Year Plan (1997-2002) says : The Indian planning process has always laid emphasis on measures to ensure sustainability of the development process not only in economic terms, but also in terms of social and environmental factors. Many of the measures adopted in the agenda 21 of the United Nations Conference on environment and development already find reflection in the Indian plans. The Ninth plan will carry this tradition further and consolidate on the creation of conditions for sustainable development.

The concern regarding environmental protection is too serious to be left to the government, NGOs and even social activists alone. Each one of us need to put in our mite, however, small it may be. Planting trees—and more important than that protecting the planted trees and looking after their growth, keeping our environment clean, discontinuation of use of plastic bags, keeping our transport vehicles within environmentally permitted specifications, use of recycled papers and adopting other environment-friendly measures would certainly help in creating a climate conducive to the protection and preservation of environment.

As developing countries struggle to forge development paths that provide both prosperity for their citizens and good stewardship of the environment, they are rejecting the old-fashioned development-versus-the-environment paradigm in favour of a new environmentalism that recognizes economic development and environmental sustainability as partners.

The report of the World Commission on Environment and Development, *our common future,* gave a new direction in which the developmental efforts need to be directed. The report pointed out that 'content of economic growth would have to change' and that 'even consumption of material goods should be ranked according to a scale of sustainability'. Another important observation in the report pertains to the holistic nature of environment. The environment does not exist as sphere separate from human actions, ambitions and needs and attempts to defend it in isolation from human concerns has given the very word "environment", a connotation of naivety in some political circles.

The report recognized the relationship of environmental and developmental concerns and proposed a number of long range steps for changing conditions and practices which threaten human survival.

Many studies have shown that clean drinking water and sanitation are important for health. It has been found that the two biggest causes of death of the poor were respiratory infections and diarrhoeal diseases. Both are linked to environmental factors dirty water and dirty air. Sixty per cent of all malaria deaths occur among the poorest 20 per cent of world's population. Another World Bank study estimates that in the Indian state of Andhra Pradesh, the Bank could reduce the burden of disease by 17 per cent with activities like providing clean drinking water and clean cooking fuel.

Carrying Capacity of Earth

It is now being increasingly realised that demography is not merely a question of numbers of people. When the carrying capacity of planet earth reaches the point of exhaustion, as is the case with countries like India, China and Indonesia, an environmental disaster is waiting to happen any moment. Essentially we need resources which provide medical care for 1 billion people in the country; and it is the earth's natural resources which provide for meeting all the above needs. As these resources deplete and population keeps growing, the rate of depletion also increases because the dwindling resources are required to cater to more people. In this context we must take note of the process of invisible destruction of resources, which constitute the basis for the survival of millions of people. Ever-expanding consumption puts strains on environment-emissions and was that pollute the earth and destroy ecosystems, and growing depletion and degradation of renewable resources that undermines livelihoods. Runaway growth in consumption in the past 50 years is putting strains on the environment never seen before.

Environmental Education and Media—The importance of environmental education was underlined in Agenda 21 of the United Nations Conference on Environment and Development held at Rio in June 1992. There has been a failure of mainstream environmental education to address the issues of environment and development which necessitates incorporating developing education as an essential part of learning. Agenda 21 of the Rio Summit incorporates development education as an integral part of environmental education, which it says, must be able to deal not only with the physical and biological but also the formal and socio-economic environment and human development. For the issue, according to the Agenda, is no longer of achieving environment awareness only but development awareness as well, in all sectors of the society. Thus, environmental education will have to go hand in hand with development education which must become an integral part of the planning and management of environmental education.

Environment and Development Education

Environmental education must widen its scope to include EDE (Environment and Development Education), and not just EE (Environment Education). This makes the planning for environment and development a daunting task. Planning for EDE has to take into consideration the country's national priorities in development, and past and current environmental and social concerns. As children move up in the educational level, i.e. at the secondary level, they should be introduced to increased knowledge about real-life situations and should be provided with adequate opportunities for environment and developmental action.

The Rio Conference emphasized the importance of education as a critical input for promoting sustainable development. It said : Education, including formal education, public awareness and training should be recognized as a process by which human beings and societies can reach their fullest potential. Education is critical for promoting sustainable development and improving the capacity for promoting address environment and development issues. While basis education provides the underpinning for any environmental and development education, the latter needs to be incorporated as an essential part of learning. Both formal and non-formal education are indispensable to changing people's attitudes so that they have the capacity to assess and address their sustainable development concerns. It is also critical for achieving environmental and ethical awareness, values and attitudes, skills and behaviour consistent with sustainable development and for effective public participation in decision-making.

World Summit on Sustainable Development—The World Summit on Sustainable Development (WSSD) held at Johannesburg, South Africa from 26 August—4 September 2002 was an other milestone is man's quest for environmental protection and sustainable development. The WSSD—also popularly called the Earth Summit, came ten years after the United Nations Conference on Environment and Development (UNCED) held at Rio de Janeiro.

In a message prior to the Earth Summit, the UN Secretary General Kofi Annan summed up the present environmental scenario quite succinctly. He said : For more than two centuries ever since the industrial revolution generated remarkable advances in living standards that the world had never seen or even imagined possible, economic development has rested in no small part on some very irresponsible activities and assumptions. We have filled the atmosphere with emissions that now threaten havoc in our life time in the form of global climate change. We have filled forests, depleted fisheries and poisoned soil and water alike. And all the while, as consumption and production continued at fever pitch, too many people—in fact, the majority of human kind—have been left behind in poverty, squalor and despair.

He pointed out : The choice is not between the environment and development, a some have framed the issue. Development that does not sensibly manage the environment will prove short-lived. Nor should this be an issue of rich versus poor. Both depend on resources and other environmental capital. One in every two jobs worldwide—in agriculture, forestry and fisheries—depends directly on the sustainability of ecosystems.

The major success of the Earth Summit was that a clear link between poverty, inequality and planet safety was established. The poor were not demonised but defended as less polluting than the rich.

India severely criticised the rich countries for unsustainable patterns of consumption and production which caused environmental degradation and poverty. It is this attachment to unsustainable consumption patterns and a determination to preserve and raise of prosperity at any cost that breeds resistance to any meaningful reform in the financial and economic structures that underpin global society today, and results in the neglect of development agenda of environment and poverty alleviation. The Indian position was that the poor were not the biggest consumers of the world's resources, the rich were. According to the Human Development Report of 2002, 2.8 billion people still lived on less than two dollars a day and the richest one per cent of the world's people received as much income each year as the poorest 57 per cent.

One of the members of UN's Eminent Person's Advisory Group for Sustainable Development, Kamla Choudhury says : The dominant patterns of production and consumption have caused serious environmental destruction and the devastation and depletion of the earth's resources. The benefits of development have been hijacked by the rich nations and the rich people within our own country. This has created widening injustice, poverty, ignorance and violent conflicts. We have no option but to reverse this trend if the earth and humanity are to survive.

Two important aspects of the Earth Summit need to be mentioned. One, environmental activist Vandana Shiva pointed out that whereas in Rio, environmental movements had been led by people, at Johannesburg, they had been hijacked by corporations and other vested interests. She said : After September 11, we see government through militarism and the containment of dissent. The second aspect was successful Indian intervention on Bhopal. Bhopal activists highlighted the plight of the survivors. Greenpeace staged a display of haunting photographs of Bhopal—from the day after the accident to the present predicament. Friends of the Earth International launched the "Bhopal Principles", calling for corporate accountability.

Centre for Science and Environment (CSE) —No discussion on environmental issues in the context of the Indian situation would be complete without reference to the outstanding contribution of CSE. CSE is one of India's leading environmental NGOs with deep interest in sustainable natural resource management. CSE's strategy of "knowledge based activism" has won it wide respect and admiration for the quality of its campaigns, research and publications which are trying to bring about change in an extremely difficult situation. CSE has provided advanced warnings, perceptive analyses and intellectual leadership in the field of environmental management. CSE's insistence on respect for democracy, people's participation, traditional knowledge and modern science make it different from other environmental organisations. CSE's research and publication work is consistently combined with advocacy and network building. Its publications like *Down to Earth* and the children's supplement *Gobar Times* help inculcate concern for environment across the nation.

Judicial Activism—The Indian judiciary—particularly at the highest levels, citizen groups, media and the CSOs have made significant contribution to the issue of environmental protection. The media played a notable part in carrying forward the message inherent in the Chipko movement. The Chipko philosophy was that the basic product of the forests are soil, water and pure air. They are not fuelwood and timber which are regarded as ultimate products from these forests in market economy. It was to save the precious heritage of forests that the women in the Garhwal hills hugged the trees from being cut at the risk of their own lives. The concerned citizen groups protested against major dams like Tehri and Narmada and against other hazardous industrial projects. The Supreme Court of India delivered landmark judgements and orders in environmental cases brought before it by the concerned citizens. According to M.C. Mehta, Supreme Court lawyer and environmentalist, some of the important laws of the land on environmental issues are : The Polluter Pays Pricnciple, the Public Trust Doctrine and the Principle of Strict and Absolute Liability. In the Vehicular Pollution case the Supreme Court directed the Indian government to provide CNG, a lead free fuel, to Delhi and other cities. The Apex Court has set down various directions for the protection of forests, biodiversity and coastal areas. Emphasising the importance of creating awareness amongst students and youth, the SC has directed the central and state governments to introduce environment as a compulsory subject in schools, colleges and at the university level. It has also directed that the radio and television networks in the country should transmit short duration programmes on environment everyday.

The Nobel Laureate economist Amartya Sen pleads for public action for the protection of environment. There are many relevant fields—land reforms, local democracy, women's action but also others including sound environmental policies, improved rural infrastructure, where the role of the state is potentially quite extensive; but at the same time standard of activity in many of these fields is abysmally related to 'public action'. India's democratic institutions provide many potential basis of public action—including not only the electoral process but also the news media, the legal system, the village panchyats etc., but an important organisational task is involved in seizing these opportunities.

REFERENCES

Dreze, Jean and Amartya Sen (1995), *India : Economic Development and Social Opportunity*, Oxford University Press.

ESCAP (1988), *Reporting on the Environment—A Handbook for Journalists*, Bangkok.

Planning Commission (2001), *Approach Paper to the Tenth Five Year Plan (2002-2007)*, Government of India, New Delhi.

10

CIVIL SOCIETY AND GOOD GOVERNANCE

The emergence of the concept of civil society is fairly recent. Most writers on the subject associate civil society with the dismantling of the former communist regimes in Eastern-Central Europe and the dismemberment of the former Soviet Union in the late 1980s and early 1990s. The people's movement that crystallized opposition to the totalitarian regimes has ben labelled as civil society. In its simplest sense it "refers to all citizens outside the government".

The term civil society has a large number of definitions, different authors offer varying definitions, interpretations and enunciations. However the basis of civil society is "openness", "voluntary action" and space for civic and political action which may not have been possible in the government sphere.

Let us examine some formulations :

1. The concept of civil society has been defined as one whose institutional core is constituted by voluntary unions outside the realm of the state and the economy. A multitude of actors outside the public sector—grassroots organisations, unions, universities, philanthropic foundations, user groups, non-governmental organisations and neighbourhood associations—influence public performance. Among other things they can help hold local governments accountable. Such groups known collectively as "civil society", can also assist local administration in search for more responsive and effective governance.
2. Civil Society can be defined as, a civic culture of generalised trust and social solidarity, peopled by citizens willing and able to cooperate in ventures; it is an important prerequiste of a vital democracy.

3. Civil Society refers to the set of institutions, orgainsations and behaviour situated among the state, the business world and the family. Specifically this includes voluntary and non-profit organisations of many different kinds, philanthropic institutions, social and political movements, other forms of social participation and engagement and the values and cultural patterns associated with them.

According to USAIDS : Civil Society is the term that best describes the non-governmental, not-for-profit, independent nature of organizations that allow for broad citizen partnership. The hall-mark of a democratic society is the freedom of individuals to associate with like-minded individuals, express their views publicly, openly debate public policy, and petition their government. Civil Society organisations include human rights groups, professional associations, religious institutions, pro-democracy groups, environmental activist organisations, business associations, labour unions, media organizations, and voluntary associations of people seeking to work for the public good.

Another interesting definition of Civil Society : Civil Society is a social dwelling place that is neither a capital building nor a shopping mall. It shares with the private sector the gift of liberty; it is voluntary and is constituted by freely associated individuals and groups. But, unlike the private sector, it aims at common ground and consensual, integrative, and collaborative action. Civil Society is thus public without being coercive, voluntary without being private.

Prof. Neera Chandhoke, Department of Political Science, University of Delhi in her book—*State and Civil Society : Explorations in Political Theory*— says : The individual as the bearer of rights in civil society has the right to work, to move from place to place, to exchange and contract, to acquire, hold and dispose of property. More importantly, he has the right to engage in political debate, discussion and even criticism of the state outside the official channels provided by the state. As individuals protected by the rights of freedom of expression, freedom of dissent, freedom of association, freedom to form and circulate public opinion, come together in civil society to debate and discuss political matters, civil society becomes an arena of political democracy, creating a community which is engaged in participative and deliberative functions. This community is located in the civil, i.e. the non-state sphere. (pp. 183-84)

CS Advocacy

Whatever be the definitions or understanding of civil society, the fact remains that the political theorists, UN organisations, social activists all have become enamoured of the concept of civil society. In this concept they see the salvation of both socialist and capitalist societies. A new stream of civil society advocacy has emerged during the last two decades. Since the 1980s, advocacy groups all over the world have begun examining public resources after realizing that either governments have not spent enough to address poverty or that government spending for pro-poor programmes have not effectively reduced poverty. There is growing evidence about the unabated and alarming increase in poverty incidence all over the world, focused primarily by the Human Development Reports of the UNDP. During the recent years there has been growing demand from CSOs and ordinary citizens for better performance and greater accountability of governments in the way it spends public money, for which objectives and the outcomes of such expenditure have been laid down. This stream of civil society advocacy is underscored by a global public management revolution, where governments, under pressure from global competition have sought to improve productivity and over-all performance while reducing costs. The revolution promotes greater public participation in governance and highlights the need for greater transparency and accountability in public management.

The Human Development Report 1996 says :

> ***An active, civil society***—Non-governmental organisations and community groups also play a vital part in enhancing human development. They not only supplement government services, extending them to people and groups who would otherwise remain unserved. They also play a vital advocacy role,

mobilizing public opinion and community action and helping shape human development priorities.

Underlining the importance of CSOs, the Secretary General of the United Nations, Kofi Annan says : The relationship between the United Nations and civil society has changed beyond all recognition.... Information technology has empowered civil society to be the true guardians of democracy and good governance everywhere. Oppressors cannot hide inside their borders any longer. A strong civil society, bound together across all borders with the help of modern communications, will not let them. In a sense, it has been the new super-power—the people determined to promote better standards of life in larger freedom.... The ideas and energy for the global Millennium Development Goals (MDGs) campaign have come largely from civil society. And on the ground, CSOs—including environmental groups, think tanks, trade unions, religious congregations, grassroots and indigenous movements and even sports clubs—have always been vital partners in helping communities build their own solutions to development challenges.

UNDP, as the UN's global development network, is working closely with CSOs at all levels to promote the MDGs and help people build a better life. The UN encourages policy dialogues between governments, CSOs and donors and advocates for legal and regulatory environments that enable CSOs to contribute to the development process; and also helps CSOs develop their own capacity by connecting them to knowledge, experience and resources from around the world, including CSOs in other countries and regions.

The World Bank and IMF have endorsed the preparation of Poverty Reduction Strategy Papers (PRSPs) by the borrowing governments with broad based stake holder participation. PRSPs will need to address accountability to the poor in three main aspects : ensuring at the formulation stage that poverty strategies reflect the needs and the priorities of the poor, ensuring during implementation that mechanisms are developed and applied whereby the poor can help contain corruption and hold government and other service providers accountable; and building into PRSP design continuous monitoring by poor people of the fulfilment of commitments in the poverty strategy more broadly. The IMF and the World Bank have taken a keen interest in participatory public expenditure management (PPEM) strategies in ensuring that PRSPs are effectively implemented. PPEM is fast becoming the standard practice in public finance. This is a new, important advocacy track that needs to be developed further. The PPEM will also encourage in increasing the "voice" of the poor as well as their representatives and intermediaries.

Apart from the role of CSOs in poverty reduction strategy projects, there is increasing recognition that international and national governments have to open up to civil society institutions. The European Union Commission initiated a Civil Dialogue to give the institutions of society—and not only governments and businesses—a voice at the policy-making levels at Brussels.

In the past, governments in many areas of the world tended to oppose civil society. The collapse of the communist regimes and of many repressive military dictatorships in Latin America and Asia, combined with the crisis of the welfare state in the North and the state-promoted development in the South, has given rise to much more open political environment.

Civil Society Organisations

A multitude of players outside of the government sector—grass-roots organisations, trade unions, universities, non-profit foundations, user groups and non-governmental organisations influence public performance. Among the things they can hold local governments and civic bodies accountable. Such groups known—collectively as "civil society", can also aid local administration in search for more responsive and effective governance. In India, the increasing role of non-governmental organisations, voluntary bodies and other organs of the civil society in advocacy and policy formulation has introduced a new element in democratic governance. In the contemporary society policy formulation is not left to governments alone. In the Foreword to a book *Public Policy, Analysis and Design*, the eminent Indian diplomat, economist and educational administrator, A.M. Khusro says : Policy need not be made by governments only, but in this country policy has been made almost wholly by governments. It may be because other segments and sectors—the commercial sector and the social sector, have been weak and are in the throes of a slow developmental process, they will acquire a degree of resilience and a policy making capability later. But to begin with they were weak and therefore, it fell to the lot of central and state governments to make policies and programmes during the last 40 years. There are NGOs like Policy Initiatives or Policy Alternatives, etc. and there are associations of industry and trade. Many people in the private sector of industry and trade, the cooperative sector, the NGO sector, the social sector and intellectual sector, are beginning to think of many policy areas and it is certain that their role will increase with time.

The special issue of *Development Dialogue,* published by Dag Hammarskjold Foundation devotes one paper to the responsibilities of civil society organisations. In the systems analysis, the paper makes fascinating study : In eighties the First System comprised princes (the politicians and the governments); while the second position fell to merchants (now transnational enterprises). Today the reality is otherwise. In several countries including USA, UK, Canada, Australia and Japan, the merchants dictate to the princes. Globalisation has become a corporate *mantra* mouthed by politicians. It is widely known that US corporations do not act for the benefit of US economy. The Second System is under attack from CSOs, which constitute the Third System. Increasingly the disenchanted sectors of civil society are asking—Why governments who cannot deliver services should be permitted to set policies. In any future dispensation CSOs will be forced to take a more aggressive policy role.

We may recall that it is because of the sustained hard work put in by organisations like NBA that today even the World Bank has agreed to revisit the claims of big dams and irrigation projects. It is only because of the critical scrutiny of the CSOs that the role of international conferences like the Earth Summit and the Beijing Conference is being evaluated for concrete results.

Erosion of rights is one area where challenge to human dignity is the greatest. CSOs are increasingly looking to constitutional and legal remedies for safeguarding human rights mechanisms to counter the force of World Trade Organisation (see the devastating effect with which the recent WTO conference in US was confronted by NGOs and VOs). The invocation of human rights (which would include freedom of expression, of the press, right to development, political opinion and education) draws together a broad spectrum of civil society and holds real promise of success.

Civil Society and Good Governance—During recent years, the issue of good governance has emerged at the forefront of the agenda for sustainable human development. Some approaches towards conceptualising governance are :

- Governance is defined as the manner in which power is exercised in the management of a country's economic and social resources. (The World Bank)
- Governance is viewed as the exercise of political, economic and administrative authority in the management of a country's affairs at all levels. It comprises mechanisms, processes and institutions through which citizens and groups articulate their interests, exercise their legal rights, meet their obligations, and mediate their differences. (United Nations Development Programme)

An article in *Media Asia* (29:1) 2002; p. 11, gives these two definitions of good governance :

- The core ideal of good governance are fairness and justice in the institution of civil society. Good governance can be characterized by high standards of transparency, accountability and access.
- Good governance means providing opportunities and the proper delivery of goods and services to the people in a fair, just, effective, responsible and open way.

From Government to Governance

The increased role of civil society marks a shift from government to governance, with governance involving a far larger group of participants and players. According to the World Bank :

> Good governance is epitomised by predictable, open and enlightened policy making, a bureaucracy imbued with a professional ethos acting in furtherance of the public good, the rule of law, transparent processes, and a strong civil society participating in public affairs. Poor governance is characterized by arbitrary policy making, unaccountable bureaucracies, unenforced or unjust legal systems, the abuse of executive power, a civil society engaged in public life, and a widespread corruption.

India's Governance—Concerns and Challenges

The National Human Development Report 2001, released in March 2002 lists, achievements, concerns and challenges in the Economic, Political and Civic Governance. No doubt there are certain definite and substantial achievements to the credit of the Indian state—India is among the ten fastest growing economies of 1998s; self-sufficiency in food grains, movement on decentralisation of power from the centre to states, districts and villages; independent and proactive judiciary on issues of larger public interest; primacy of human and civic rights, freedom of expression, free press and electronic media and considerable non-governmental and civil society initiatives in varioius spheres of social and public life. However in the area of political and economic governance there have matters of serious concerns for the policy planners, administrators and political leadership.

Some of the glaring concerns and challenges that the NHDR 2001 lists are :—

Political Governance

1. Criminalisation of public life, politics of vote bank, communal violence and corruption constitute major challenges for improving governance in the country.

2. Recourse to competitive, populism, the use of money power, particularly during elections, compromising decisive political action.
3. Disruptions in parliamentary proceedings delaying timely and informed legislative work.

Economic Governance

1. About 260 million perons or about 26 per cent of population still below the normative poverty line,
2. Population growth still high, unsustainable and persisting adverse sex-ratios in some states,
3. Pockets of hunger and deprivation still an unfortunate reality.

Corruption and Good Governance

The overriding issue of corruption has emerged as problem number one in the country. It is now being accepted all over that one of the major drawbacks of the process of development planning has been corruption in rural development works and even at high levels of bureaucracy and political leadership. Three instances of all pervading corruption from three different quarters will go on to illustrate as to how endemic the issue of corruption has become.

I. Approach Paper to the Tenth Five Year Plan (2002-2007):

> Almost the entire social sector programme is implemented by State level field machinery and, therefore, we should be vitally concerned with falling standards of performance and integrity among the field officials. As corruption is on the increase even in higher echelons of bureaucracy, the fear in the minds of lower level officials has declined and corruption at all levels, as the Prime Minister put it, has become a 'low risk and high reward activity.' Even honest civil servants are disheartened by the uncertainty of tenure and lack of support from the top for innovative ideas. This has generated a growing feeling among the civil servants that honesty, impartiality and concern for public welfare are at a discount today.

II. India: From Midnight to Millennium—Shashi Tharoor states :

> Whatever headway India makes in reforming its economy, however, the biggest enemy of the country's economic progress—corruption—must be tackled. It is important to stress that the sight of a small minority in positions of privilege conspicuously consuming undeclared assets—even though this is a phenomenon that precedes liberalisation is not a good advertisement for the policy of economic reforms; indeed, it is likely to create a sense of alienation from the market among people who feel they are denied access to it. Indian economists have estimated that only 15 per cent of governmental expenditure actually actually goes to the intended beneficiaries. It is impossible to overstate the importamce of eradication, with all the ruthlessness of law, governmental corruption if the economic reforms are to succeed, because only people who are convinced that they hold within their own hands the capacity for self-advancement will create the savings and production that the reforms aim to generate. And as long as the ordinary citizen of India believes that only those who know how to cheat and decieve, who have the means to bribe and suborn, and who have bureaucratic access or political clout, can succeed, that faith will never take root in the mass of the population.

III. Everybody Loves a Good Drought— P. Sainath, gives a graphic account of rampant corruption prevailing at the grassroots level of development bureaucracy. He refers to one such instance which is better reproduced in his own words :

> A corrupt Block Development Officer (BDO) came. And what he said you cannot hear that even in a Bollywood film. He was asking for bribes from a few young people. He takes 25 per cent. If the work to be done in your village costs Rs. 10,000, then he should be given Rs. 2,500. This is the rate, it has to be given. He went to one village, Eshak village, a communist village. There was a young boy. He became emotional, it was the question of his pride, self-respect. Next day they came to

> the BDO's office and called him out. He had demanded 25 per cent, isn't it? Twenty-five young men came there and beat him 25 times with their *chappals*. Then the BDO filed a case of dacoity, brigandry, murder, etc., against these boys. When the case was in the process, I was there. The BDO was telling them, "I am willing to drop the cases, I bear you no grudge", he is a businessman. He was telling the leader of the group, "*are yarr, sir ko mara, dil ko mara, izzat ko mara arre hai pet me math maro,* give me my 25 per cent, I will do your work and withdraw my case against you, I have got my transfer already." These kinds of negotiations were going on in the court right in front of everybody.

One can imagine what type and quality of development work is possible in the villages, under the given cirumstances of open, flourishing and rampant corruption.

Therefore, the disclosures made by the *Indian Chapter* of the Transparency International, which listed India in the bottom rung of corruption index with a rating of 2.7 on a scale of 10, did cause concern. Admiral R.H. Tahiliani, head of the *Indian Chapter* says : Corruption is personal gain at public expense. It is largesse at public expense to near and dear ones. Once you have filled your own pockets, you like to fill the pockets of your family and members of your own political party. We have mastered the art of doing this. The silver lining is that people are getting sensitised. The only thing that will eventually change things drastically is that little man who refuses to paya bribe (*The Indian Express,* 6 September 2002).

The World Development Report 2002, *Building Institutions for Markets,* says that corruption has large costs for economic development. Across countries there is strong evidence that higher levels of corruptions are associated with lower growth and lower levels of per capita income. Corruption can be thought of a force that undermines well functioning markets in three ways : as a tax, as a barrier to entry, and by subverting the legitimacy of the state and its ability to provide institutions that support markets. Corruption can be seen as a tax, which distorts the choice between activities and lowers the returns to public and private investments. But corruption is much worse than a tax because the revenues do not contribute to the public budget, to be spent on socially useful activities.

Lack of Accountability and Transparency—Lack of accountability and transparency in the conduct of government business is another important factor inhibiting good governance. According to one definition [*Media Asia* : 29 (1)], transparency means openness in laws, rules and procedures, and decision-making processes of government and its public institutions. And, equally important, it empowers the civil society, individually or through their associations, as well as the media, to correctly assess the performance of their government in all major sectors, such as economic, social, security and the like.

Likewise the concept of accountability means a government and its institutions must be duty bound to honestly give account to the public and the media in relation to their performance in carrying out their responsibilities.

Lack of accountability of the implementing agencies either to the government or to the people has been the single major cause for misappropriation of funds in development programmes. In this context the observations in the Approach Paper to the Ninth Five Year Plan are quite pertinent : "It is well known that implementing agencies and programme managers can get away easily with time and cost overruns or non-fulfilment of targets by attributing these to factors beyond their control. In many cases they are indeed justified as most programmes leave too many loose ends at the planning stage. Nevertheless several cases of misappropriation of funds meant for anti-poverty programmes have also come to light. In one of the employment generating schemes, it was found that the muster roles were not maintained at the grassroots level. An NGO has unearthed several cases of misappropriation of funds in rural development programmes in four districts of one state. This happened because of lack of people's participation in the implementation of the programmes, lack of transparency in the operation of schemes and inadequacy of the monitoring mechanism. Suitable institutional reforms—involvement of the people and grassroots level NGOs in formulation and implementation are needed to overcome this problem."

Commenting on this aspect of rural development schemes, the well-known social activist Bunker Roy says : Because the system is so corrupt, because there is no accountability and no fear of being caught and suspended, every year millions of rupees of funds earmarked for building schools, dispensaries, houses, drinking water schemes, planting saplings in forest land, and construction of dams, community centres, go into the pockets of *gram sewaks* (village workers), *patwaris* and village level officials in league with touts and politicians. This is the situation in all the South Asian region, without exception, where the governments have taken the responsibility to deliver development schemes to the poor in villages.

The problems enunciated here however remain; in fact in some cases these problems have aggravated. The cases of corruption, lack of accountability, non-functioning of Parliament for days together, lack of political will at the highest level and a general attitude of passivity and permissiveness have added to the problems of good governance.

Right to Information **:** It is only to curb the rampant corruption and ensure transparency in rural development works that the campaign for Right to Information has been gathering strength in several states in the country. In Rajasthan the campaign has metamorphosed into a movement from grassroots embedded in the protest by villagers in several districts. The movement essentially aims at ensuring accountability in development projects. The campaign, which was basically to obtain photocopies of bills, receipts, muster rolls and other documents concerning project accounts got its inspiration from several *Jan sunwayis* (open public hearings) organised by the Mazdoor, Kisan Shakti Sangathan (MKSS) where hundreds of the poorest from far off villages came to speak, listen and share their experiences. Since the bureaucracy found such a movement challenging its authority, a stalemate ensued in getting any access to information legislation through. The Bill for Right to Information was passed by the Parliament in its session which concluded in December 2002. It is, however, yet to be seen as to what extent the Bill will be successful in ensuring transparency in the conduct of public affairs.

The NHDR underlines the role of civil society which is to facilitate mobilization of people's opinion and participation in economic, social and political activities for sustaining an efficient and productive social order. There have been a number of successful civil society initiatives in community development in various parts of the country, founded on a unique partnership of the local people with the State Governments, often catalysed and mediated by some motivated individuals and Non-Governmental Organizations. The success of such initiatives, particularly in the area of water shed management and minor irrigation in the States of Gujarat, Rajasthan and Maharashtra, to name a few, have considerably improved the income levels of the people. It has also strengthened the capacities of the communities to become self-reliant in addressing their development concerns locally. It has fostered a sense of 'ownership', 'responsibility' and 'progress' among the people.

To hope that NGOs, VOs and CSOs will succeed where the political leadership is reluctant to act through administrative and legislative measures is indeed a tall order. Let us hope that Civil Society, as a movement, and as it emerges in a stronger mould, would be able to retrieve the situation which at present looks rather disappointing.

The former BBC Correspondent in South Asia, Mark Tully in his book, *India in Slow Motion,* launched in November 2002, finds a civil society which is vibrant in India. He says : Indian democracy has brought a social revolution. India has become the NGO capital of the world. Let us hope civil society helps India solve many of its social and economic problems, as well as problems of good governance that the country is confronted with at present.

REFERENCES

Approach Paper to the Ninth Five Year Plan, (1997) Planning Commission, Government of India, New Delhi.

Approach Paper to the Tenth Five Year Plan, Planning Commission (September 2001), Government of India, New Delhi.

Chandhoke, Neera, (2000) *State and Civil Society : Explorations in Civil Society*, Sage Pulication, New Delhi.

Media Asia, (2002) *Media and Civil Society*, AMIC Singapore.

National Human Development Report 2001, (March 2002) Planning Commission, Government of India, New Delhi.

World Bank, World Development Report 2000—*Building Institutions for Markets*, The World Bank, Washington.

ANNEXURES

Annexure-I

DECLARATION ON THE RIGHT TO DEVELOPMENT

A landmark development in the formulation and recognition of new human rights is the Declaration on the Right to Development which was adopted by the General Assembly of the United Nations on 4 December 1986. This Declaration is particularly significant for its importance to the developing countries, even though the necessary means for enforcing it are lacking. The text of this Declaration is reproduced below :

The General Assembly

Bearing in mind the purposes and principles of the Charter of the United Nations relating to the achievement of international co-operation in solving international problems of economic, social, cultural or humanitarian nature, and in promoting and encouraging respect for human rights and fundamental freedoms for all without distinction as to race, sex, language or religion.

Recognizing the development is a comprehensive economic, social, cultural and political process, which aims at the constant improvement of the well-being of the entire population and of all individuals on the basis of their active, free and meaningful participation in development and in the fair distribution of benefits resulting therefrom.

Considering that under the provisions of the Universal Declaration of Human Rights everyone is entitled to a social and international order in which the rights and freedoms set forth in the Declaration can be fully realized.

Recalling the provisions of the International Covenant of

Economic, Social and Cultural Rights and of the International Covenant on Civil and Political Rights.

Recalling further the relevant agreements, conventions, resolutions, recommendations and other instruments of the United Nations and its specialized agencies concerning the integral development of the human being, economic and social progress and development of all peoples, including those instruments concerning decolonization, the prevention of discrimination, respect for and observance of human rights and fundamental freedoms, the maintenance of international peace and security and the further promotion of friendly relations and cooperation among States in accordance with the Charter.

Recalling the right of peoples to self-determination, by virtue of which they have the right freely to determine their political status and to pursue their economic, social and cultural development.

Recalling also the right of peoples to exercise, subject to the relevant provisions of both International Covenants of Human Rights, full and complete sovereignty over all their natural wealth and resources.

Mindful of the obligation of States under the Charter to promote universal respect for and observance of human rights and fundamental freedoms for all without distinction of any kind such as race, colour, sex, language, religion, political or other opinion, national or social origin, property, birth or other status.

Considering that the elimination of the massive and flagrant violations of the human rights of the peoples and individuals affected by situations such as those resulting from colonialism, neo-colonialism, apartheid, all forms of racism and racial discrimination, foreign domination and occupation, aggression and threats against national sovereignty, national unity and territorial integrity and threats of war would contribute to the establishment of circumstances propitious to the development of a great part of mankind.

Concerned at the existence of serious obstacles to development, as well as to the complete fulfilment of human beings and of peoples, constituted, *inter alia*, by the denial of civil, political, economic, social and cultural rights, and considering that all human rights and fundamental freedoms are indivisible and interdependent and that, in order to promote development, equal attention, and urgent consideration should be given to the implementation, promotion and protection of civil, political, economic, social and cultural rights and that accordingly, the promotion of, respect for and enjoyment of certain human rights and fundamental freedoms cannot justify the denial of other human rights and fundamental freedoms.

Considering that international peace and security are essential elements for the realization of the right to development.

Reaffirming that there is a close relationship between disarmament and development and that progress in the field of disarmament would considerably promote progress in the field of development and that resources released through disarmament measures should be devoted to the economic and social development and well-being of all peoples and, in particular, those of the developing countries.

Recognizing that the human person is the central subject of the development process and that development policy should therefore make the human being the main participant and beneficiary of development.

Recognizing that the creation of conditions favourable to the development of peoples and individuals is the primary responsibility of their States.

Aware that efforts at the international level to promote and protect human rights should be accompanied by efforts to establish a new international economic order.

Confirming that the right to development is an inalienable human right and that equality of opportunity for development is a prerogative both of nations and of individuals who make up nations.

Proclaims the following Declaration on the Right to Development :

Article 1

1. The right to development is an inalienable human right by virtue of which every human person and all peoples are

entitled to participate in, contribute to and enjoy economic, social, cultural and political development, in which all human rights and fundamental freedoms can be fully realized.

2. The human right to development also implies the full realization of the right of peoples to self-determination, which includes, subject to the relevant provisions of both International Covenants on Human Rights, the exercise of their inalienable right to full sovereignty over all their natural wealth and resources.

Article 2

1. The human person is the central subject of development and should be the active participant and beneficiary of the right to development.
2. All human beings have a responsibility for development, individually and collectively, taking into account the need for full respect for their human rights and fundamental freedoms as well as their duties to the community, which alone can ensure the free and complete fulfilment of the human being and they should therefore promote and protect an appropriate political, social and economic order for development.
3. States have the right and the duty to formulate appropriate national development policies that aim at constant improvement of the well-being of the entire population and of all individuals, on the basis of their active, free and meaningful participation in development and in the fair distribution of the benefits resulting therefrom.

Article 3

1. States have the primary responsibility for the creation of national and international conditions favourable to the realization of the right to development.
2. The realization of the right to development requires full

respect for the principles of international law concerning friendly relations and cooperation among States in accordance with the Charter of the United Nations.

3. States have the duty to cooperate with each other in ensuring development and eliminating obstacles to development. States should realize their rights and fulfil their duties in such a manner as to promote a new international economic order based on sovereign equality, interdependence, mutual interest and cooperation among all States, as well as to encourage the observance and realization of human rights.

Article 4

1. States have the duty to take steps, individually and collectively, to formulate international development policies with a view to facilitating the full realization of the right to development.
2. Sustained action is required to promote more rapid development of developing countries. As a complement to the efforts of developing countries, effective international cooperation is essential in providing these countries with appropriate means and facilities to foster their comprehensive development.

Article 5

States shall take resolute steps to eliminate the massive and flagrant violations of the human rights of peoples and human beings affected by situations such as those resulting from apartheid, all forms of racism and racial discrimination, colonialism, foreign domination and occupation, aggression, foreign interference and threats against national sovereignty, national unity and territorial integrity, threats of war and refusal to recognize the fundamental right of peoples to self-determination.

Article 6

1. All States should cooperate with a view to promoting,

encouraging and strengthening universal respect for an observance of all human rights and fundamental freedoms for all without any distinction as to race, sex, language or religion.

2. All human rights and fundamental freedoms are indivisible and interdependent; equal attention and urgent consideration should be given to the implementation, promotion and protection of civil, political, economic, social and cultural rights.
3. States should take steps to eliminate obstacles to development resulting from failure to observe civil and political rights, as well as economic, social and cultural rights.

Article 7

All States should promote the establishment, maintenance and strengthening of international peace and security and, to that end, should do their utmost to achieve general and complete disarmament under effective international control, as well as to ensure that the resources released by effective disarmament measures are used for comprehensive development, in particular that of the developing countries.

Article 8

1. States should undertake, at the national level, all necessary measures for the realization of the right to development and shall ensure, *inter alia*, equality of opportunity for all in their access to basic resources, education, health services, food, housing, employment and the fair distribution of income. Effective measures should be undertaken to ensure that women have an active role in the development process. Appropriate economic and social reforms should be carried out with a view to eradicating all social injustices.
2. States should encourage popular participation in all spheres as an important factor in development and in the full realization of all human rights.

Article 9

1. All the aspects of the right to development set forth in the present Declaration are indivisible and interdependent and each of them should be considered in the context of the whole.
2. Nothing in the present Declaration shall be construed as being contrary to the purposes and principles of the United Nations, or as implying that any State, group or person has a right to engage in any activity or to perform any act aimed at the violation of the rights set forth in the Universal Declaration of Human Rights and in the International Covenants on Human Rights.

Article 10

Steps should be taken to ensure the full exercise and progressive enhancement of the right to development, including formulation, adoption and implementation of policy, legislative and other measures at the national and international levels.

Annexure-II

THE JOHANNESBURG DECLARATION ON SUSTAINABLE DEVELOPMENT

From Our Origins to the Future

1. We, the representatives of the peoples of the worid, assembled at the World Summit on Sustainable Development in Johannesburg, South Africa from 2-4 September 2002, reaffirm our commitment to sustainable development.
2. We commit ourselves to build a humane, equitable and caring global society cognizant of the need for human dignity for all.
3. At the beginning of this Summit, the children of the world spoke to us in a simple yet clear voice that the future belongs to them, and accordingly challenged all of us to ensure that through our actions they will inherit a world free of the indignity and indecency occasioned by poverty, environmental degradation and patterns of unsustainable development.
4. As part of our response to these children, who represent our collective future, all of us, coming from every corner of the world, informed by different life experiences, are united and moved by a deeply-felt sense that we urgently need to create a new and brighter world of hope.
5. Accordingly, we assume a collective responsibility to advance and strengthen the interdependent and mutually reinforcing pillars of sustainable development— economic development, social development and environmental

protection— at local, national, regional and global levels.

6. From this Continent, the Cradle of Humanity we declare, through the Plan of Implementation and this Declaration, our responsibility to one another, to the greater community of life and to our children.
7. Recognizing that humankind is at a crossroad, we have united in a common resolve to make a determined effort to respond positively to the need to produce a practical and visible plan that should bring about poverty eradication and human development.

From Stockholm to Rio de Janeiro to Johannesburg

8. Thirty years ago, in Stockholm, we agreed on the urgent need to respond to the problem of environmental deterioration. Ten years ago, at the United Nations Conference on Environment and Development, held in Rio de Janeiro, we agreed that the protection of the environment, and social and economic development are fundamental to sustainable development, based on the Rio Principles. To achieve such development, we adopted the global programme, Agenda 21, and the Rio Declaration, to which we reaffirm our commitment. The Rio Summit was a significant milestone that set a new agenda for sustainable development.
9. Between Rio and Johannesburg the world's nations met in several major conferences under the guidance of the United Nations, including the Monterrey Conference on Finance for Development, as well as the Doha Ministerial Conference. These conferences defined for the world a comprehensive vision for the future of humanity.
10. At the Johannesburg Summit we achieved much in bringing together a rich tapestry of peoples and views in a constructive search for a common path, towards a world that respects and implements the vision of sustainable development. Johannesburg also confirmed that significant progress has been made towards achieving a global consensus and partnership amongst all the people of our planet.

The Challenges We Face

11. We recognize that poverty eradication, changing consumption and production patterns, and protecting and managing the natural resource base for economic and social development are overarching objectives of, and essential requirements for sustainable development.
12. The deep fault line that divides human society between the rich and the poor and the ever-increasing gap between the developed and developing worlds pose a major threat to global prosperity, security and stability.
13. The global environment continues to suffer. Loss of biodiversity continues, fish stocks continue to be depleted, desertification claims more and more fertile land, the adverse effects of climate change are already evident, natural disasters are more frequent and more devastating and developing countries more vulnerable, and air, water and marine pollution continue to rob millions of a decent life.
14. Globalization has added a new dimension to these challenges. The rapid integration of markets, mobility of capital and significant increases in investment flows around the world have opened new challenges and opportunities for the pursuit of sustainable development. But the benefits and costs of globalization are unevenly distributed, with developing countries facing special difficulties in meeting this challenge.
15. We risk the entrenchment of these global disparities and unless we act in a manner that fundamentally changes their lives, the poor of the world may lose confidence in their representatives and the democratic systems to which we remain committed, seeing their representatives as nothing more than sounding brass or tinkling cymbals.

Our Commitment to Sustainable Development

16. We are determined to ensure that our rich diversity, which is our collective strength, will be used for constructive

partnership for change and for the achievement of the common goal of sustainable development.

17. Recognizing the importance of building human solidarity, we urge the promotion of dialogue and cooperation among the world's civilizations and peoples, irrespective of race, disabilities, religion, language, culture and tradition.
18. We welcome the Johannesburg Summit focus on the indivisibility of human dignity and are resolved through decisions on targets, timetables and partnerships to speedily increase access to basic requirements such as clean water, sanitation, adequate shelter, energy, health care, food security and the protection of bio-diversity. At the same time, we will work together to assist one another to have access to financial resources, benefit from the opening of markets, ensure capacity building, use modern technology to bring about development, and make sure that there is technology transfer, human resource development, education and training to banish for ever underdevelopment.
19. We reaffirm our pledge to place particular focus on, and give priority attention to, the fight against the worldwide conditions that pose severe threats to the sustainable development of our people. Among these conditions are: chronic hunger; malnutrition; foreign occupation; armed conflicts; illicit drug problems; organized crime; corruption; natural disasters; illicit arms trafficking; trafficking in persons; terrorism; intolerance and incitement to racial, ethnic, religious and other hatreds; xenophobia; and endemic, communicable and chronic diseases, in particular HIV/AIDS, malaria and tuberculosis.
20. We are committed to ensure that women's empowerment and emancipation, and gender equality are integrated in all activities encompassed within Agenda 21, the Millennium Development Goals and the Johannesburg Plan of Implementation.
21. We recognize the reality that global society has the means and is endowed with the resources to address the challenges of poverty eradication and sustainable development confronting all humanity. Together we will take extra steps

to ensure that these available resources are used to the benefit of humanity.

22. In this regard, to contribute to the achievement of our development goals and targets, we urge developed countries that have not done so to make concrete efforts towards the internationally agreed levels of Official Development Assistance.
23. We welcome and support the emergence of stronger regional groupings and alliances, such as the New Partnership for Africa's Development (NEPAD), to promote regional cooperation, improved international co-operation and promote sustainable development.
24. We shall continue to pay special attention to the developmental needs of Small Island Developing States and the Least Developed Countries.
25. We reaffirm the vital role of the indigenous peoples in sustainable development.
26. We recognize sustainable development requires a long-term perspective and broad-based participation in policy formulation, decision-making and implementation at all levels. As social partners we will continue to work for stable partnerships with all major groups respecting the independent, important roles of each of these.
27. We agree that in pursuit of their legitimate activities the private sector, both large and small companies, have a duty to contribute to the evolution of equitable and sustainable communities and societies.
28. We also agree to provide assistance to increase income generating employment opportunities, taking into account the International Labour Organization (ILO) Declaration of Fundamental Principles and Rights at Work.
29. We agree that there is a need for private sector corporations to enforce corporate accountability. This should take place within a transparent and stable regulatory environment.
30. We undertake to strengthen and improve governance at all levels, for the effective implementation of Agenda 21, the Millennium Development Goals and the Johannesburg Plan of Implementation.

Multilateralism is the Future

31. To achieve our goals of sustainable development, we need more effective, democratic and accountable international and multilateral institutions.
32. We reaffirm our commitment to the principles and purposes of the UN Charter and international law as well as the strengthening of multilateralism. We support the leadership role of the United Nations as the most universal and representative organization in the world, which is best placed to promote sustainable development.
33. We further commit ourselves to monitor progress at regular intervals towards the achievement of our sustainable development goals and objectives.

Making it Happen!

34. We are in agreement that this must be an inclusive process, involving all the major groups and governments that participated in the historic Johannesburg Summit.
35. We commit ourselves to act together, united by a common determination to save our planet, promote human development and achieve universal prosperity and peace.
36. We commit ourselves to the Johannesburg Plan of Implementation and to expedite the achievement of the time-bound, socio-economic and environmental targets contained therein.
37. From the African continent, the Cradle of Humankind, we solemnly pledge to the peoples of the world, and the generations that will surely inherit this earth, that we are determined to ensure that our collective hope for sustainable development is realized.

We express our deepest gratitude to the people and the Government of South Africa for their generous hospitality and excellent arrangements made for the World Summit on Sustainable Development.

GLOSSARY

Accountability: The concept of accountability means a government and its institutions must be duty bound to honestly give account to the public and the media in relation to their performance in carrying out their responsibilities.

Acid Rain: This should correctly be called acid precipitation because it includes rain, snow, sleet, fog and any other form of precipitation. It is produced as industrial by-products in emissions of sulphur and nitrogen oxides from burning coal and petroleum products. Found throughout the world, its heaviest concentrations are in urban areas. Among other things, it harms aquatic wildlife, corrodes monuments and bridges, destroys exterior paint, kills forests and damages some agricultural soils, makes drinking water toxic by leaching lead from pipes and reduces visibility.

Air Pollution: The introduction of substances into the air which makes it impure in comparison with pure air.

Appropriate Technology: A low-cost technology using mainly local or easily available materials and skills to meet a recognized need.

Biodegradable: Matter that can be decomposed by nature's living organisms, especially bacteria.

Carrying Capacity: The amount of life and exploitation that a biological system can support without suffering damage and becoming degraded.

Civil Society: (1) A civic culture of generalized trust and social solidarity, peopled by citizens willing and able to co-operate in ventures; it is an important prerequisite of a vital democracy. (2) 'Civil Society' is the term that best describes the non-governmental, not for profit, independent nature of organizations that allow for broad citizen participation. The hallmark of a democratic society is the freedom of individual to associate with like-minded individuals, express their view publicly, openly debate public policy, and petition their government. Civil society organizations (CSOs) include human rights groups, professional associations, religious institutions, province—democracy groups, environmental activist organizations, business associations, labour unions, media organizations and voluntary associations of people seeking to work for the public good.

Communication Technology: It is the hardware equipment, organizational structures, and social values by which individuals collect, process, and exchange information.

Deforestation: (1) The loss of tropical forests due to collection of fuel wood, commercial logging, shifting cultivation, grazing, road construction, ranching, mining and fire. Leads to soil erosion and flooding and endangers wildlife through habitat destruction. (2) The permanent clearing of forest land for all agricultural uses and for other land uses such as settlements, other infrastructure and mining. It does not include other alterations such as selective logging.

Development Communication: (1) It is the process of using communication to further development. (2) Type of journalism practiced by many Third World countries that stresses national goals and economic development. (3) It is purposive and the intention here is to help in socio-economic development. It aims at educating people, not simply passing along information to them. It takes into account a variety of media forms, both human and non-human and mass-media. An appropriate combination of mass-media and inter-personal communication channel is considered more prudent. Use of localized medium with control in hands of users seems quite befitting as in local radio, local television, community based cable TV networks etc.

Development: (1) Development is a widely participatory process of directed social change in a society, intended to bring about both social and material advancement (including greater equality, freedom, and other valued qualities) for the majority of people through their gaining greater control over their environment. (2) The conventional understanding of development as some form of improvement is no longer tenable. Improvement as a concept has different connotations economic growth, modernization, nation building, industrialization, betterment of life opportunities, enlarging people's choices, and enhancement of capacities, good governance, sustainability, and poverty alleviation. It is polycentric in meaning, objectives and methods of implementation. (3) Economic growth cannot be the only objective for national planning and indeed over the years, development objectives are being defined not just in terms of increases in GDP or per capita income but broader in terms of enhancement of human well-being.

Disasters: Includes natural and technological disasters. Natural disasters include avalanches, cold waves, cyclones, hurricanes, typhoons, drought, earthquakes, epidemics and famine (but do not include famine relating to conflict because of a lack of reliable data). Technological disasters include accidents, chemical accidents and urban fires.

Disinfection: The killing of the larger portion (but not necessarily all) of the harmful and objectionable microorganism in, or on, a medium by means of chemicals, heat, ultraviolet light, etc.

Economic Reforms : The term is used to refer to stabilization and structural adjustment measures. Stabilization usually refers to the policies initiated by the International Monetary Fund (IMF) and has been defined as 'the correction of imbalances which are held to be unsustainable'. Structural adjustment, on the other hand, is associated with World Bank lending for the medium term to enable reorienting the economy for greater efficiency. The World Bank defined structural adjustment as 'reforms' of policies and institutions—micro-economic (such as taxes), macro-economic (such as fiscal imbalance) and institutional (public sector inefficiencies).

Ecosystem : (1) Any segment of nature, or community of organism, in which organisms interact one with the other and with their environment, and are therefore interdependent. (2) The interacting system of a biological community and its non-living environment.

Ecumenopolis : A world city. The hypothetical final stage of urbanization where most of the world becomes a part of a single megalopolis.

Education Index: One of the three indicators on which the human development index is built. It is based on the combined primary, secondary and tertiary gross enrolment ratio and the adult literacy rate.

Education Level: Education has been categorized as primary, secondary or tertiary in accordance with the International Standard Classification of Education (ISCED), *Primary Education* (ISCED level 1) provides the basic elements of education at such establishments as primary or elementary schools. *Secondary Education* (ISCED level 2 and 3) is based on at least four years of previous instruction at the first level and provides general or specialized instruction, or both, at such institutions as middle school, secondary school, high school, teacher training school at this level and vocational or technical school. *Tertiary Education* (ISCED level 5-7) refers to education at such institutions as universities, teachers' colleges and higher-level professional schools— requiring as a minimum condition of admission the successful completion of education at the second level or evidence of the attainment of an equivalent level of knowledge.

Effluent: (1) A liquid that flows out of a containing space, (2) Sewage, water, or other liquid partially or completely treated, or in its natural state, as the case may be, flowing out of a reservoir, basin, or treatment plant, or part thereof.

Environment: The sum of all external influences and conditions affecting the life and the development of an organism.

Environmental Reporting: Communicating information about interrelationships between man and his environment— between man and the natural and man-made environment, events or conditions.

Erosion: The loss of surface soil through the action of precipitation and wind. Leads to sedimentation and siltation of water-ways, which destroy aquatic and marine habitats, make water undrinkable and clog water-dependent industrial machinery and other intake equipment.

Extension Education: (1) The aim of all extension work is to teach people living in rural areas how to raise their standard of living, by their own efforts, using their own resources of manpower and materials, with minimum of assistance from government. (2) It points out the common fundamental principles, philosophy and procedures which are applied in different technological disciplines or problem areas. Extension education is the core with universal application. (3) The concept of extension has combined the concern for the overall development of man with methodology and efficiency of a systematically organized educational programme. It is also known as a form of adult education. Extension education is largely non-formal in nature.

Food Chain: The feeding relationship described by a series of plants and animals each of which serves as food for the next in the chain.

Global Village: (1) It is a world that is increasingly interconnected by communication technologies and that is tending towards a global culture. (2) A phrase which is used to describe the ways in which modern electronic media have spread around, interconnected and 'shrunk' the world, making possible seemingly immediate forms of communication and cultural relationship.

Good Governance: Good governance means providing opportunities and the proper delivery of goods and services to the people in a fair, just, effective, responsible, and open way. The core ideals of good governance are fairness and justice in the institution of civil society. Good governance can be characterized by 'high standards of transparency, accountability and access'.

Greenhouse Effect: The theory that continued burning of fossil fuels will increase concentrations of carbon dioxide in the atmosphere, thereby trapping additional heat and moisture. In time, this could create a hothouse effect, raising the temperature of the earth, causing glaciers to melt and the sea level to rise.

Gross Domestic Product (GDP): The total output of goods and services for final use produced by an economy by both residents and non-residents, regardless of the allocation to domestic and foreign claims. It does not include deductions for depreciation of physical capital or depletion and degradation of natural resources.

Gross National Product (GNP): Comprises GDP plus net factor income from abroad, which is the income residents receive from abroad for factor services (labour and capital), less similar payments made to non-residents who contribute to the domestic economy.

Habitat: The sum total of environmental conditions of a specific place that is occupied by an organism, a population or a community.

Heavy Metals: These include such toxic metals as mercury, lead, and cadmium, which are biologically harmful, even in very small doses.

High Technologies: These are capital and energy intensive technologies designed in developed nations to reduce labour and cater to market. In general, high technologies have some common features as below: They create work opportunities for highly trained work forces, they depend on large, centralized, hierarchical organizations that require large capital investments and create dependency of uses on suppliers, they generate large volume of toxic wastes and they require heavy use of non-renewable resources.

High-Technology Industry: It is an industry at the cutting edge of technology, whose core technology changes rapidly.

Human Capital: 'Stock of skills and productive knowledge embodied in people'. The expenditure on schooling, health, on-the-job training, and searching for information about job opportunities and migration constitutes an investment that people make in themselves. Investment in these sectors is emphasized as a means to higher productivity of the labour force and is justified on the basis of either financial rates of return (as in the case of education) or estimates emerging from production functions (as in the case of health).

Human Development Index (HDI): A composite index based on three indicators: longevity, as measured by life expectancy at birth; educational attainment, as measured by a combination of adult literacy (two-third weight) and the combined gross primary secondary and tertiary enrolment ratio (one-third weight); and standard of living, as measured by GDP per capita (PPP US$)

Human Development: The term has been defined by the UNDP as 'The process of the enlarging people's choices'. The concept encompasses empowerment, co-operation, equity in basic capabilities and opportunities, sustainability and security. In this approach people occupy centre stage, and measures such as education, health and nutrition are emphasized for their intrinsic value and for their role in enhancing the basic capabilities of people. The emergence of the concept of human development can be traced to efforts by economists such as Amartya Sen who define standard of living in terms of functionings and capabilities rather than in terms of commodity possession.

Human Poverty Index (HPI): The human poverty index for developing countries (HPI-1) measures deprivations in three dimensions of human life—longevity, knowledge and a decent standard of living. The HPI for industrialized countries (HPI-2) includes, in addition to these three dimensions, social exclusion.

Infant Morality Rate: The probability of dying between birth and exactly one year of age times 1,000.

Information Societies: The countries in which information workers are more numerous than such occupational categories as farmers, industrial workers, or service workers.

Information Workers: The individuals whose main job responsibilities are to gather, process, or distribute information, or to produce information technologies like computers or telecommunications equipment that are used by other information workers.

Information: is patterned matter-energy that affects the choices available to an individual making a decision.

Informatization: is the process through which communication technologies are used as strategies for furthering socio-economic development.

Innovation: It is an idea perceived as new.

Interactive Participation: People participate in joint analysis, development of action plans, and formation or strengthening of local institutions. Participation is seen as a right, not just the means to achieve project goals.

Intermediate Technology: It refers to such small scale technologies emerging out of a gradual process of technological innovations sustainable in the communities. It avoids pitfalls of high technologies especially exploitation of natural and human resources. Such technologies are more natural, non-polluting and can be locally owned and produced in small units. They have respect for ecology, food, energy, and shelter and water need of the communities.

Life Expectancy at Birth: The number of years a newborn infant would live if prevailing patterns of mortality at the time of birth were to stay the same throughout the child's life.

M.N.C.: Multinational Corporations considered to be very large companies with production units in several countries. Several MNCs have made their presence felt in T.V., advertising and film production.

Mass Media/Mass Communication: Organized and specialized modern media institutions such as the press, cinema and broadcasting, whose principal business involves the supply of different forms of information and entertainment. Mass-communication is used to describe what these agencies do what they produce. (2) Mass Media Communication includes all those means of transmitting messages such as radio, television, newspapers, and film, which enable a source of one or a few individuals to reach a large audience. (3) The process by which messages are communicated to a large number of people by a mass-medium.

Mega city: A city with a population of five million or more.

Megalopolis: A city created when two or more cities merge via urban infilling.

New Media Technologies: The large scale technical developments in communication systems and their cultural consequences. The term is also used to refer to cable, satellite, and digital and other computer based media in the current phase.

Participation: (1) It includes people's involvement in decision-making processes, in implementing programmes, their sharing in benefits of development programmes and their involvement in efforts to evaluate such programmes. (2) People's participation is essentially to do with economic and political relationships within the wider society; it is not just a matter of involvement in project activities but rather the process by which rural people are able to organize themselves and trough their own organization, are able to identify their own needs, share in design, implement, and evaluate participatory action. (3) Community participation is an active process by which beneficiary or client groups influence the direction and execution of a development project with a view to enhancing their well-being in terms of income, personal growth, self-reliance, or other values they cherish.

Pluralism: The theory that power is exercised by interest groups in society, and is reflected in the diversity of ideas and views found in the media.

Pollutant: Any introduced gas, liquid, or solid that makes a resource unfit for its natural function or for a specific purpose.

Polluter Pays Principle (PPP): Commonsense idea that the cost of putting right pollution damage should be borne by the person or organization causing that damage, for example, in the form of pollution taxes.

Pollution: (1) Contamination of air, water, land or other natural resources that will or is likely to create a nuisance or render such resources harmful to public health or which is harmful to domestic, municipal, commercial, industrial, agricultural, recreational or other legitimate beneficial uses, or to livestock, wild animals, birds, fish or other life. (2) Release of sewage, industrial wastes, or other harmful or objectionable material into water.

Runoff: Water that does not soak into the ground but runs into a river, lake, or ocean.

Soap opera: It is a dramatic serial that is broadcast mainly in order to entertain audience members.

Social Sector: It refers to education, health and nutrition as well as to poverty alleviation programmes and social assistance measures such as old age pensions. Often, the term social security is linked to the rights of citizens in a country. In this sense the provision of a minimum level of income, education, health and nutrition may be considered to be the basic rights of individuals in a society.

Sustainable Development: (1) The concept of using resources in an ecologically sound manner so that they will be sustainable over the long term. (2) It is an approach to progress that meets the needs of the present without compromising the ability of future generations to meet their needs.

Technological Determinism: It is an approach that considers technology as the main cause of social change.

Technology: (1) Application of science to the practical aim of human life. It refers to the transformation of scientific laws into machines, tools, mechanical devices, instruments, innovations, procedure and techniques to attain tangible ends or manipulate environment for practical purposes. Technology has been taken from Greek language. 'Techno' means art of doing or systematic way of working whereas 'logus' means knowledge or study. So technology is used for all those procedures or systematic ways of working by application of scientific law. (2) Technology refers to both the hardware, viz. machines, equipment and software such as programmes or procedure of working or running machines. (3) It is defined as information that is put to use in order to accomplish some task.

Toxic Substances: Poisonous substances known or believed to be harmful to people's health, often producing chronic, irreversible physical problems and possibly harming subsequent generations. Examples are acrylonitrile, arsenic, asbestos, benzene, beryllium, cadmium, chloroform, chromates, EDB, Ethylene oxide, mercury, PCBs and many others.

Toxic Waste: A waste that poses a substantial present or potential hazard to human health or the environment when improperly managed. It includes wastes that are poisonous, carcinogenic, mutagenic, teratogenic, phytotoxic or toxic to aquatic species.

Transfer of Technology (TOT): TOT refers to the entire process of technology development, processing, dissemination and integration through research, extension and farming systems (in case of agriculture) and capabilities of the three systems to solve the problem of society.

Transparency: Transparency means openness in the laws, rules and procedures, and the decision-making processes of government and its public institutions. And, equally important, it empowers the civil society, individually or through their associations, as well as the media, to correctly assess the performance of their government in all major sectors, such as economic, social, security and the like.

Urban Infilling: The process of urbanizing areas between urban centres to create a continuous urban area.

Urban Planning: The study and profession of developing urban areas.

Urbanization: The process of transforming land into and a densely populated city environment.

Waste Recycling: The reuse of material that diverts it from the waste stream, except for recycling within industrial plants and the reuse of material as fuel.

Water Pollution: The introduction of substances which make water impure compared with undisturbed water. Usually this comes from soil erosion, introduction of poisonous chemicals from industries and spills, domestic sewage or industrial and agricultural wastes.

Water-logging: Soaking of agricultural land caused by a rising water-table or excessive irrigation. Compacts soil, deprives roots of oxygen and contributes to salinization.

BIBLIOGRAPHY

APJ Abdul Kalam with Y.S. Ranjan (1998). *India 2020 : A Vision for the New Millennium*, Penguin Books, New Delhi.

Asian Mass Communication Research and Information Centre (1996). *Opening Windows—Issues in Communication*, Singapore.

Asian Media Information and Communication Centre (1997). *Water : Asia's Environmental Imperative*, Singapore.

Birender Kumar and B.S. Hansra (2000). *Extension Education for Human Resource Development*, Concept Publishing Company.

Chandhoke, Neera (1995). *State and Civil Society : Exploration in Political Theory*, Sage Publications, New Delhi.

Chandra, Bipan (1993). *Essays on Contemporary India*. Har-Anand Publications, New Delhi.

Dreze, Jean and Sen, Amartya (1995). *India : Economic Development and Social Opportunity*. Oxford University Press, Oxford and New Delhi.

Dreze, Jean and Sen, Amartya (eds.) (1996). *Indian Development : Selected Regional Perspectives*, Oxford University Press, Delhi.

ESCAP (1988). *Reporting Environment : A Handbook for Journalists*, Bangkok.

Gowariker, Vasant (ed.) (1993). *The Inevitable Billion Plus*. National Book Trust, New Delhi.

Gupta, V.S. (1995). *Third Revolution in Indian Perspective—Contemporary Issues and Themes in Communication*. Concept Publishing Company, New Delhi.

Gupta, V. S. (1996). *Media Strategies for Rural Development. Kurukshetra* XLIV (4-5). Publications Division, New Delhi.

This bibligraphy contains a list of only those sources which have been actually used in the book, and not the many others which have been consulted by the author but not specifically used. Minor references in the text, such as references to newspapers and internet have been omitted.

Gupta, V. S. (1999). *Communication Technology, Media Policy and National Development*. Concept Publishing Company, New Delhi.

Gupta, V.S. (2001). *Literacy and Technology of Rural Development*, Kurukshetra, October, Publications Division, New Delhi.

Gupta, V. S. and Aggarwal, Vir Bala (1996). *Media Policy and Nation Building, Select Issues and Themes*. Concept Publishing Company, New Delhi.

Gupta, V.S. and Dyal, Rajeshwar (eds.) (1995). *Rural Press : Problems and Prospects*. Concept Publishing Company, New Delhi.

Gupta, V. S. and Dyal, Rajeshwar (eds.) (1996). *National Media Policy*. Concept Publishing Company, New Delhi.

Haq, Mahbub ul (1976). *The Poverty Curtain : Choices for the Third World*, Oxford University Press.

Human Rights—The New Consensus (1994). Regency Press, Golden House, London.

Independent Commission on Population and Quality of Life (1996). *Caring for the Future*. Oxford University Press, Oxford.

India 2002 (A Reference Annual). Publications Division, Ministry of Information and Broadcasting, Government of India, New Delhi.

India Today (1998). Vol. XXIII, No. 43. *Poverty's Philosopher*—Amartya Sen, New Delhi.

Johnson, Kirk (2000). *Television and Social Change in Rural India*, Sage Publications, New Delhi.

Joshi, P.C. (1986). *Communication and Nation-Building : Perspective and Policy*, Sardar Patel Memorial Lectures, Publications Division, New Delhi.

Kunczik, Michael (1992). *Development and Communication*. Friedrich-Ebert Stiftung, Bonn.

Media Asia (29.1), Media and Civil Society, AMIC, Singapore.

Melkote, Srinivas R. and H. Leslie Steeves (2001). *Communication and Development in the Third World—Theory and Practice*, Sage Publications, New Delhi.

Mody, Bella (1991). *Designing Messages for Development Communication*, Sage Publications, New Delhi.

Nair, K.S. and White, S.A. (1993). *Perspectives on Development Communication*, Sage Publications, New Delhi.

Narayanan, V.N. and Sabharwal, Jyoti (1997). *India at 50, Bliss of Hope and Burden of Reality*. Sterling Publishers, New Delhi.

Phadnis, Umashanker (ed.) (1998). *Exploring the Heartland—An Agenda for the Media*, Gyan Publishing House, New Delhi.

Pieterse, Jan Nederveen (2001), *Development Theory : De-Constructions/Reconstructions*, Vistaar Publication, New Delhi.

Planning Commission (2001), *Approach Paper to the Tenth Five Year Plan (2002-2007)*, Government of India, New Delhi.

Planning Commission (2002), *National Human Development Report 2001*, Government of India, New Delhi.

Prabhu, K. Seeta (2001). *Economic Reform and Social Sector Development*, Sage Publications, New Delhi.

Proceedings of the D. T. Lakdawala Memorial Symposium (1994). *Decentralised Planning and Panchayati Raj*, Concept Publishing Company, New Delhi.

Rao, U.R. (1996). *Space Technology for Sustainable Development*. Tata McGraw Hill Publishing Company, New Delhi.

Sainath, P. (1996). *Everybody Loves a Good Drought—Stories from India's Poorest Districts*, Penguin Books, New Delhi.

Samirendra, N. Ray (1995). *Communication in Rural Development : A Public Policy Perspective*, Indian Institute of Advanced Study, Shimla.

Shariff, Abusaleh (1999). *India : Human Development Report*, National Council of Applied Economic Research, New Delhi.

Shiva Vandana (1991). *Ecology and the Politics of Survival—Conflicts over Natural Resources in India*, Sage Publications, New Delhi.

Singhal, Arvind and Rogers, Everett, M. (1989). *India's Information Revolution*, Sage Publications, New Delhi.

Singhal, Arvind and Rogers, Everett, M. (2001). *India's Communication Revolution*, Sage Publications, New Delhi.

Somesh Kumar (2002), *Methods for Community Participation*, Sage Publications, New Delhi.

Teheranian Majid, Hakimzadeh, Farhad and Vidale, Marcello L. (eds.) (1977). *Communication Policy for National Development*. Routledge and Kegan Paul, London.

Toffler, Alvin (1980). *The Third Wave*, William Collins, London.

UNDP (1993). *Human Development Report* (1993). Oxford University Press, Oxford.

UNDP (1996). *Human Development Report* (1996). Oxford University Press, Oxford.

UNDP (2000). *Human Development Report* (2000). Oxford University Press, Oxford.

UNDP (2001). *Human Development Report* (2001). Oxford University Press, Oxford.

UNESCO (1982). *Many Voices, One World*, The International Commission on the Study of Communication Problems, Paris.

UNESCO (1996). *Learning : The Treasure Within*, Paris.

UNESCO (1997). *Public Service Broadcasting : The Challenge of the Twenty-first Century*, Paris.

UNESCO (1997). *World Information Report* 1997-98, Paris.

Venkateswaran, Sandhya (1995). *Environment, Development and the Gender Gap*, Sage Publications, New Delhi.

Voices (1997). *Media Policy and Community Radio*, Bangalore.

World Bank (1996). *From Plan to Market*, Oxford University Press, Oxford.

World Bank (1998/99). *World Development Report, Knowledge for Development,* Oxford University Press, Oxford.

World Bank (2000). *World Development Report 1999/2000, Entering the 21st Century,* Oxford Unviersity Press, Oxford.

World Bank (2000). *World Development Report 2000/2001, Attacking Poverty,* Oxford University Press, Oxford.

World Bank (2002). *World Development Report 2002, Building Institutions for Markets,* Oxford University Press, Oxford.

INDEX